GOTHIC
MASCULINITY

The Bucknell Studies in Eighteenth-Century Literature and Culture

General Editor: Greg Clingham, *Bucknell University*

Advisory Board: Paul K. Alkon, *University of Southern California*
Chloe Chard, *Independent Scholar*
Clement Hawes, *The Pennsylvania State University*
Robert Markley, *West Virginia University*
Jessica Munns, *University of Denver*
Cedric D. Reverand II, *University of Wyoming*
Janet Todd, *University of Glasgow*

The Bucknell Studies in Eighteenth-Century Literature and Culture aims to publish challenging, new eighteenth-century scholarship. Of particular interest is critical, historical, and interdisciplinary work that is interestingly and intelligently theorized, and that broadens and refines the conception of the field. At the same time, the series remains open to all theoretical perspectives and different kinds of scholarship. While the focus of the series is the literature, history, arts, and culture (including art, architecture, music, travel, and history of science, medicine, and law) of the long eighteenth century in Britain and Europe, the series is also interested in scholarship that establishes relationships with other geographies, literatures, and cultures of the period 1660–1830.

Titles in This Series

Regina Hewitt and Pat Rogers, eds., *Orthodoxy and Heresy in Eighteenth-Century Society*
Edward Jacobs, *Accidental Migrations: An Archaeology of Gothic Discourse*
Catherine Jones, *Literary Memory: Scott's Waverley Novels and the Psychology of Narrative*
Ellen Brinks, *Gothic Masculinity: Effeminacy and the Supernatural in English and German Romanticism*
Tanya Caldwell, *Time to Begin Anew: Dryden's Georgics and Aeneis*
Mita Choudhury, *Interculturalism and Resistance in the London Theatre, 1660–1800: Identity, Performance, Empire*
James Cruise, *Governing Consumption: Needs and Wants, Suspended Characters, and the "Origins" of Eighteenth-Century English Novels*
Ziad Elmarsafy, *Freedom, Slavery, and Absolutism: Corneille, Pascale, Racine*
Sarah Jordan, *The Anxieties of Idleness: Idleness in Eighteenth-Century British Literature and Culture*
Deborah Kennedy, *Helen Maria Williams and the Age of Revolution*
Chris Mounsey, *Christopher Smart: Clown of God*
Chris Mounsey, ed., *Presenting Gender: Changing Sex in Early Modern Culture*
Roland Racesvkis, *Time and Ways of Knowing Under Louis XIV: Molièr, Sevigne, Lafayette*
Laura Rosenthal and Mita Choudhury, eds., *Monstrous Dreams of Reason*
Katherine West Scheil, *The Taste of the Town: Shakespearian Comedy and Early Eighteenth-Century Theater*
Philip Smallwood, ed., *Johnson Re-Visioned: Looking Before and After*
Peter Walmsley, *Locke's Essay and the Rhetoric of Science*
Lisa Wood, *Modes of Discipline: Women, Conservatism, and the Novel after the French Revolution*
http://www.departments.bucknell.edu/univ_press

GOTHIC MASCULINITY

Effeminacy and the Supernatural in English and German Romanticism

Ellen Brinks

Lewisburg
Bucknell University Press
London: Associated University Presses

Associated University Presses
2010 Eastpark Boulevard
Cranbury, NJ 08512

Associated University Presses
Unit 304
The Chandlery
50 Westminster Bridge Road
London SE1 7Q4, England

Associated University Presses
P.O. Box 338, Port Credit
Mississauga, Ontario
Canada L5G 4L8

The paper used in this publication meets the requirements of the American National Standard for Permanence of Paper for Printed Library Materials Z39.48-1984.

Library of Congress Cataloging-in-Publication Data

Brinks, Ellen, 1957–
    Gothic masculinity : effeminacy and the supernatural in English and German romanticism / Ellen Brinks.
        p.   cm. — (The Bucknell studies in eighteenth-century literature and culture)
    Includes bibliographical references and index.
    ISBN 0-8387-5524-0 (alk. paper)
    1. English literature — 18th century — History and criticism.   2. Masculinity in literature.   3. German literature — 18th century — History and criticism.   4. Literature, Comparative — English and German. 5. Literature, Comparative — German and English.   6. Gothic revival (Literature) — Great Britain.   7. Gothic revival (Literature) — Germany. 8. Romanticism — Great Britain.   9. Supernatural in literature.   10. Romanticism — Germany.   11. Men in literature.   I. Title.   II. Series.
    PR448.M37B75   2003
    823'.709 — dc21   2003001836

PRINTED IN THE UNITED STATES OF AMERICA

Contents

5

Acknowledgments

THIS BOOK COULD NOT HAVE BEEN WRITTEN WITHOUT THE ASSIS-
tance of more people than I can name. My greatest debts are to April
Alliston, Claudia Brodsky Lacour, and Susan Wolfson, who have given
so generously of their critical intelligence over so many years and fostered this project from its beginnings. I simply cannot imagine how the
finished product would have looked without them. Special thanks go to
the Whiting Foundation for a year-long dissertation grant and to
Princeton University (especially the Comparative Literature and English departments), for providing such a supportive and intellectually
stimulating community of graduate students and faculty, including
Susan Bernofsky, Adrienne Donald, Anne-Lise Francois, Ann Gaylin,
Jen Kates, Karen McPherson, Eun Min, Earl Miner, Jeff Nunokawa,
Eric Santner, Lee Talley, David Thurn, and Ellen Wayland-Smith.

At Colorado State University's English department, I have benefited
from release time and encouragement from Pattie Cowell, Judy
Doenges, David Milofsky, Laura Mullen, Chip Rhodes, Barbara
Sebek, and Paul Trembath. Greg Clingham at Bucknell University
Press has been a pleasure to work with; reports from their anonymous
readers asked me challenging and rewarding questions. Julien Yoseloff,
Christine Retz, and Mary Cicora at Associated University Presses were
always available with their professional expertise and assistance at various stages of the production process. Heartfelt appreciation goes to
Claudia Johnson and Jane Garrity for their discerning feedback at an
especially critical moment in the revision of the manuscript.

An earlier version of the Keats chapter first appeared as an essay. I
would like to thank *Nineteenth-Century Literature* for permission to re-
print material from "The Male Romantic Poet as Gothic Subject:
Keats's *Hyperion* and *The Fall of Hyperion: A Dream*."

During the long time it takes to complete a book, I have benefited
from the love and steadfast support of my father, my sister, my friends
Annette Clark, Leslie Dwyer, Lou Lasson, Bruno Navasky, and Lee
Talley, and from the daily presence of Julie Horton, the companion and
partner I had always hoped to find.

GOTHIC
MASCULINITY

Introduction

Bᴇᴀʀɪɴɢ ᴛʜᴇ ɢɪɢᴀɴᴛɪᴄ ꜱᴡᴏʀᴅ ᴏꜰ ᴛʜᴇ ᴀɴᴄᴇꜱᴛᴏʀ ᴀʟꜰᴏɴꜱᴏ ᴛʜᴇ Good, a procession of one hundred young men "[seem] to faint under the weight of it." In this fashion Horace Walpole stages the public cere-mony of paternal inheritance in *The Castle of Otranto* (1764), designated the first gothic novel.[1] These young men falter in their designated "manly" role: carrying the past—the sword inscribed with the name of the legitimate heir—into the present. *The Castle of Otranto*, the "original" gothic, dramatizes the difficulty of the Father's legacy, his emblematic sword, for a younger generation of men. If Alfonso's sword stands for phallic masculinity as real and symbolic legitimacy, this inheritance or entailment can be said, literally, to overbear a younger generation of men. Without putting too much interpretive pressure upon this scene, the young men's loss of physical control, articulated through an "un-manly" response, the swoon, recasts the difficulty with this legacy as a problem with its implied gender demands. It is unleashed by the super-natural presence and display of Alfonso's sword, which, like his tremen-dous helmet and armor, intrudes into a startled present.[2]

Gothic Masculinity: Effeminacy and the Supernatural in English and Ger-man Romanticism situates itself in the decades shadowed by Walpole's novel and explores richer, more complex stagings of *Otranto*'s "dis-tressed masculinity" in works of Hegel, Keats, Byron, Coleridge, and, in a leap forward, in the early work of Freud. These authors do not write full-fledged Gothic novels, but they do write highly gothicized narratives where a male protagonist encounters an effeminizing super-natural force. He finds himself divested or dispossessed of his real and symbolic masculine estate within the imaginary, interiorized, or fantas-tic spaces of these narratives. What interests me particularly is that the gothic is the discourse that comes to these authors' minds when gender stress is under discussion.[3] Gothic tropes and tableaux cross a range of genres and perplex social and "natural" distinctions concerning mascu-linity and male sexuality to produce multiple, often contradictory, iden-tifications.

Thus, I shall be concerned with some canonical instances of gothic

11

imagination—Byron's *Oriental Tales* and Coleridge's *Christabel*—but also works such as Hegel's *Phenomenology of Mind*, Keats's *Hyperion* fragments, and Freud's letters and scientific writings, insofar as they report, from various sites, increasing anxieties about male effeminacy or the emergence of a male "homosexual" identity within the fraught cultural desires during the Romantic period and its Freudian afterlife.[4] While the eighteenth century often accommodated same-sex desire through discourses of melancholy or friendship that recontained it within a closet-like framework, gothic languages and figures report anxieties that require supernaturalized fantasy formations, especially for the masculine subject whose psychosexual coherence is at risk or voluntarily sacrificed.[5] Dispossessed masculinity raises an insidious question regarding the basis of gendered identity: if a male subject can be inhabited, displaced, or self-alienated, even temporarily, by uncanny forces that unleash, precipitate, or coincide with effeminizing effects, in what sense does he possess a masculine identity?[6]

As we shall see, this dynamic of a male subject evacuated and possessed by an "alien" femininity bears scrutiny in relation to contemporary critical constructions of male authorial subjectivity during the Romantic period. These encounters stand as an allegory for a male Romantic subjectivity whose identity or vocation is staked on the repudiation of oedipal or phallic power. The disruption of patriarchal culture's symbolic order from a place seemingly out of bounds—the place of the marginalized, effeminate male—instead of being a liability or loss, ironically becomes a part of culture's highest symbolic functioning. Instead of a male Romantic subjectivity established at the expense of the feminine, I shall argue that a shadow plot exists, wherein the effeminizing force of the gothicized, alien, and the uncanny within the male subject's psyche, far from exiling the feminine as other, refers to (and even requires) the feminine to describe divergences within itself which cultural strictures have occluded.[7] If Romanticism repeatedly stages the failure to master and complete the developmental narratives it inherits as a condition of insight, in certain gothic forms this "failure" includes the gender demands of such a development, a refusal that, as each chapter will suggest, promises or intuits imaginative strength.[8]

It will help, at this point, to clarify the possessions of *Gothic Masculinity*: what are the central concerns of the gothic that inform this study, especially at its point of articulation in the late eighteenth century? and how does this articulation involve shifting sex-gender roles during the period? With its affinity for the monstrous, the uncanny, and the unspeakable, the gothic offers a stage for all manner of cultural and psychological abjections—those wishes, fears, and fantasies seemingly alienated but insistently returning in distorted, displaced, and magnetically terrifying guises.[9] Through the gothic, heterosexual culture would cast off its own homoerotic yearnings, representing them in supernatural guise as "other," where the struggle to deny or normalize shapes the narrative dynamic. Yet by illuminating fears about the "unclear, though often asserted, boundaries between 'licit' and 'illicit' sexual behavior or orientations," the gothic also can and has been used to explore the individual desires that such culturally mandated distinctions would render unacceptable.[10] As a symbolic place of othering as well as the site of its ghostly or uncanny longings, the gothic disturbs fantasies of self-evident or certain self-knowledge.[11]

By force of this disturbance, the history of the gothic is controversial.[12] In representing the disalignment of conventional masculinity as a gothicized "disinheritance," this study condenses—or collapses—what critics have identified, separately, as central concerns of the gothic during the second half of the eighteenth century: the impediments to the legitimate transmission of the father's estate; the rupture of masculine and feminine psychosocial development and its conventional telos, marriage; and the subject's capacity to be altered, temporarily suspended, or radically alienated.[13] Let us briefly consider each of these concerns in turn, as reflected in gothic works of the period. Possession, the prerogative of patriarchal power, finds itself shadowed by dispossession and unofficial history in the plots of Clara Reeve's *The Old English Baron*, Richard Warner's *Netley Abbey*, the anonymous *Mort Castle*, Sophia Lee's *The Recess*, Ann Radcliffe's *The Castles of Athlin and Dunbayne*, and Matthew Lewis's *The Castle Spectre*, which, like *Otranto*, foreground lost "real" estate, a literally alienated paternal estate. At the same time, castles figure as material emblems of an enduring patriarchal line. As "embodied fate," such estates assume great symbolic weight in the transmission of cultural ideologies, felt as burdens placed upon their inhabitants, as Walpole, albeit in campy fashion, literalizes in the scene already described from *Otranto*.[14] The inheritors of this fate are made "[captive] of the past, while the characters of the past live on as spirits only to be their vigilant captors."[15] This double play of alienation and captivation anticipates Hegel's discussion of "haunted": a past that looms as overwhelming authority—an authority whose longevity is measured by its repeated returns in phantasmatic form—yet is present only as a ghost—hollowed out or evacuated of real presence, alien and alienating.

This contest of past and present determines a network of related topics: castles as prisons or places of entrapment; children rebelling against autocratic fathers or father figures; heroes or heroines estranged from their family of birth; primogeniture subverted; the next generation deferred or not produced at all. Across works as diverse in overt purpose as *The Castle of Otranto*, Radcliffe's *The Italian*, Charles Maturin's *Melmoth the Wanderer*, as well as the political writings of Edmund Burke, Thomas Paine, and Mary Wollstonecraft during the early 1790s, gothic tropes stage psychologized, intergenerational conflict or alienation.[16] In *Otranto*, for example, although the legitimate son Theodore regains the rights to his father's estate and the novel concludes with his marriage, the success is undone as soon as it is accomplished: instead of anticipating a promising future with his bride Isabella, Theodore succumbs to an enduring melancholic fixation on Matilda, the usurper Manfred's deceased daughter. Wollstonecraft's *A Vindication of the Rights of Men*, Burke's *Reflections on the Revolution in France*, and Paine's *The Rights of Man* all resort to gothic metaphors to foreground the direct links between psychosexual development, patriarchal family dynamics, and political tyranny in the revolution against entailed property.[17] When Vivaldi of Radcliffe's *The Italian*, veiled like a gothic heroine, stands before the Inquisition and refuses to speak the "truth" that the Inquisition's "Fathers" are willing to extract by torture, he relinquishes his role in patriarchal culture. The interlocking narratives in *Melmoth the Wanderer* (1820) replay scenes where intergenerational male emasculation interrupts the transmission of patriarchal values: young John Melmoth rejects his legacy by burning the portrait and manuscript relating the ancestral Melmoth's history; illegitimate Moncada, terrified at the prospect of never escaping the monastery's subterranean chambers where his parents have incarcerated him (usually a female fate in the gothic), imagines he could "feed on a parent, . . . gnaw[ing] out [his] passage into life and liberty"; and Melmoth flirts with a homoerotic passion (before it is revealed that his beloved is really a woman).[18] Estates are frequently not restored to the rightful heir: in Sophia Lee's *The Recess*, Charlotte Smith's poem *The Emigrants*, and Wollstonecraft's *Maria*, women dispossessed of their fortunes remain exiled from the living; in Radcliffe's *The Italian*, Ellena recovers her name, but her patrimony has been squandered away by her uncle; and in Godwin's *Caleb Williams*, Poe's *The Fall of the House of Usher*, and Shelley's *Frankenstein*, patrilineal property and values are ultimately removed from the possession of the male protagonists.[19]

Gothic dispossession thus breaks or impedes the symbolic functioning of patriarchal culture — especially those matters concerned with property, heirs and kinship ties, names and titles, marriage systems, and, most important for this study, masculinity and male sexuality. When Locke announced in his *Second Treatise on Government* that "every Man has a Property in his own Person"; when, with his panopticon, Bentham presumed the visibility of each person; and, when Godwin made private judgment an absolute moral arbiter, each argues for masculine self-possession. Yet the necessity of so arguing implies the unstable ground.[20] Possession is notoriously slippery as a metaphor: who possesses/dispossesses whom? Who owns, or is subjected to, whom?

These questions pervade the prose, epistolary, and poetic narratives in this study. If Edmund Burke saw identity as fixed, immutable, and tied to real property as the guarantor of character, emergent bourgeois ideologies favored the self as unfixed, "in-the-making," subject to speculation, sudden reversals, and in gendered terms, struggling with effeminizing fantasies and appetites.[21] Gothicized tales of dispossession as effeminization report this conflict again and again, interrogating the very metaphor of property for male personhood by force of a fascination with the alterity, even fragmentation, of subjectivity.

Dissolving the ordinary boundaries of masculinity thus constitutes the key actions of these narratives and the key scenes of interiority. In Hegel, Mind watches his spectral incarnations; in Keats, a poet-narrator records sadomasochistic initiatory rituals within a visionary space; in his Eastern tales, Byron orientalizes and ironizes the rhetoric of the "open secret"; in *Christabel*, Coleridge's narrator reveals a dream- or trance-like exchange of identities; and in his letters and early scientific writings, Freud hysterically identifies with his "other," Fliess.[22] These literary conceptions coincide with the shift between the seventeenth and twentieth centuries in definitions of masculinity as public reputation to masculinity as subjective self-possession. Along with cultural determinations, masculinity comes to be felt as an "authentic" expression of the self, "up to a point a matter of individual choice, no matter how tormenting or liberating."[23] Insecurity or anxiety about masculinity takes the form of internal doubts, particularly about sexuality. The dream-like and visionary spaces of these tales, I shall be arguing, articulate the emergence of masculinity as an aspect of subjectivity, but known only negatively, through the repeated stagings of its dispossession.

~

When the Romantic narratives I treat in *Gothic Masculinity* express considerable urgency about domestic gender roles, they do so in ways strikingly akin to the anxieties accompanying the shift in familial organization and sex and gender roles during the eighteenth century in Great Britain and Western Europe. Concomitant with the moral demand for equality fostered by the idea, if not the practice, of the companionate marriage, an increasing polarization of the sexes charted separate but equal social roles *and* biology.[24] The contemporary science of the eighteenth century, Thomas Laqueur argues, no longer saw the female body as an inferior copy or model of the male; the emphasis was on their difference.[25] Gender differences could thus be naturalized.[26] Women "naturally" desired their complement in men, and men in women. The biological purpose of sexuality, reproduction, reflected a larger moral purpose, while all non-reproductive forms of sexuality were regarded as deviant, especially male homosexuality.[27]

Because discourses about "sexuality" as such were nonexistent, same-sex desire was discussed in the notoriously slippery languages of gender and gender inversion. During the eighteenth century, masculinity was continually being redefined. After 1700, however, as Randolph Trumbach has outlined, some culturally salient features of the "third" gender, or "effeminate male," emerge. Any man who engages in sex with another man is assigned to this third gender, whether he takes an active or passive role in the relationship (in the preceding centuries only the male adopting the passive role was "effeminate"). Whereas in earlier centuries adolescent boys were allowed a "grace" period for sexual experimentation with (usually) older men, the eighteenth century took a dimmer view. And even though third gender practices involve patterns of behavior common to both male and the female, it is effeminacy of character and manner that is now the hallmark of the "sodomite."[28]

Effeminacy alone, however, did not identify a male as a "sodomite." Rather, it characterized much more than sexual practices: deviation from the ideal of a manly religion; slander, a "female" vice; overfastidiousness in politeness; frivolous behavior; French affectation; and licentiousness.[29] Yet the associations of effeminacy with that social identity did make it a nexus that generated profound concern about gender identity and sexuality, especially for those seeking definitional control over homosexual and homosocial bonding.[30] Although effeminacy had "a long complicated history that gave it a possible but never certain link to homosexual behavior," suspicions of sodomy could and often did cluster around any expression or use of the term effeminacy.[31]

The socially "acceptable" channel for "effeminate" sensibility by the late eighteenth century was the "cult of sensibility," epitomized in works such as Laurence Sterne's *A Sentimental Journey through France and Italy* and Henry Mackenzie's *The Man of Feeling*, and later, in the Romantic ideal of androgyny.[32] Terry Castle describes the "female man" as follows:

> The Western image of masculinity has altered strikingly over the past two centuries, gradually absorbing many once exclusively feminine modes of experience. Characteristics once seen as belonging only to women — moodiness, heightened sensitivity, susceptibility to hysteria, and so on — have come increasingly to be perceived as belonging to both sexes. In the eighteenth century, the cult of sensibility was an early sign of the weakening of sexual polarities. . . . [33]

Not simply condoning feminine characteristics, the cult of sensibility encouraged close bonds or friendships between men which, to our eyes, appear remarkably "homosexual." As Claudia Johnson and Michael McKeon suggest, eighteenth-century writers took pains to normativize feminine qualities in men, making previously negative or disregarded characteristics (due to their association with women) into positive ones of patriarchal power.[34] "The vexed relation between visible signs and assumed practices," Andrew Elfenbein observes, meant, however, that while an effeminate male was not necessarily a sodomite, sodomites were described as feminine.[35] In reading male effeminacy as more than sodomy, one may neglect specific textual representations of effeminacy that do imply different varieties of same-sex desire.[36]

Historical studies are just beginning to trace some of the competing and conflicting discourses of gender inversion during this time with their implications of same-sex desire. Traditional literary and cultural stereotypes of male homosexuality inherited from the period, including the rake, the fop, and the effeminate aristocrat, a connoisseur-collector with an interest in high religion and Catholic Europe, are too limiting.[37] The historians Bray and Trumbach expand on these earlier models and identify the molly, or transvestite, role. Andrew Elfenbein has charted how the character of the genius functions during the eighteenth century and Romantic period as a metaphor for the homosexual character.[38] Beyond these roles often circumscribed by class, homoerotic experiences have been identified in the context of casual encounters or specific situations, such as within court and theater culture, on ship or in the (military) field, abroad (especially during the Grand Tour), in boarding

schools, in all-male societies, prisons, or in close, emotional male friendships.[39] In some eighteenth-century literature, same-sex desire is re-
thought in terms of Greek love, which celebrates male-male desire as
eroticized friendship, defusing the hierarchical implications of the liber-
tine model. This classical model of male homoerotics, free of the eighteenth-century stigma of corruption and effeminacy, comes to
predominate in Victorian England, as studies by Richard Dellamora,
Christopher Craft, and Linda Dowling further substantiate.[40] It goes
without saying that same-sex desire did not inevitably lead to the adoption of the sodomite role, nor did heterosexual activity or marital status
prove to be an indication of sexual preference. Many arrested for sodomy were married.[41] The point at which male effeminacy crosses over
or implies sexual "deviance" in such a fluid spectrum is not clear, nor
will it be the aim of this study to redraw some already phantasmatic line
between the hetero- and the homosexual male.

Rather, I would argue that concomitant with increasingly codified
gender norms, both literary representations of the period, as well as historical records, disclose a plethora of transgressive figures that manage
to "escape" these confines. And by virtue of its fantastic or non-mimetic
mode, gothic conventions accommodate powerful affective or erotic
energies identified with an "unrepresentative consciousness," without
undermining the "reality" of the sex-gender binarism expressed in dominant cultural ideologies of the time. These gothicized tales reaffirm that
heterosexuality needs homosexuality as its other, even as this mode also
produces a disciplinary regime: a risk of "illegitimacy," corporeal punishment, and social/linguistic exclusion in a stigma of morbidity, imma-
turity, illegibility, or pathology.[42] Imperiled in this double-bind of
transgression and discipline, of subversion and containment, is subjectivity itself. Gothic subjectivity oscillates dramatically between extremes of dissolution and rigidity.

Gothic Masculinity marks this complex fate across a historical span
from the late Enlightenment to early modernism, wherein the gothic
imaginations of English Romanticism recur, with theoretical power, in
Hegel's *Phenomenology* and Freud's epistolary and scientific writings a
century later. The sustained focus of this study on British and German
Romanticism makes visible rich, though relatively unknown, ties of
cross-cultural exchange. While English literature and culture enjoyed
great respect in Germany beginning in the mid-eighteenth century, English gothic literature first assumed a dominant presence there in the

late 1780s.[43] Works by Clara Reeve, Sophia Lee, Charlotte Smith, and Ann Radcliffe were tremendously popular and commercially successful. The German term for the gothic novel—*der Schauerroman* (tale of horror)—was first applied by German critics to Radcliffe's works. A widespread knowledge of German literature in England came with translations of German romances called *Schauer-* and *Ritterromane* (tales of horror and chivalry), many of which were published by William Lane's Minerva Press). These overtly gothic works for a popular audience reached an English reading public in huge numbers during the 1790s, in what was the first significant influx. (They are best known as Catherine Morland's required reading in Jane Austen's *Northanger Abbey*). Two writers in this study, Coleridge and Byron, both read widely in German literature. Keats read writers such as Lewis, Scott, and Byron, whose works are heavily indebted to the German literary tradition. Matthew Lewis and Sir Walter Scott drew on German sources for their own work, besides translating a large number of them for the British audience.[44] Lewis's fiction, substantially indebted to German models, may have been the single most significant factor in creating a Germanized gothic taste in the British reading public. His own work, especially *The Monk*, exercised a considerable influence upon an English gothic Romantic imagination, to which the frequent allusions in Byron and Coleridge testify. Sir Walter Scott can be said to have done the same for a second or later generation of writers.[45]

After a brief period of praise by British reviewers, and despite their huge popular success, these contemporary German gothic novels and dramas, as well as folk and literary ballads, all of which drew upon the supernatural and evinced a strong interest in transgressive figures, the psychology of mystery and horror, and in states of psychic fragmentation, came increasingly under attack. The periodical *The Antijacobin* made a move to denounce these tales and dramas (many of which belong to the *Sturm und Drang* movement), indeed German literature in general, as politically radical, freethinking, and aesthetically marred by a focus on violence and psychologically extreme states. Coupled with the political conservatism provoked by the Terror in France, this critical brand was most likely the cause of a lull in the translation of German literature during the first decade of the nineteenth century. In the formation of the British national character, as David Simpson has argued, Germany gradually replaces France during the 1790s as despised and demonized other. German gothic literature, as much for its perceived "Germanness" as for its gothicism, was said to exhibit and promulgate the worst vices of the country: an imbrication of political radicalism and sexual frankness, expressed as women's involvement in revolutionary politics and their "degraded" commitment to marriage and the principles of feminine "delicacy."[46] (A similar response occurred in Germany, with English gothic works stigmatized as infectious and immoral influences). Regardless of whether these nationalizing impulses generated a rejection of the gothic or whether the debate about the gothic was translated or transmuted into debates about the respective qualities and worth of German and English national character(s), the terms of the debate are relevant to this study. For critics in both countries recognized that the gothic, German or English, encompassed or synthesized by the end of the 1790s a shared set of values. These values are those emphasized in the narratives explored in this study: radical, anti-paternal sentiments or a willed departure from patriarchal values, and their framing in a rhetoric of gender deviance, as an inclination to resist maturation and to throw "away the character of [one's] sex."[47]

Ten to fifteen years later the furor over the "germanizing" influences of the gothic had completely subsided, perhaps due to the recognition that English gothic literature could manage such proclivities quite well on its own, despite the vilification of German literature. In 1813, Germaine de Staël's essayistic study of German Romanticism, *De l'Allemagne*, appeared in English translation. (A good deal of German literature came into Great Britain by way of France and French mediation, as translations from the French. The ghost stories that Mary Shelley, Percy Shelley, and Lord Byron read at Villa Diodati, for example, were from the volume *Phantasmagoria*, a translation from the French of German ghost stories). Great Britain thus witnessed a resurgence of interest in the German gothic and a large increase in published translations. Two periodicals, *Blackwood's Magazine* in 1815, followed by the *Literary Gazette*, proved very receptive to German literature and published many works from German over the next decade.

As the overarching trope in this book, gothic dispossession reveals previously unglimpsed connections between a diversity of discourses, literary, philosophical, and scientific, in Hegel's preface to *The Phenomenology*, Keats's *Hyperion* fragments, Byron's *Oriental Tales*, Coleridge's *Christabel*, and Freud's early hysteria case studies and letters to Wilhelm Fliess. Chapter 1 reads the supernatural tropes that surface in Hegel's *Phenomenology of Mind* as evidence of a suppressed gothic narrative that disrupts the protagonist's — that is, mind's or spirit's — masculine *Bildungsroman*. In the concluding section of the *Phenomenology*, Hegel represents mind imagining self-consciousness as a successive negation of spectral figures. These specters from the past, like "portraits in a gallery," Hegel writes, eye the spectator who views them. They anticipate and present in literary, mimetic form the supernaturalized terror of the dialectic's recurring negative turn, a dispossessing, effeminizing moment for the masculine subject. The very structure of the dialectic prohibits the direct inheritance of the cultural property—*das Eigentum des Geistes*—which Hegel gives as the aim of his narrative phenomenology. The protagonist must repeatedly reject all given models and histories of a masculine education and undergo instead the vivifying activity of the horrific (*das Furchtbarste*), the unfamiliar (*das Ungeheure*), or the uncanny.

An epic project of *Bildung* is at stake as well in Keats's fragmentary works on poetic election, *Hyperion* and *The Fall of Hyperion: A Vision*. This is the subject of the second chapter, which calls attention to the previously unnoticed gothic subtext of Keats's attempts at Miltonic, then Dantean epic. Whether it is Saturn, Apollo, or himself that the narrator witnesses, his returns to scenes where an effeminized male body is subjected to pain and domination become a way to explore questions of legitimation and empowerment when they can no longer be presupposed by the writing subject. While recent readings of these poems have tended to align their fragmentation with Keats's refusal of mastery, I argue that Keats identifies male masochism and effeminacy as the perverse condition of, rather than the impediment to, the attainment of symbolic power. Apollo's eroticized submission in *Hyperion* and the poet's self-castigating trials in the *Fall of Hyperion* (as well as his return to the Titans) stage the very experience they supposedly stand in the way of: legitimation. Not only does bodily dispossession directly measure symbolic possession, but through his doubles Keats recognizes himself in this loss of power.

Two verse narratives of Byron's *Oriental Tales*, *The Giaour* and *Lara*, explore the male protagonist's dispossession through a carefully cultivated gothic rhetoric of the secret and the mysterious. Ostensibly referring to his unknown past and concealed identity, this rhetoric more interestingly accrues around the ambiguously gendered and sexed page figure, a person whose fate and identity are inextricable from his and through whom the community measures his alienation from a patriarchal narrative of succession. This chapter focuses on how the narrators and characters within these tales cultivate "open secrets," a form of power around which they constitute their own difference. Paradoxically, the "empty"—unknown or unexpressed—content of the secret transforms it into a valuable symbolic presence wherever it circulates, and the implied threat it represents to the cultural order "from outside" guarantees the ordinary workings and stability of the communities in which these figures play a part. Byron thus fashions a more extensive intersection between the rhetoric of the secret and prevailing cultural mystifications of homosexuality and non-normative gender identities than previous critical readings of *The Giaour* and *Lara* have granted. At the same time, he converts the gothic secrets surrounding male effeminacy and same-sex desire into a metaphor for critical reading. As he maps the socius's attempts to read surfaces for meaning as a strategy of coercive knowledge, he suggests a different kind of reading, one that necessarily misses or fails to possess its object.

As in Keats, gender deviance and same-sex desire are more explicitly tied to aesthetic creation in Samuel Taylor Coleridge's *Christabel*. The female homoeroticism at the center of *Christabel* is troped through a gothic discourse of "the unspeakable." Impelling Geraldine's and Christabel's lovemaking, doubling, and ventriloquism, mimetic, identificatory, and supernaturalized energies also extend to enchant the entire represented social realm. Being spoken by an other or as the other wishes, a disruption of signification figured as the uncanny effect of same-sex desire, is retroped in Part Two of the poem as an affinity for mimicry, or repetition compulsion, that underlies the symbolic order. Drawing on Coleridge's critical writings on the gothic, the contested critical reception of the poem, and the poem's preface, the chapter connects the poem to larger issues of aesthetic creation and reception. Through the poem's parodic tone, Coleridge performs his own formal identification with the gothic, supposedly suspect for male writers because of its reliance on borrowing. Exploring the import for a male artist who identifies with conventional and feminized forms, Coleridge homoeroticizes formal questions even as he mediates literary relations between men. Mirroring or mimesis not only determines aspects of aesthetic form, but, as Coleridge shows, produces the performative, reiterative nature of the reader's pleasure in the gothic—that willing dispossession of self in favor of identification—that so vexed male critics.

This study concludes in the 1890s, at the beginnings of Freud's theoretical construction of a gendered and sexed subject, and more specifically, of the "achievement" of a masculine, heterosexual subject. This is less an extreme jump than it may at first appear, for Freud adopts gothic conventions to write a counternarrative to this developmental one. Drawing on his writings on hypnosis, the early hysteria case studies, and above all, his correspondence with Wilhelm Fliess, this chapter argues that the gothic fantasy material Freud retrieves from his female patients under hypnosis infiltrates the epistolary representations of his homoerotic impulses toward Fliess. The narrative of their friendship situates itself apposite to the emerging science of psychoanalysis with its tales of demonic possession, foreign bodies, phobic formulas, and phantom pregnancies. Instead of normalizing the achievement of heterosexual masculinity as he may have intended, Freud pathologizes it, as a symptom or outcome of a specifically male hysteria. In Freud's versions of the history of psychoanalysis, mention of his relationship to Fliess, which occupied a central place in the first seventeen years of that history, are so rare as to be nonexistent. This early affair of psychoanalysis is forgotten, until the science establishes its own legitimate dynasty. Yet through the self-alienating and self-transferring exchanges that take place between doctor and patient, or between Freud and Fliess, a Freud emerges who inherits the gothic Romantic paradigm of a dispossessed male subjectivity and incorporates it within his science of the self. This chapter, together with the others, dramatizes how non-normative masculinity and sexuality are repeatedly drawn in figures of the gothic supernatural and gothic dispossession.

1

Hegel Possessed:
Reading the Gothic in *The Phenomenology of Mind*

*La pensée est, en somme, le travail qui
fait vivre en nous ce qui n'existe pas.*

—Paul Valéry

THE PHENOMENOLOGY OF MIND TELLS A STORY. AS A JOURNEY OF BE-
coming and maturation, Hegel's narrative bears a strong resemblance
to the literary coming-of-age fictions known as *Bildungsromane*. Critics
and theorists as diverse as M. H. Abrams and Judith Butler have emphasized the symbolic debt the *Phenomenology* owes to that genre, seeing
it as a philosophical *Doppelgänger* of Goethe's *Wilhelm Meister* and his
Faust.[1] And in part they are right, for Hegel traces the development of
the protagonist Mind (*der Geist*) through "his" development—our protagonist is gendered masculine—and calls it explicitly a *Bildung* (education). Charting the *Stufen eines Weges* (stages/steps of a way, path, or
passage), the narrative labor of the text becomes one of exhuming, re-
figuring, projecting, and staging. It is memory (*Er-innerung*) that externalizes the forgotten, faded, or alienated content of experience or history as "figures" or "shapes" (*Gestalten*) in order to allow Mind to
reclaim them as his own:

> . . . was vorher die Sache selbst war, ist nur noch eine Spur; ihre Gestalt ist
> eingehüllt und eine einfache Schattierung geworden. Diese Vergangenheit
> durchläuft das Individuum . . . Er [der Geist] ruft die Erinnerung derselben
> zurück . . . Der Einzelne muß auch dem Inhalte nach die Bildungsstufen
> des allgemeinen Geistes durchlaufen, aber als vom Geiste schon abgelegte
> Gestalten, als Stufen eines Wegs. . . .[2]

> [. . . what was previously the matter itself is now only a trace; its shape is
> veiled and has become a mere shade. This past passes through the individual
> . . . Mind recalls the memory of these (shades) . . . Each man must go

24

through, in their content too, the formative steps of universal Mind, but as figures already performed by Mind, as the stages of a passage. . . .]

Through these representational and performative acts of memory, the various errors and blindnesses of self-consciousness are worked through as our subject proceeds toward Absolute Knowing: the culminating point and goal in which Mind has become conscious of himself in his own labor (*der sich als Geist wissende Geist*).[3]

This story of veiled shades that Hegel alludes to above turns out to be a ghost story as well. Incorporating into its preface and conclusion ghosts or spectral figures, the spirit-realm, an ancestral hall, the unreal, the dead, the undead, and acts of reanimation, the *Phenomenology's* monstrous task (die *"ungeheure* Arbeit," 33–34) turns weirdly gothic.[4] Hegel gives us to understand that the *Geist* of the *Phenomenology* finds himself part of a *Geisterroman* (supernatural or gothic novel). In his essay *Das Unheimliche* ("The Uncanny"), Sigmund Freud notes that

> many people experience the feeling [of the uncanny] in the highest degree in relation to death and dead bodies, to the return of the dead, and to spirits and ghosts . . . There is scarcely any other matter . . . upon which our thoughts and feelings have changed so little since the very earliest times, and in which discarded forms have been so completely preserved under a thin disguise, as of our relation to death.[5]

If Hegel disturbs the naturalized discourses in the *Phenomenology*, whether they be those of philosophy or the *Bildungsroman*, with an anticipatory eruption of the Freudian uncanny, we could say as well that Freud finds his own scientific discourse on the death drive equally disturbed by a return to the Hegelian uncanny. The "discarded forms [that] have been so completely preserved under a thin disguise," as we shall see, bear their own unsettling resemblance to a procession of shadowy figures in a key passage of Hegel's text. In both cases, what is discarded returns—first to Hegel, and then more than one hundred years later, to Freud—in an insubstantial disguise.

That disguise is a gothic narrative, one that haunts and disturbs these progressive and rational fictions, whether it is the dialectic or Freudian psychoanalytic theory. Pierre Bourdieu calls attention to the languages of "academic aristocratism" as discursive attempts to suppress oppositional double meanings within a text: "'vulgar' . . . readings . . . highlight the meanings that are negated but not refuted, and doomed by *philosophical sublimation* to the absent presence of a spectral existence."[6] In the interest of such negated readings, this chapter seeks to conjure up the oppositional presence of such spectres ignored in studies of the *Phenomenology* by reading the many ghosts back into Hegel's story of "Geist." In his choice of gothic tropes and scenes, as well as the adoption of a narrative of dispossession and the blocked transmission of history, Hegel redefines male Romantic subjectivity. One of the most significant terms of this redefinition is the feminizing uncanny—figured, in Hegel, as the negative.

Mind is dispossessed of his sexual and cultural identity, inheritance, and property—in other words, his symbolic estate. Opposing the prevalent "masculinist" philosophical language which would establish its exclusive proprietorship of symbolic capital, in other words, reify itself and its objects in the interest of control, the gothic multiplies the effeminizing languages of dispossession. It not only negates the seeming rationality of what is considered the real of the masculine subject's experience, but the rationality of its articulation. In its gothic discourse, mind or reason confronts the extent to which it insists on remaining unreasonable. As representations of the mind knowing or constituting itself, reason finds itself in a position where an unreasonable discourse with gothic narrative becomes a subjective necessity.[7]

While it is crucial to ask why the dead return to Hegel's narrative, for the moment it seems important to stress that their return is, of course, dependent on someone being able to see them. And here we find that Hegel's hero is not alone as a *Geisterseher* (a ghostseer). The post-Enlightenment philosopher finds his project haunted, not in order to be exorcised, but perversely, *motivated* and *constituted* by that which he cannot dispel. In other words, Hegel's protagonist is not the only philosopher-as-ghostseer of his time. One of Immanuel Kant's earliest treatises on metaphysics is his *Träume eines Geistersehers, Erläutert durch Träume der Metaphysik* (Dreams of a Ghostseer, clarified through the Dreams of Metaphysics).[8] Ostensibly in the service of enlightenment rationality, Friedrich Schiller's novella *Der Geisterseher* takes the reading public by storm with its phantasmagoria and Radcliffean supernaturalism, causing Schiller to exclaim in exasperation about the work: "welcher Dämon hat mir ihn eingegeben!" [what demon possessed me to do this!].[9]

Hegel's narrative *Phenomenology* reflects a particularly Romantic fascination with both psychology and the fantastic.[10] John Russon has written of Hegel's counterenlightenment interest in "images of darkness, of night, of the cunning and deceptive powers that operate out of sight," and John Smith has argued that Hegel makes rhetorical use of such phenomena as animal magnetism, phrenology, and clairvoyance in order to tutor the reader's comprehension of Mind.[11] Terry Castle describes the science and philosophy of the late eighteenth century in terms of a shift away from theological explications of apparitions from the spirit world to explicitly psychological theories. As she argues, "the world of ghosts [is relocated] in the closed space of the imagination."[12] While Castle's work treats the supernatural and psychological of the Gothic novel within the empirical project of eighteenth-century British psychology, this essay looks at the *Phenomenology* as a Romantic assimilation and revision of the gothic. Gothic conventions and tropes inform these moments which configure a supernaturalized subjectivity. By interiorizing the uncanny experience, Hegel represents those moments in which the mind and its functioning, that which counts as the masculine self's most intimate core, turns radically alien to itself as the subject of representation and/or knowledge.

What interests me particularly is that Hegel, by writing and reading the gothic into his own narrative, lodges a disturbance in what by now have become standard readings of Hegel's *Phenomenology* as an epic education, as a progression to the synthesizing totality of Absolute Knowing. The gothic *Phenomenology*, in fact, impedes the successful *Bildung* of our masculine subject by preventing the secure claim of an *inheritance*. A stated discursive aim of the text, the claim to inherit history as *his* history, is something the absolute masculine bourgeois subject is bent on achieving. At the same time, the figurative mode of the gothic, aligned, as I will show, with the negative turn of the dialectic, signals Mind's willed disinheritance of his subjective and cultural content. Further, the negative functions not only as the recurring moment and momentum of the narrative but is a metaphor for the very idea of narrativity. This chapter, then, will explore: Hegel's use of gothic tropes, such as doubling, life-in-death, and reanimation, to characterize the subject's experience of the negative moment in the labor of subjective "constitution"; how the inconclusiveness informing conventional gothic narratives structures the dialectic and functions as a condition of possibility for narrative or history, in other words, for culture's highest symbolic functioning; and finally, how the gothic, as this and other Romantic narratives in this book suggest, is experienced as the "emasculating" impediment to the full possession of what Hegel designates as a specifically masculine prerogative: the claim to inheritance or possession of cultural property.

In the last section of the *Phenomenology*, Hegel presents the reader
with an extended figure suggestive of how his project is to be seen, read,
and remembered. This passage runs as follows:

> Die andere Seite aber seines Werdens, die *Geschichte*, ist das *wissende*, sich
> *vermittelnde* Werden—der an die Zeit entäußerte Geist; aber diese Entäußer-
> ung ist ebenso die Entäußerung ihrer selbst; das Negative ist das Negative
> seiner selbst. Dies Werden stellt eine träge Bewegung und Aufeinanderfolge
> von Geistern dar, eine Galerie von Bildern, deren jedes, mit dem vollständi-
> gen Reichtume des Geistes ausgestattet, eben darum sich so träge bewegt,
> weil das Selbst diesen ganzen Reichtum seiner Substanz zu durchdringen
> und zu verdauen hat. . . . Er [verläßt] sein Dasein und [gibt] seine Gestalt
> der Erinnerung über. . . . (590)

> [The other side however of his becoming, *history*, is *knowing* and *self-mediat-
> ing* becoming—Mind that is given over to time; but this giving over is also
> the giving up of himself; the negative is the negative of himself. This becom-
> ing re-presents a slow movement and succession of spirits, a gallery of por-
> traits, in which each, attired with the entire wealth of Mind, moves slowly
> because the self has to penetrate and digest the full riches of his
> substance. . . . He leaves his existence behind and entrusts his shape to
> memory.]

As the spectator of his own Absolute Knowing, the protagonist Mind
takes in the entire dialectical passage as a slowly moving procession of
ghostly figures: "Dies Werden stellt eine träge Bewegung und Aufein-
anderfolge von Geistern dar, eine Galerie von Bildern" [This becoming
re-presents a slow movement and succession of spirits, a gallery of por-
traits]. These spectres from the past, like portraits in a gallery, eye the
spectator who views them. For the subject, watching the ancestral
phantasmagoria is to encompass visually, in literary mimetic form, the
unfolding of his genealogical narrative: the passage through multifari-
ous, inadequate stages of consciousness. Yet it is precisely the voyeur's
controlling distance and will-to-mastery, implicitly assumed by the subject in this scene, that Hegel calls into question. The "reality" of Absolute Knowing posits the eerie "unreality" of its fantasy, i.e., of its
represented relation to itself.

This projected event not only undermines the self-possession of our
voyeur but bears witness to the narrative's radical inconclusiveness.
Mind must "be sunk into the night of self-consciousness": in effect, beginning the *Phenomenology* all over again. In other words, the distance
measuring the distinction between the subject's real mastery and the

superseded reality of these plural, alien figures collapses, and Mind invites or undergoes an ongoing negation:

> Das Geisterreich, das auf diese Weise sich in dem Dasein gebildet, macht eine Aufeinanderfolge aus, worin einer den anderen ablöste . . . der sich als Geist wissende Geist hat zu seinem Wege die Erinnerung der Geister, wie sie an ihnen selbst sind. . . . (591).

> [the realm of spirits which inform themselves into his existence by these means is a succession where one spirit takes the place of the other . . . the mind knowing himself as mind has as its path the remembrance (or interiorization) of spirits, as they are in themselves. . . .]

By dwelling in the position of otherness to himself, through his own death-like suspension, Mind labors to reanimate these deceased figures. Other passages confirm this subjective displacement:

> . . . die Substanz des Individuums, . . . sogar der Weltgeist [hat] die Geduld gehabt, diese Formen in der langen Ausdehnung der Zeit zu durchgehen und die ungeheure Arbeit der Weltgeschichte, in welcher er in jeder den ganzen Gehalt seiner, dessen sie fähig ist, herausgestaltete, zu übernehmen . . . (33–34)

> [the substance of the individual, . . . even World Mind has had the patience to pass through these forms in the long stretch of time and take on the monstrous labor of world history, in which he embodies each to its utmost extent. . . .]

> Andernteils ist bei jedem [Moment] zu verweilen, denn jedes ist selbst eine individuelle ganze Gestalt. (33)

> [On the other hand, it is necessary to linger in each moment, because each moment is itself an individual, entire figure.]

> . . . in diesem Bewegung [des Werdens] geht jedes ruhende Subjekt selbst zugrunde (57).

> [. . . in this movement (of becoming) each resting subject itself is destroyed.]

The "casting" of spectres underlies the dialectical performance of the subject: "I" becomes "not-I."

In making negation constitutive of identity, Hegel recognizes an occult force: self and strange Other meet in *Er-innerung* (memory), the subject's uncanny residence. *Er-innerung* designates both the experience of estrangement and the privileged conceptual space that serves, historically and culturally, as its container. With this experience shifted to the mind, a position of safety becomes increasingly difficult to maintain; instead of providing a home for himself, Hegel's Mind includes frightening others who undermine his substantial security.[13] An experience where two opposed meanings coincide, where the *un-*, or the negative aspect of *unheimlich*, does not count, defines the uncanny event for the subject, according to Freud.[14] This is the case in Hegel, where the *not* at home, the *un*heimlich, finds itself very much at home in Mind. Blurring the distinctions between supposedly stable conceptual pairs, this event points

> neither to the interior nor to the exterior, but . . . there where the most intimate interiority coincides with the exterior and becomes threatening . . . The [uncanny] is simultaneously the intimate kernel and the foreign body.[15]

Unsettling a privatizing fantasy of domesticity and property in the person, an unfamiliar presence emerges repeatedly as the innermost self, though the subject resists this dispossession, claiming it is inflicted upon him by a foreign force (*eine fremde Gewalt*). His difference, however, is to himself.[16] Projection as a psychic response to the terror of internal division defines or characterizes the "male gothic," so that a predominant feature of "male gothic" fictions is the monster outside trying to reclaim its space inside.[17] Self-possession—the masculine subject's complacent investment in a self-contained, substantial, and inalienable interiority as that with which he feels at home (*bei sich*)—is foreclosed by what Hegel calls negation.

It is in the *Phenomenology*'s preface that Hegel first presents this capacity for self-understanding as a *negative* capacity:

> Sie [die lebendige Substanz] ist als Subjekt die reine *einfache Negativität*, eben dadurch die Entzweiung des Einfachen; *oder* [italics mine] die entgegengesetzte Verdopplung, welche wieder die Negation dieser gleichgültigen Verschiedenheit und ihres Gegensatzes ist. (23)

> [As subject, living substance is pure, *simple negativity*, and for this reason, the division of what is single; *or*, in opposition to this simple negativity, subject is the doubling, the negation of this indifferent difference of simple negativity, its contrary.]

Hegel positions the subject between two forms of negation: an *entzweien* (to divide in two) and a *verdoppeln* (to double). While *entzweien* means to divide or split what is single into two (i.e., simple negation), *verdoppeln*, the negating of this simple negative, implies a mirroring. As he fixes the idea of the subject, Hegel's words curiously unfix themselves. It is not clear whether the subject arises through simple negativity *or* through double negativity. In this oscillating ambiguity of Hegel's "or," I would suggest, we find a symptom of the subject's own restlessness with his definition. Is it a rhetorical "or," indicating a progression, a self-reflexive correction of the first position? Or does it also mean "and": a double-take of the same event, a splitting of his own perspective? To be a subject is to experience the self in an odd simultaneity of separation and recognition, an oscillation between difference and identity. Mind projects his representation as a gothic *Doppelgänger*, or double, and gets a "deadly" glimpse *of himself as an other*.[18]

In fact, Hegel's description of the dialectic's negative moment dramatizes this confrontation as a dying or death:

> denn nur darum, daß das Konkrete sich scheidet und zum Unwirklichen macht, ist es das sich Bewegende . . . Der Tod, wenn wir jene Unwirklichkeit so nennen wollen, ist das Furchtbarste . . . Das Leben, . . . das ihn [den Tod] erträgt und in ihm sich erhält, ist das Leben des Geistes. Er gewinnt seine Wahrheit nur, indem er in der absoluten Zerrissenheit sich selbst findet . . . Er ist diese Macht nur, indem er dem Negativen ins Angesicht schaut, bei ihm verweilt. Dieses Verweilen ist die Zauberkraft, die es in das Sein umkehrt. (35–36)

> [Only for this reason, that the concrete (life) passes away and makes itself (one of the) unreal, is it that which moves . . . Death, if we want to call that unreality by this name, is the most horrific . . . the life . . . that bears (death) and maintains itself in it, is the life of Mind. He (Mind) achieves his truth only to the extent that he finds himself in absolute division (or dismemberment). . . . He is the power (of truth) only insofar as he looks the negative in the face, and remains with it. This lingering is the magic power that transforms it (the face of the negative) into essence.]

What is concrete *scheidet sich*, a reflexive verb which, among its other meanings, signifies to split, or to part from something or someone. Euphemistically, it also means "to die" (as in "to pass away"). According to Hegel, this "passing away" exemplifies the dialectic as *das sich Bewegende*, that which moves into the unreal (*zum Unwirklichen*). Experiencing a gap in the present—that is, an inconsistency between his concrete, substantial immediacy and his self-representation, self-consciousness makes that immediacy look as unreal as his past (shapes). This split *constitutes* mind as a subject: "Er gewinnt seine Wahrheit nur, indem er in der absoluten Zerrissenheit sich selbst findet" (He achieves his truth only to the extent that he finds himself in absolute division). Because his identity is paradoxically "proven" in an experience of non-identity, Hegel can speak of the negative dialectic of consciousness as precisely such a supernaturalized experience of "living death": "Das Leben, . . . das ihn [den Tod] erträgt und in ihm sich erhält, ist das Leben des Geistes" (the life that bears death and maintains itself in it, is the life of Mind).[19] Literalizing the metaphor, Hegel's subject must repeatedly "give up the ghost." The *Phenomenology*'s ending addresses the necessity of always having to begin over again in the face of this returning limit: "he must begin unconstrainedly and let it [the ghostly shape] raise him up again, as if all that came before were lost to him . . . Mind begins his education again from the beginning" [*er (hat) ebenso unbefangen von vorn . . . anzufangen und sich von ihr auf wieder großzuziehen, als ob alles Vorhergehende für ihn verloren wäre . . . dieser Geist (fängt) seine Bildung . . . wieder von vorn (an)*] (590–91).

As readers, then, we could ask Hegel: why is the *Phenomenology*'s conclusion haunted with ancestral ghosts? Why have the dead returned? The presence of a ghost signifies an improper burial or an improper memorialization by the living:

> . . . something went wrong with [the] obsequies. The return of the dead is a sign of a disturbance in the symbolic rite, in the process of symbolization; the dead return as collectors of some unpaid symbolic debt.[20]

The *Phenomenology* acknowledges Mind's failed interment of his history—in other words, its narrative insufficiency.

On the one hand, this insufficiency is symptomatic of the subject's entry into reflexivity or self-consciousness, into being able to think about himself in time, which is necessarily an entry into the universalizing network of language, of culture's symbolic.[21] As such, it always entails the "death" of the concrete and particular individual in a universal language (nur darum, daß das Konkrete sich scheidet und zum Unwirklichen macht).[22] To know himself, the subject becomes enmeshed in a discursive medium which, while making him a social subject, subsumes his singular experience. Symbolization fails to compensate the subject for the perceived loss of immediacy. Some *thing* is irrevocably lost, set adrift, made homeless: namely, the subject's unity with his immediate or concrete experience. This *thing* is the ghost that returns to haunt the subject, reminding him of his failure to memorialize adequately the richness of experience. Thus, Hegel refers to the wealth of substance that these "insubstantial" figures carry: "[Geister] . . . mit dem vollständigen Reichtume des Geistes ausgestattet, . . . diese[m] ganzen Reichtum[e] seiner Substanz" [spirits arrayed with the complete wealth of Mind, the whole wealth of his substance] (590). Faced with this plenitude of substance and responding to this lack, memory clings to the reminders of what is unrecuperated—the individual's full, positive immediacy—and acknowledges that something will not have been transformed symbolically, always.[23]

A purely melancholic interpretation of *Erinnerung* is insufficient, though, because of its failure to accomplish a dialectical turn. If negation evokes the horrors of a subjective death, it is because the subject captured by "the face" of the negative (*er [schaut] dem Negativen ins Angesicht*, 35–36) imagines he sees a physiognomy emerging at the expense of his own. Just as in the passage where *entzweien* entails a *verdoppeln*, division here too is recast as a doubling. It is the self-conscious moment that guarantees to the subject, however, that a self has been effaced. Hegel construes the negative, alienating moment as the moment of substance *and* subject: an insight that helps illuminate the paradox of why those *insubstantial* ghosts of the concluding passage move so heavily (*träge*) with their *substantial* weight. The positive content—the immediacy of being a fully self-identical substance—does not correspond to any actual experience, since the subject is always already in language (and thus, in lack). It is a belated fantasy.

It may help to imagine the dialectic's negative moment as the subject's "phobic" confrontation with himself. Adam Phillips describes how the *reliability* of the phobic's terror acts as a form of self-protection, a way of insuring that the self (and the past) continue to exist.[24] Securing knowledge—especially of the most unbearable experience in an uncertain world—provides the subject with control. Because its terror never changes and because it is never surprising, the phobic object relays the sense of a secure self. When the self feels most threatened, it "freezes." With its insistence on sameness, the phobia is the psyche's way of refuting explanation, skepticism, and opportunity.

Phobias install a clear boundary between a threatened self and what is projected as a threatening external world. The subject, "as a victim of terror[,] is as far as possible, in his own mind, from being the one who terrorizes."[25] In Hegel, the negative's terror elicits from Mind the reactionary, habitual response of the phobic: confronting him from the outside (as a *fremde Gewalt*, an alien force, 54), the not-I of the negative proposes to displace what the subject can then hold onto "for dear life"—the idea of himself. The phobic object only looks like an unbearable meeting with non-identity. What the subject experiences as the "outsideness" or externality of the negative is, as Hegel proposes, only the unacknowledged, unmediated part of himself.[26] It is a place that holds a part of the subject that he has not known or spoken about but comes to recognize as his own.[27]

The negative as phobia dramatizes the desire for what one does not yet know how to say about oneself, and the desire that there will always be something that one has not yet managed to say.[28] If the negative (or phobia) were to be mastered, if the narrative were to end, how would one live without ghosts—the symbolic wealth that *das Furchtbarste* offers? The uncanny negative suggests an idea of significance that Hegel counts on to return. Just as the phobic irrationally refuses to relinquish his phobia, the Hegelian subject chooses to dwell (*verweilen*) with his terror. The phobic refusal to give up what feels most unbearable about oneself is a way to honor one's promise.[29]

Negation is central to the dialectic, since it is that which moves it, the motor, *das sich Bewegende*. It is the possibility of a narrative, and at the same time, that which prevents conclusion. Like the recurrent discoveries of lost or hidden manuscripts in gothic tales, the negative keeps resurfacing, and its reappearance implies the absence of a conclusive story (as well as the illusion that one is there to be told). Readers familiar with the eighteenth-century gothic know how the recovered, barely decipherable manuscripts promise more than they deliver. They divert as much as direct, and they fail to produce conclusive knowledge. It is not only the villain who, by usurping another's title and inheritance, usurps identity; these fragmentary manuscripts postpone the revelation of identity and thereby, the social recognition or authenticity vouchsafed by the establishment of a line of inheritance. Partial as these manuscripts are, the negative measures Hegel's skepticism of movement as equivalent to progress.[30]

A position of rest is not attained, and what counts as philosophy in the *Phenomenology* is structured by the interminability and formal repetition characteristic of the gothic novel. The *Phenomenology*'s closing lines articulate the implicit irony of its narrative achievement, the *telos* of Absolute Knowing, by misquoting the final lines of Schiller's poem "Die Freundschaft" ("Friendship"):

Schiller's lines: Hegel's lines:

Fand das höchste Wesen schon kein
gleiches,
Aus dem Kelch des ganzen Seelenreiches   aus dem Kelche dieses Geisterreiches
Schäumt ihm—die Unendlichkeit.[31]   schäumt ihm seine Unendlichkeit.

[If the highest being as yet has found no
equal,
Out of the chalice of the whole realm of   [Out of the chalice of this realm of
souls   spirits
Spumes forth for him—infinitude]   Spumes forth for him—his
                                                infinitude.]

Quoting only the last two lines of these three, Hegel's phenomenological protagonist stands as their subject, not Schiller's "highest being."
The particularity of *dieses Geisterreiches* (*this* realm of *spirits* or *spectres*)
replaces Schiller's abstract and transcendent totality of the *ganzen Seelenreiches* (the *whole* realm of *souls*). Consistent with this deflation, the possessive pronomial adjective *seine* (his) modifies, and limits, infinity: "aus
dem Kelche dieses Geisterreiches / schäumt ihm seine Unendlichkeit"
[out of the chalice of this realm of spirits / Spumes forth for him *his*
infinitude] (my italics). Unlike Schiller's highest being, who, without a
friend or equal (*kein gleiches*), expresses a hopeful patience commensu-
rate with the eternity of souls available for consolation, Hegel's subject
has no friend except, ironically, the skeletal remains he finds himself
surrounded by. The "place" of Absolute Knowing, according to Hegel,
is the place of remains, literally of skulls (*Schädelstätte*). Schiller's chalice
with its future promise becomes Hegel's chalice of history. The *Phenomenology*'s subject hymns (toasts) to the infinity of an interminable conversation with the dead.[32]
    The insistence, then, of Hegel's subject that, while he may not be
Schiller's highest being, he is not a "lifeless solitary" (*leblose Einsame*)
appears grounded on uncertainty:

    . . . beide zusammen [die Geschichte und die Wissenschaft des erscheinen-
    den Wissens], die begriffene Geschichte, bilden die Erinnerung und die
    Schädelstätte des absoluten Geistes, die Wirklichkeit, Wahrheit und Gewiß-
    heit seines Throns, ohne den er das leblose Einsame wäre (591).

    [. . . both together [history and the science of knowing in the realm of ap-
    pearances], history comprehended, inform memory and the places of the

skulls of absolute Mind, the reality, truth and certainty of his throne, without which he were a lifeless solitary.]

Does Hegel "protest too much," when he boasts of the reality, truth, and certainty of his throne? By conjuring up the lifeless solitary as, syntactically, the final shape of the *Phenomenology*, does he implicitly suggest a negative truth to Absolute Knowing? Following his triumphal claim, three negatives appear in close succession: the preposition of dispossession, "without" (*ohne*); the negated adjective, "life*less*" (*leblos*); and the suspension of the indicative mode with the subjunctive "were" (*wäre*), a mode which negates reality in favor of an imagination of the unreal. Describing what "would have been" had he had not achieved his throne, Hegel's hero projects an "other" image of himself as a kind of photographic negative: the usurped and lifeless sovereign, alienated from his authority and community.

This "other" who disturbs the triumphal conclusion is in fact resurfacing after a prior appearance. When Hegel describes narrative conclusion in his preface, he indicates that, were his subject to arrive at that point, his final entrance would be as a corpse (*Leichnam*):

> denn die Sache ist nicht in ihrem Zwecke erschöpft, sondern in ihrer Ausführung, noch ist das Resultat das wirkliche Ganze, sondern es zusammen mit seinem Werden; der Zweck für sich ist das unlebendige Allgemeine, wie die Tendenz das bloße Treiben, das seiner Wirklichkeit noch entbehrt, und das nackte Resultat ist der Leichnam, der die Tendenz hinter sich gelassen. (13)

> [for the matter is not exhausted in its goal, but in its unfolding, nor is the result the true whole, but together with its becoming; the goal by itself is the lifeless universal, just as the tendency is mere activity which renounces its reality, and the bare result is a corpse, one that has left behind the tendency.]

Hegel expresses anxiety about narrative progression *and* closure through the metaphors of the automaton and the corpse, respectively. The subject defined only through its movement is like an automaton. The subject beyond process and becoming, past the necessity of movement, is at a dead end: "the goal [der Zweck] by itself is a lifeless universal. . . . the bare result [das Resultat] is a corpse."[33] For Hegel, what does not move itself is what is dead: "denn das Tote, weil es sich selbst nicht bewegt, kommt nicht zu Unterscheiden des Wesens, nicht zur wesentlichen Entgegensetzung oder Ungleichheit" [since it does not move itself, what is dead does not come to differentiate its essence, does not come to any essential opposition or inequality] (45).

This kind of stasis characterizes the unmediated absolute as well. Hegel writes that it is impossible to say more about absolutes than a word or two, since they go by names such as "the divine" or "the eternal": "die Worte des Göttlichen, Absoluten, Ewigen, usw. [sprechen das nicht aus], was darin enthalten ist; —und nur solche Worte drükken in der Tat die Anschauung als das Unmittelbare aus" [the words of the divine, the absolute, the eternal, and so on, do not express that which is contained within them; and only such words express in fact the viewpoint of the immediate] (24). Because an absolute has no (self-relating) predicates, it does not allow for difference and hence, cannot reflect its own development. It lacks a narrative. To generate a narrative is to move from a word to a sentence, to move into particular discourses. As Hegel writes, it is to move into difference:

> Was mehr ist als ein solches Wort, der Übergang auch nur zu einem Satze, enthält ein *Anderswerden*, das zurückgenommen werden muß, ist eine Vermittlung. Diese aber ist das, was <u>perhorresziert</u> wird, als ob dadurch, daß mehr aus ihr gemacht wird denn nur dies, daß sie nichts Absolutes und im Absoluten gar nicht sei, die absolute Erkenntnis aufgeben wäre.
>
> Dies <u>Perhorreszieren</u> stammt aber in der Tat aus der Unbekanntschaft mit der Natur der Vermittlung und des absoluten Erkennens selbst. Denn die Vermittlung ist nichts anderes als die sich bewegende Sichselbstgleichheit, oder sie ist die Reflexion in sich selbst, das Moment des fürsichseienden Ich, die reine Negativität oder auf ihre reine Abstraktion herabgesetzt, das *einfache Werden*. (24–25, my underlining)

[Whatever is more than such a word, the transition even to a single sentence is a mediation, contains a *becoming different*, which must be taken back. This becoming different is what provokes horror, as if thereby nothing were to come of it other than that absolute knowledge (Erkenntis) would be surrendered, since mediation is not absolute and does not exist within the absolute.

This provoked horror, however, stems from an ignorance of the nature of mediation and absolute knowledge itself. For this reason: mediation is nothing other than self-continuity which moves itself, or reflection in itself, the moment of the I being for itself, pure negativity, or reduced to its pure abstraction, *simple becoming.*]

Negation as narrative movement unleashes a gothic dread because it confronts the subject of absolute knowing with the shifting ground between the transforming subject of narration and the narrated subject.[34]

The fear of relinquishing a quasi-divine status inspires horror, that is, the impulse to resist alienation and the provisional.

To literalize this fear, Hegel suggestively inserts a foreign word (*Fremdwort*) —*perhorreszieren*—into his German. The alien word mocks, even as it stands for, this emotional and intellectual resistance to change.[35] Derived from the Latin *perhorresco, perhorreszieren* is translated with the verbs *zurückschrecken, von sich weisen, aufschrecken, sich entsetzen* and *schauern*—to recoil in terror from, to repel, to be startled, to stand in awe or dread of, and to tremble greatly.[36] Sounding a catalog of the affective responses of gothic protagonists, it is perhaps *schauern* (to shudder) that most closely suggests the Hegelian affinity for the gothic, since German gothic novels go by the name *Schauerromane* (novels that provoke shuddering).

When he is surveying all his mediated content, the subject of Absolute Knowing rests, like God, satisfied with the view. The complacency of the enthroned subject arises from his sense of familiarity (*Bekannt-sein*) with his content. His mastery of difference ends with indifference. If the absolute subject asserts that he has brought history to a conclusion, he exists as a lifeless universal without a narrative. For Hegel, the universal and the absolute both are results: "Es ist von dem Absoluten zu sagen, daß es wesentlich *Resultat*, daß es erst am *Ende* das ist, was es in Wahrheit ist . . . das Absolute, wie es zuerst und unmittelbar ausgesprochen wird, ist nur das Allgemeine" [one can say about the absolute that it is essentially a result, that it is only at the end that which it truly is . . . the absolute, when it is immediately and first spoken of, is only the universal] (24). And if the subject of Absolute Knowing is "self-conscious freedom that is at rest" (*die selbstbewußte Freiheit, die in sich ruht*), then his rest reflects the corpse-like immobility of the universal, as Hegel himself has figured it. The absolute subject mirrors the subject as universal mind with no past left to be mediated.[37] Since mediation is not absolute and does not exist within the absolute, the lifeless solitary emerges as the negative moment of Absolute Knowing. It is the point where the subject is lifeless (*leblos*), because he is no longer moving. He is a solitary (*Einsame*), because the "universal subject" of absolute knowing represents individualism taken *to its absolute limit*, to the point where he confuses his particular standpoint with universality, where everything opposed to him is effaced.[38]

In accordance with this negative dialectic of universals and absolutes, Slavoj Žižek draws attention to the parallel between the universal negation of the conclusion and the absolute negation exercised during the French Revolution's regime of Terror.[39] To see this parallel, we should turn briefly to Hegel's discussion of Absolute Negation in the *Phenome-nology*'s section on the French Revolution. Absolute Negation is the moment when

> alle diese Bestimmungen sind in dem Verluste, den das Selbst in der absoluten Freiheit erfährt, verloren; seine Negation ist der bedeutungslose Tod, der reine Schrecken des Negativen, das nichts Positives, nicht Erfüllendes in ihm hat. (439)

> [all these determinations vanish in the loss experienced by the self in absolute freedom; his negation is the death that is meaningless, the pure terror of the negative that holds nothing positive, holds nothing that satisfies it.]

The negation that corresponds to the French Revolution is characterized by an absolute freedom. Hegel maintains that the abstract universal will characteristic of the French Revolution represents a "negative" freedom: *a universal freedom from* the subjection to another's will. As a purely formal freedom, however, Hegel links it to the Terror (*das reine Schrecken des Negativen, das nichts Positives . . . in ihm hat*). The Terror prevents the enduring effects of any individual will, since the performance of any individual will reintroduces substantial or positive difference: the real social divisions of class, power, properties, rights, and privileges.[40] Absolute Freedom is Absolute Negation—in other words, the Terror. It obliterates all substantial differences between individual wills by destroying individuals who attempt to exercise theirs. The Terror leads to annihilating individuals *en masse*. At the same time, the truth of the Terror is that the actions of its universal will are always only the will of an individual.

Hegel attempts to distinguish the experience of Absolute Negation from that of Absolute Knowing: a significant distinction for him, since the latter corresponds to German idealism, and hence, his philosophical project. Yet the mind at the conclusion of the *Phenomenology* exercises its absolute capacity for negation *ideally* upon itself as it goes into the "night of self-consciousness." The *reine Schrecken* of the French Revolution becomes aligned with what Hegel calls the *Furchtbarste* of the negative moment. Absolute Knowing reflects the internalized power of the negative.[41]

Pairing the rhetorical strategies of gothic novels and the political writings of the French Revolution, Ronald Paulson points to their shared motifs of *justification* and *excess*. Both the novels and the pamphlets foreground the justifiable, if excessive, breaking of unjust restraints and the unjustified assumption of the oppressor's excessively tyrannical role by the erstwhile oppressed.[42] If the French Revolution and the gothic point to both the liberatory divestment of particular identities, powers, and properties, *and* to an illegitimate resurfacing of a kind of absolute tyranny, Hegel's narrative representation of Absolute Knowing encapsulates these aspects as well. "Mind knowing itself as mind" justifies the destruction of each determinate, discursive incarnation. Exercising his absolute freedom, he relegates it to history. The subject of Absolute Knowing achieves his universality in this absolutely negative capacity to divest narratively, to be liberated from each "tyrannizing" discursive interpretation of his history or memory, each stage of his passage.

The French Revolution becomes the paradigmatic event and figure for narrative momentum, for the freedom to remember things differently by representing them differently in discourse. Such freedom to remember implies, however, the terror of forgetting.[43] Revolutionary narrative is neither exempted from its failures nor is it identical to them. That such narrative transformation is not redemptive, that it ends up frustrated, is part of the burden of absolute freedom. Hegel's subject finds himself situated in a gothic narrative of mastery and revolt (the absolute is defined as its incommensurability with substance). Since the negative is unceasing, the narrative (and the embodiment of its will, our protagonist) shall continue, even though he, as a former executioner, will himself be executed. The *Phenomenology*'s ongoing labor consists in the freedom to reject, compulsively, each memory of its history: to forget each appropriation and investment in a particular discourse, one whose subject is destined to fall victim to the revolutionary terror of his own negative capacity.

The negative face of Absolute Knowing, the lifeless solitary, reminds the subject of Absolute Knowing of his throne's illegitimacy. What is illegitimacy if not a figure for unreadability—what cannot be recognized *and* maintained in narrative? As the lifeless solitary, the subject becomes illegitimate because he is illegible in the present of Absolute Knowing—in the absence of a living other, a not-I.[44] He locates himself somewhere between those barely legible ghosts and the materiality of the superseded skull. By making the constitutive principle of the subject a negative one of freedom, his tarrying (*Verweilen*) with the negative is the ironic countermoment to the corpse-like reality of self-conscious freedom that falsely imagines itself at rest and at home with its already narrated memories. Instead, with movement and with the unreal, those transformative experiences of subjective loss, he finds his narrative, his history in the act of telling: "das Bestehen des Daseins . . . ist selbst seine Ungleichheit mit sich und seine Auflösung" [the continuance of existence . . . is his difference to himself and his dissolution] (53).[45]

In Hegel, the subject's efforts to write a legitimizing history are doomed. The heir creates his precursors retroactively from what he no longer is. In exile, the solitary denies the subject's possession of his throne, his position of dominance, and an empire over which to dominate. His re-introduction of alienation and difference to the subject of Absolute Knowing expresses the free production of discourse that such uncanny presences compel. The ghosts of *Geist* are the concepts that haunt his new science; a philosophy of knowing what can neither be symbolically captured nor forgotten. As he compulsively remembers, trying to grasp the "figures of the mind . . . [who] are negative and pass away" [*Gestalten des Geistes . . . sind . . . Momente . . . (die) negativ und verschwindend (sind)*, 46], his narrative keeps forgetting, i.e. losing "its path . . . the remembrance of spirits . . . and the organization of their realm" [*Das Ziel, das absolute Wissen, oder der sich als Geist wissende Geist hat zu seinem Wege die Erinnerung der Geister . . . und die Organisation ihres Reiches*, 591].

~

. . . *in der That, Sie müssen von Zeit zu Zeit nach Ihrem Gute sehen, es fällt sicher sonst alles in Ruinen . . .*

[*. . . You must really look after your estate from time to time, or else it will surely fall into ruins . . .]*

Hegel to Niethammer, 10 December 1804

As outlined in the introduction of this study, the gothic is the genre of real and symbolic dispossession: focusing on the separations from the paternal estate, the blockages that impede the transmission and inheritance of patrilineal property.[46] It is in this concern with inheritance that Hegel's *Phenomenology* more fully allies itself with the gothic genre. Having studied the supernatural procession Hegel views as a narrative of the ongoing (de)constitutive work of subjectivity and as a figure for narrativity in mimetic form, it should be addressed in its relation to what Hegel understands as a cultural estate or property. As the narrator remarks of the passing silhouettes (*Schattenrisse*) of history: "Dieses vergangene Dasein ist bereits erworbenes Eigentum des allgemeinen Geistes" [This past existence is the already attained property of universal mind] (32).[47] Our hero's dilemma is that this accumulated property (*Eigentum*) of universal mind is striking not only for its plenitude, its weight and accumulation, but paradoxically, due to Hegel's choice of metaphor, for its insubstantiality.[48]

From his spectatorial position, our hero cannot see anything but life-less things in the property of universal mind which, since it belongs to all, does not belong to him. It is only when a thing is *needed* that it can become the property of a particular individual.[49] A kind of "unclaimed freight," the advertisement of the dialectic would create a personal need or desire to invest in it. Designating the past (these spectral figures) as culture's "unclaimed freight," Hegel places his masculine subject in the position to appropriate it as his own, rightful inheritance:

> Die Bildung in dieser Rücksicht besteht, von der Seite des Individuums aus betrachtet, darin, daß es *dies Vorhandene erwerbe*, . . . *für sich in Besitz nehme*. (33, my italics).

> [In regard to this, from the standpoint of the individual, education consists in appropriating what is at hand . . . to acquire it as one's own property.]

> Die Wissenschaft stellt sowohl diese bildende Bewegung in ihrer Ausführ-lichkeit und Notwendigkeit als [auch] das, was schon zum Momente und *Eigentum* des Geistes herabgesunken ist, in seiner Gestaltung dar. (33, my italics)

> [Through its figures, [Philosophy] represents not only this educative move-ment in its entirety and necessity, but also that which has already been re-duced to moments and property of Mind.]

As the movement of the dialectic, education (*Bildung*) is transformed grammatically into an active verb, a taking-into-possession (*in Besitz nehmen*), whereby the protagonist becomes the individual proprietor of culture and landlords history, storing or collecting in his own house the riches of its reanimated spirits.[50]

Throughout the preface, Hegel consistently sustains this distinction between *Eigentum* (property) and the will as it expresses itself through the act of appropriation (*in Besitz nehmen, übernehmen, erwerben*). *Eigentum* stands for culture's symbolic property, a social inheritance or treasury (*Kulturgut*), and as such, it belongs to the abstract "universal Mind" (*bereits erworbenes Eigentum des allgemeinen Geistes*). The social subject is determined (positioned) in relation to this treasury, even without the work of reflection.[51] Hegel aligns this *bereits erworbenes Eigentum* (already inherited property) with simple, i.e., unmediated, negation as the point where the subject of history has not yet reflected upon what he has inherited in the form of cultural property: "Das . . . Dasein ist durch jene erste Negation nur erst *unmittelbar* in das Element des Selbsts versctzt; dieses ihm erworbene Eigentum hat also noch denselben Charakter unbegriffener Unmittelbarkeit, unbewegter Gleichgültigkeit wie das Dasein selbst; dieses ist so nur in die *Vorstellung* übergegangen" [Through this first negation, existence is only just displaced *immediately* into the element of the self; this his acquired property still has the same quality of uncomprehended immediacy, unmoving indifference just like existence itself; this existence has just passed over into a *representation*] (34–35).

As such representations, the spectral figures are alienating abstractions without subjective content: "In der neueren Zeit hingegen findet das Individuum die abstrakte Form vorbereitet; . . . jetzt besteht . . . die Arbeit . . . darin, . . . das Allgemeine zu verwirklichen und zu begeisten" [In contrast, in modern times the individual finds the abstraction already prepared; now his work consists in this, that the universal become realized and subjectivized] (37). If, as we noted before, the mind "goes" supernatural, we can also say that property goes mental. The subject's desire to invest in this *Bildung* bears witness not only to the symbolic and subjectivized nature of cultural capital but the refusal to relegate commodification and property to an objective marketplace or an objectified dimension.

Hegel's interest in possession can be traced to his reading of Karl Friedrich von Savigny's *Treatise on Possession* in 1803.[52] A number of Savigny's concerns directly relate to the *Phenomenology*. Savigny traces the enduring inheritance of Roman law in modern times by examining its critical distinction between property or *Eigentum* (the use of a thing at will) and possession or *Besitz* (the acquisition or loss of the possession of property). His treatise considers only possession, with sections on the concept of possession, on acquiring and losing possession, on remedies for protecting possession, as well as on contemporary modifications of Roman legal thought. His emphasis on Roman law is critical, since through a will or testament, the Romans were the first to practice dispossession and to allow for a *nonnatural* inheritance (bequeathing property to someone not related by blood). They thereby severed the individual from tradition and nature.[53] Further, Savigny emphasizes possession as the will to possess, as an *animus possidendi*. More than a corporeal relation to an object or the exercise of a superior force over a thing, Savigny's references to the consciousness of the possessor turn upon the necessity of a mental *act* of desiring.[54]

Seen from this angle, the dialectic becomes the accumulative act of cultural *investiture*. It is education as the reflexive work through which Mind mentally grasps and situates himself where culture's symbolic property has already positioned him. In the desire to give a home to the perceived otherness of culture's version of history, Hegel's appropriative gestures imply a conservative strain. The entropic principle of recuperation becomes a kind of death wish, a desire for convention, a belief in assimilation—what, in our time, we might express with the exclusionary idea of a culture's "family values." When Hegel says that the subject "brings home" his property, he imagines the dialectic as a massive domestication of history. The subject undoes his difference to culture by making it familiar, native: "the 'becoming native' of the concrete content" (*das einheimische Werden des konkreten Inhalts*). This internal assimilation is his symbolic investiture.[55]

The seignorial, distant pose of the invested subject implies a past made into a kind of historical collection or museum.[56] The offer of the museum, of course, is that its contents belong to the visitor (as collective property), thereby consoling him for the degradation of culture to lifeless property. If, to use Herbert Marcuse's words, the unfree subject is the one who conquers matter and objectifies the world, then in Hegel he must carry the dead weight of his conquest.[57] And in fact, when he looks at that procession of spirits as a spectator, the subject is in a position where Absolute Knowing begins to feel like unfreedom. Like Nietzsche's nihilist, his eye

> is unfaithful to his memories—it lets them drop, lose their leaves. It does not protect them from fading to a corpselike pallor like that which debility casts over what is distant and past. And what the nihilist fails to do for himself he neglects to do for mankind's entire past—he lets it drop.[58]

Every spectator remains a nihilist. The veil over the past reflects a subject who, without facing the animating and terrifying uncanny, condemns the past to fade to ghostliness, divorced from its proximity. The slow movement (*träge Bewegung*) of what the spectator sees bears witness to the heavy weight of a past he has reduced to the mortality that clings to property. The spectator must enter the procession, abandoning nihilism in favor of negation. In other words, he must give up the dominating, leisurely position from which he considers whether the past is relevant.

Hence, the dialectic's negative moment unleashes a desire for *divestiture*. Here we should pause a moment on the Hegelian word *Entäußerung*, because Hegel designates the manifold activity of the negative with

this word. The usual English translation of *Entäußerung* is externalization or alienation, but in its legal usage, *Entäußerung* is the divestment
or alienation of property. Giving oneself up to that night of self-consciousness is to be dispossessed. This is not only because one loses *oneself*, the wealth of a concrete and particular substantiality.[59] Negation
defamiliarizes by making the known (what is *bekannt*) look alien. Culture's symbolic property becomes unreal (*unwirklich*) at the moment it
is re-cognized (*erkannt*) as such. Reduced in his own sight to symbolic
reification, to inherited property (*bereits erworbenes Eigentum*), or inclusion under an abstract universality, the subject negates the given and
spins into a state of dispossession. Following Savigny, by a new and
contrary mental act, Hegel's subject refuses his inheritance. The negating subject is not identical or reducible to his mental property. Hegel
makes this willed dispossession the positive condition wherein the historical subject emerges. He is a subject insofar as he is an *animus nonpos-
sidendi*. And though he is reimbursed with different cultural property,
supposedly "of a higher value," it too will prove inadequate and lead to
another divestment.

Importantly, the act of dispossession poses a particular threat to gender identity, as a passage in the preface suggests:

> so sehen wir . . . was in früheren Zeitaltern den reifen Geist der Männer
> beschäftigte, zu Kenntnissen, Übungen und selbst Spielen des Knabenalters
> herabgesunken und werden in dem pädagogischen Fortschreiten die wie im
> Schattenrisse nachgezeichnete Geschichte der Bildung der Welt erkennen.
> (32)

> [so we see that what in former ages engaged the attention of men of mature
> mind, has been reduced to facts, exercises, and even games for boys; and in
> the boy's progress through school, we recognize the history of the cultural
> development of the world traced, as it were, in a silhouette.]

Although it once engaged "the attention of men of mature mind," the
wealth of these spectral figures appears to do so no longer. *Bildung* is
degraded to "facts, exercises, and even games for boys." Yet the mind
of Hegel's subject must become immature, a boy. He plays those boys'
games (*Spiele des Knabenalters*) in which he sees the silhouettes of "the
cultural development of the world." If it seems that we are straying far
from the gothic, I would point to the connotative affinity of the German
word for silhouette or shadow figure, *Schattierung*, with *Schattenreich*
(the realm of spirits), the semantic field of Hegel's gothic. When the
male protagonist perceives that he is acting out a less than mature mas-

culinity, the dialectical fantasy of possessing the past or mastering history becomes a gothic tale of gender- and gendered dispossession. A
crisis ensues for the male who, by interacting with these shadowy figures, simultaneously stakes a claim to possess property while he continuously wills his own dispossession.

The masculine prerogative to property is jettisoned in the divesting
activity of negation.[60] The subject is compelled to give up inherited
wealth as the identification with given masculine sociosymbolic roles,
affixing the horrific quality of the negative to the emasculating effect of
dispossession, the loss of any stable, "proper" position of authority. In
a slightly different context, when Hegel anticipates resistance to the
Phenomenology, he speaks of the "shame" (*Schande*) the reader will experience when he finds himself having to give up his authority:

> Eine solche Aufnahme pflegt die erste Reaktion des Wissens, dem etwas
> unbekannt war, dagegen zu sein, um die Freiheit und eigene Autorität gegen
> die fremde (denn auch unter dieser Gestalt erscheint das jetzt zuerst Auf-
> genommene) zu retten, — auch um den Schein und die Art von Schande, die
> darin liegen soll, daß etwas gelernt worden sei, wegzuschaffen . . . (55)

> [Such an inclusion [of what is new] tends to produce an oppositional reac-
> tion, first in the knowing for which something is unknown, in order to save
> its own freedom and its own perspective, one's own authority in the face of
> what is foreign (for what is first taken in appears in this shape [of foreign-
> ness]) — also in order to dismiss the appearance and kind of shame which
> supposedly adheres to having learned something . . .]

This passage makes clear that to learn (the dialectic is a *Bildung*) is to
risk feeling ashamed, because the protagonist (as Hegel's diegetic
reader) must acknowledge the interpretive limits of the knowledge he
possesses along with the freedom and authority it confers. He must relinquish his maturity in favor of what amounts to a "shameful" emasculation in the face of the unknown.

The Hegelian subject is only belatedly a male subject through his
identifications with prior shapes, who themselves have no prior ontological truth. The protagonist's distress might be called, after Lacoue-
Labarthe, a specifically male hysteria:

> . . . that kind of pluralization and fragmentation of the "subject" [is] pro-
> voked from the outset by its linguistic or "symbolic" (de)constitution: an
> effect of discourses, the "self"-styled "subject" always threatens to "consist"
> of nothing more than a series of heterogeneous and dissociated roles, and to

fraction itself endlessly in this multiple borrowing. . . . Let us say that the "subject" *de-sists* in this, and doubly so when it is a question of man (of the male). . . . [61]

The Hegelian protagonist "acts out" the negative dialectic as the symptom of a symbolic failure, a failure that repeatedly produces the male subject as a man of less than mature mind, an unmanly man.[62] Like children trapped in the familial castle, that hereditary enclosure falling into ruin and haunted by its ghosts, our subject interiorizes the flaws in the transmission of culture's discursive estate. Because he recognizes that the possession of cultural capital is dependent upon his mastery of these dispossessing figures, they provide him with a powerful motivation to recuperate a singular ego or property in the person. As the subject of Absolute Knowing, the Mind imagines itself collecting, possessing, or ruling over them all together, under his authoritative aegis or throne. The failure of this attempt becomes the "monstrous" labor of *Bildung*, its phantasmagoric claim to masculinity as self-mastery.

Since this developmental achievement is paradoxically predicated on his ability to negate, to find himself continually other than his determinate incarnation or *more than* any cultural projection, the subject of Absolute Knowing can be said to have mastered only one thing absolutely—failure. He fails insofar as each escape from a sociosymbolic incarnation repeatedly situates him in a new enclosure, and thus he falls short of meeting the exorbitant demands of the "male plot of ambition," to use Peter Brooks's phrase. This plot, in contrast to the gothic one of repeated entrapment and escape, is linear and goal-oriented, concerned with the coherence and shaping of time.[63] When Hegel's subject attains Absolute Knowing, all positive content is "behind" him as a series of failed escapes. His "final" exit is into the night of self-consciousness, into radical divestiture.

Why does Hegel "go gothic," as it were, when he represents the dialectic? Why is the negative's work an uncanny narrative? If we conceive the dialectic's negativity as the challenge to the power of what exists, to the status quo, then the shift to the gothic first and most obviously signals a discursive disruption; it supplants the *Phenomonology*'s philosophical language and introjects what we could call the uncanny of a highly figurative mode, a discourse of the supernatural, the irrational, and the contrived. Hegel negates philosophy's traditional, self-important language, its claim to a monopoly on truth. Further, the adoption of the gothic constitutes a kind of gender deviance for the male writer, since, by the end of the eighteenth century, the gothic imagination is discredited as excessive, sickly, and overly feminized. Related to these questions of gender and genre, Hegel's negative dialectics brings another, more dangerous charge: if the male protagonist is repeatedly dispossessed by the effeminizing negative, in what sense does he retain his proper masculine identity? These supernatural figures of the negative make it impossible for him to mature—to inherit and collect—his cultural or symbolic property, or the given discursive models and histories of a masculine education.

2

The Male Romantic Poet as Gothic Subject:
Keats's *Hyperion* and *The Fall of Hyperion: A Dream*

The drama of terror has the irresistible power of converting its audiences into its victims.

—*Melmoth the Wanderer*

Language is a body technique.

—Pierre Bourdieu

Power is only pain,
Stranded, through discipline

—Emily Dickinson

HEGEL'S PROTAGONIST, EMBARKED ON AN EPIC PROJECT OF *BILDUNG* in *The Phenomenology*, found himself repeatedly dispossessed of culture's sociosymbolic legacy. *Hyperion: A Fragment* and *The Fall of Hyperion: A Dream*, Keats's two failed attempts at an epic of poetic election, also dramatize their (poet-)protagonist's troubled engagement with developmental narratives and assertions of mastery.[1] Developmental narratives that claim to be an election, like Hegel's and Keats's, call attention to their particular sociocultural purpose: the legitimation of an individual by a community (here, philosophers and poets, respectively). Within such real or imagined cultural communities, legitimation bestows a higher, often exclusive, status upon the one who is chosen and successfully initiated.[2] In *The Phenomenology*, Hegel underscores the subject of Absolute Knowing's fantasy of reigning over the past through his mastery of prior incarnations or discourses of masculine authority, and in both *Hyperion* fragments, Keats also underscores the element of discursive status, since he draws on the elevated rhetorical modes of Dantean and Miltonic epic, Greek myth, and the tropes of universal history and allegory. As Marlon Ross has shown, this rite of passage is an epic of poetic election, one that would confer upon its male participant, the

49

poet-narrator, an ability to speak from a position of discursive dominance. When and if he imagines his passage complete, he assumes a
place within an elite masculine cultural tradition, able to transform it
through the creative authority of his own subjectivity.[3] Keats's inability
to imagine the completion of that rite of passage resonates strongly with
Hegel's because both undo a typical, figurative "equivalence": the idea
that poetic—or philosophical—maturation is aligned with physical maturation. Instead, poetic election for Keats—or philosophical election for
Hegel—takes the form of a recurring refusal to assume a "mature" masculinity, formally inflected as the negative moment of the dialectic in
Hegel and as the production of fragments in Keats.[4]

The irony of Keats's "failure" has not gone unnoticed: not only the
grounds for the placement of these works at an interpretive center of
the Keatsian canon, poetic failure can be said to elevate their status to
works that define a specifically Romantic ideology. Many recent analyses of *Hyperion* and *The Fall of Hyperion* focus on the *productive* contradic-
tions between the poems' formal fragmentation and Keats's allegory of
poetic election.[5] Marjorie Levinson, for example, sees in Keats's fragmentation the achievement of an autonomy based, ironically, on the
fragment's "dependent" form. John Whale argues that the "appropriat-
ing power of Romantic ideology occurs alongside . . . claims of its own
incapacity," while for Marlon Ross, Keats's fragmented discourse reflects a conflict between a culturally determined will-to-power and a
desire to undertake a revolutionary reordering of discourse.

What critics have thus far not examined is Keats's adoption of the
gothic mode to express the gendered stakes of his ambivalence regarding the conditions underlying the possession of symbolic power. Before
doing so, however, let us briefly consider some general gothic features
in the following scene from *Hyperion*. The Titan Hyperion, ignorant of
his family's fate, succumbs to a premonition of doom:

> For as among us mortals omens drear
> Fright and perplex, so also shuddered he—
> Not at dog's howl, or gloom-bird's hated screech,
> Or the familiar visiting of one
> Upon the first toll of his passing-bell,
> Or prophesyings of the midnight lamp;
> But horrors, portion'd to a giant nerve,
> Oft made Hyperion ache. . . .

(I, 169–76)

The narrator presents a conventionalized gothic scenario—the screech-
ing of the owl, the ghostly visitation, and superstitious dread. While he

seems to reject the gothic as an inadequate mode of rhetorical accommodation ("*Not* at dog's howl, or gloom-bird's hated screech"), he nonetheless cites its features and encourages the reader to imagine a gothic of enormous magnitude: one, as he says, "portion'd to a giant nerve."[6] Hyperion then envisions his family as spectres:

> O monstrous forms! O effigies of pain!
> O spectres busy in a cold, cold gloom!
> O lank-eared Phantoms of black-weeded pools!
> Why do I know ye? why have I seen ye? why
> Is my eternal essence thus distraught
> To see and to behold these horrors new?
>
> .   .   .   .
>
> Am I to leave this haven of my rest,
> This cradle of my glory, this soft clime,
> This calm luxuriance of blissful light,
>
> .   .   .   .
>
> Of all my lucent empire? It is left
> Deserted, void, nor any haunt of mine.
>
> (I, 228–33; 235–37; 239–40)

Hyperion as gothic protagonist dwells among ruins, surrounded by the presence of ancestral figures whose fate will bear upon his own. Here, Hyperion is cast into this role as his narcissistic home or "cradle" becomes peopled with the superseded Titans. In a place he can no longer own, he reduces himself to the ghostliness his family has already assumed ("it is . . . nor any *haunt* of mine," my italics).

Keats's employment of the gothic goes beyond his reliance on an imagery of hallucinatory "spectres in a cold, cold gloom," the alternation between pastoral and sublime landscapes, or his emphasis on affective states of distress, anxiety, melancholia, and hysterical questioning.[7] More importantly for this study, *Hyperion* and *The Fall of Hyperion* represent the constitution of the male Romantic poet as an effeminized gothic subject. Against the inherited reading of gothic subjectivity as flat and lacking in depth, Michelle Massé redirects attention to the gothic subject as one who is known in and through a sadomasochistic dynamic, either as a giver or receiver of pain.[8] In Massé's study, the subjects involved in that dynamic are almost invariably male (sadistic) and female (masochistic); in the *Hyperion* fragments, sadomasochism between men seems to be the norm, with its hierarchical positions and opportunities for shifting gender and sexual identifications (situated within a Keatsian oeuvre that itself so often embodies a norm of blurred gender). The demand for narrative, in these fragments, as in other gothic works, is made under duress or compulsion, often under a kind of torture.[9] Central in this representation is the victim's body, for, as Chloe Chard writes, "the victims in Gothic fiction are frequently presented weak, collapsing or in chains, as emblems of oppression, and attention is focused . . . on the body."[10] The major figures (of poetic agency) in the *Hyperion* and *The Fall of Hyperion*—the fallen Titans, Hyperion, Apollo, the poet-narrator of *The Fall of Hyperion*—repeatedly receive a physical or psychological beating as they attempt to narrate the origin of poetry.

Besides signaling a structural affinity for the gothic, the extensive tableau that opens Book Two of *Hyperion*, to be repeated in other tableaux, illuminates the fragment's representational arrangement and its vexed relation to the constitution of subjectivity in and through pain. The Titans find themselves in a gothicized torture chamber, a place where each vividly rehearses his or her agony:

> *Dungeon'd* in opaque element, to keep
> Their clenched teeth still clench'd, and all their limbs
> *Lock'd up like veins of metal, crampt and screw'd* . . .
> Each one kept shroud, nor to his neighbour gave
> Or word, or look, or action of despair.
> Creus was one; his ponderous iron mace
> Lay by him, and a shatter'd rib of rock
> Told of his rage, ere he thus sank and pined.
> Iapetus another; in his grasp,
> A serpent's plashy neck; its barbed tongue
> Squeez'd from the gorge, and all its uncurl'd length
> Dead; and because the creature could not spit
> Its poison in the eyes of conquering Jove.
> Next Cottus: prone he lay, chin uppermost,
> As though in pain; for still upon the flint
> He ground severe his skull, with open mouth
> And eyes at horrid working. . . .
>
> (II, 23–25, 39–52; my emphasis)

Critics have remarked on Keats's Dantean frieze-like accumulation of "effigies of pain." This framing device achieves two contrary effects: 1) it condenses the pain through crowding, an aestheticizing effect, and 2) the containment in objectified figures distances it, an *an*aesthetizing effect. This move allows for the ambivalence of identification and separation, crucial for Keats's emphasis on the priority of the viewer's or reader's response.[11] The Titans suffer, not for the benefit of each other's gaze or for someone else within the tableau, *but for an onlooker situated outside*: "Each one kept shroud, nor to his neighbor gave / Or word, or look, or action of despair" (II, 39–40). The proximate distance of the spectator to an unfolding scene of pain is more self-consciously and reflexively adopted in *The Fall of Hyperion*. There the poet witnesses his rite of passage from the outside, as the scribe of his own dream, and within it, when he transcribes Moneta's vision.

The repeated tableaux of pain present an opening onto male authorial subjectivity: the masochistic bodies figure as doubles representing his own subjective dispossession (as Geoffrey Hartman has noted, these spectral figures somehow "mean the poet").[12] The poet-spectator-scriptor of the *Hyperion* fragments finds barely concealed versions of himself mirrored in the various characters spectralized or entrapped in gothic scenarios, whose feminized positioning contests the notion of an inalienable male subjectivity within a self-containing body. Through recurrent displays of physical and psychic shattering in pain and/or pleasure, Keats abdicates the power associated with an agential and autonomous masculine self. Such receptivity is, according to Lee Edelman, a figure for "the death of the subject"—another name for the effeminizing effect of dispossession on the male subject.[13] Whereas in *Hyperion*, Books I and II, the Titans' loss of mastery is a masochistic display not overtly eroticized, Apollo's swooning or painful submission to the cultural order in Book III brings distinctly (homo)eroticized pleasures into view—and poetic legitimacy, through the unlikely coincidence of passivity and power. The inability to assume a position of mastery in relation to the symbolic order, in Keats as well as Hegel, is posited nonetheless as a moment of culture's highest functioning. The narrator of *The Fall of Hyperion* organizes his desire around the "perverse" position of submission to a system that punishes and rewards that submission with election—the investiture with symbolic power. The fragments' conjunction of masochism, male effeminization, homoeroticism, and homophobia as the conditions for poetic legitimation articulate Keats's gothic insight into the literary as both a sexual and a social body.[14]

For his epic of election, Keats revises Hesiod's *Theogony*, a genealogical epic of the Titan and Olympian conflict whose narrative impulse is driven by generational violence and suppression.[15] Like election, genealogy establishes legitimate succession. In Hesiod, three generations of sons claim their right to succession through paternal castration and usurpation, triumphing over oppressive fathers who have refused to recognize or pass on their power to their sons. A violent logic underlies history: sons repeat their fathers' errors, initiating their own downfall, and fail to bequeath peacefully or to guarantee intergenerational succession. Hesiod ends the repetitive pattern of rebellion, wounding, and castration by installing Zeus and the Olympian hierarchy in power. Zeus is a son who violently supplants his father, but his sons will not supplant him. If the fathers have been the target of castration up to this point, now the sons accept symbolic castration, as they permanently concede their power to their eternal-father Zeus. The oedipal conflict and violence ends, but so does succession. Sons never mature in Hesiod, as mythic history stalls in a timeless stasis whose legitimacy is never called into question.

Like Hesiod, Keats depicts a secure Olympian hegemony. Yet whereas Hesiod represents the three generations at war, the narrative chronology of the *Hyperion* fragments limits itself to the conflict's aftermath. Given the Titans' incapacity to launch a counterattack in *Hyperion* and *The Fall of Hyperion*, the war is essentially concluded, and the narrator repeatedly calls attention to their suffering and impotence. Being beaten is overexposed, while its necessary correlative—the fact that there must be someone or something administering it—seems deliberately concealed. Keats presents the heightened spectacle of suffering without making a spectacle of its sadistic counterpart.

Representationally, the Olympian victors are what the narrative visibly and visually represses. Without being exposed—even in their power—they possess the capacity to make others seen in their powerlessness. By neither subjecting Jupiter to another's gaze nor showing him wield physical force, Keats magnifies his power. In *Hyperion*, power is inversely proportional to embodiment. Without a body, face, or voice, Jupiter is elevated to the status of an abstract, necessary principle or truth.[16] (Except Enceladus, the defeated Titans confer this sublimated status upon him.). The Olympian order is not only depersonalized, but experienced as an objective, if unseen, reality. The political power underlying culture transmutes into symbolic forms whose dispersion attests to the successful working of its ideology. Altering Oceanus's claim that Saturn was made "blind from sheer supremacy," we could say that Oceanus and Saturn remain blind to the real (and vulnerable) body behind Jupiter's sheer supremacy. They cannot see him, nor can the narrator. Like them, the narrator reinforces a conservative response to the existing hierarchy.[17]

In an epic of poetic election, the poet desires recognition from Apollo, the "Father of all Verse" (III, 13). As Apollo's would-be legitimate son, he stands to benefit from a justification or acceptance of the Olympian victory. It has been and could be argued, however, that the narrator records his ambivalence by a sustained, sympathetic focus on the marginalized Titans: those who, like himself, find themselves excluded from the exercise of both embodied and symbolic power. If dominance and submission structure the relationship between victor and vanquished, between the present and the past, then the narrator critically reckons the cost of progress by his calculation of the resulting pain. The Titans' wracked bodies become the focal point where the reader sees what is wrong with the Olympian hegemony, with history, and with discursive mastery. They do so by eliciting the viewer's sympathy. Further, by empathizing with the beaten, the poet would atone for his own will-to-power, his position as would-be heir, and his desire to achieve mastery—all of which are predicated on the Olympian overthrow.

It is perversely the unmoving, passive Titans to whom Keats gives the burden of narrative progression in *Hyperion* and in *The Fall of Hyperion*. They are held responsible for telling a history that will culminate with their illegitimacy and the poet's legitimation. Yet impossible, broken, or impeded speech—a feature of countless gothic narratives—is foregrounded from *Hyperion*'s beginnings: "far from the healthy breath of morn" denies the poet any inspirational possibility, while the Naiad's prohibitory gesture precludes an epic invocation.[18] These inhibitions directed at the poet's speech are an introduction to *Hyperion*'s frozen discursive landscapes; they carry over to the Titans' failure to use language to transform what exists into an imagination of the possible. The opening speech of Thea to Saturn is only the first example of paralyzed rhetoric. After rehearsing Saturn's loss of power, she concludes: "O thoughtless, why did I / Thus violate thy slumberous solitude?" (I, 68–69). By denying any necessity for her speech and retracting it, Thea retreats as a subject. The gratuity or insignificance of language becomes a reflexive mode of violation.[19]

This experience at the beginning of *Hyperion* prefigures other forms of incommunicability. Language is troped as sickness (a "palsied tongue," I, 93) and self-inflicted pain ("I am smother'd up," I, 106); most radically, it becomes the experience of bodily dispossession, of choking, at the moment when change is imagined:

> He spake, and ceas'd, the while a heavier threat
> Held struggle with his throat but came not forth;
>
> . . . .

> So at Hyperion's words the Phantoms pale
> Bestirr'd themselves, thrice horrible and cold;
>
> . . . .
>
> . . . through all his bulk an agony
> Crept gradual, from the feet unto the crown,
> Like a lithe serpent vast and muscular
> Making slow way, with head and neck convuls'd
> From over-strained might. . . .
>
> (I, 251–52; 255–56; 259–63)

Instead of overcoming segregation through its empathetic potential, the
Titans' language intensifies privation: ". . . the laden heart / Is *persecuted*
more, and *fever'd* more, / When it is nighing to the mournful house /
Where other hearts are sick of the same bruise" (II, 101–4, italics mine). The
consciousness of a shared misery does not enable the Titans to alter it.
By rendering suffering as a kind of bad mimesis, empathetic words simply double the negative effects by reproducing them. Pain undoes social
relationships, and the Titans' speech regresses into preverbal cries and
noises, or into silence—a reflection of its own unfreedom. Saturn's syn-
tactic repetitions become one figure for this destructive mirroring:

> . . . Moan, moan,
> Moan, brethren, moan, for thy pernicious babes
> Have chang'd a God into a shaking palsy.
> Moan, brethen, moan; for I have no strength left,
> Weak as a reed—weak—feeble as my voice—
> O, O, the pain, the pain of feebleness,
> Moan, moan. . . .
>
> (*FH*, 424–30)

Even Hyperion's visual brilliance mirrors the Titans' present torture,
instead of the difference of his unfallen potential. Like their words, he
betrays their misery "to the most hateful seeing of itself" (II, 370).

The poet not only chooses a subject—pain—that is difficult to represent, but insofar as he succeeds in its representation, he too will fall into
the same trap as the Titans: he replicates it. This statuary needs a different reader, if its story is to be told. Yet all the readers in the *Hyperions*
fall into modes of identification which, instead of mobilizing a narrative,
freeze them into attitudes of Titanic fixity. Apollo sits with numb limbs
(III, 89), while Hyperion winds up "like the bulk / Of Memnon's image
at the set of sun" (II, 373–74). Mnemosyne's face is fixed in "eternal
calm" (III, 60), and in *The Fall of Hyperion* we are presented with "the

chambers of [Moneta's] skull" (I, 278), her "broad marble knees" (I, 214), as well as the poet's leaden attempts to mount the altar steps or bear the burden of the Titans' pain himself, without going away.

Whether narrative or psychological, the increasing petrification of the protagonists and the viewers forecloses movement as a figure for transition. As long as Keats makes the Titans responsible for the narrative, this gothic problem persists: how is he to alter these accumulating resemblances into difference?[20] Having inherited the same history, the Titans cannot see any point of transformation. Their recurring trauma points instead to the mounting pressure of an unresolved crisis or conflict, one as immoderately generated as their figures are gigantic. Being unable to challenge the violent rules that underlie their defeat, the Titans' exclusive attention to their pain ultimately seems to prove the inevitability of the Olympian hegemony. If they become their own "illegible manuscript," it is because their pain is never legitimized within a discursive context that would give it meaning. Unable to construct a new language out of illegitimacy, they are reduced to "hieroglyphics old . . . their import gone" (I, 227, 282). Similarly, in *The Fall of Hyperion*, the narrator's inability to console Moneta halts his tongue and the narrative:

> I had no words to answer; for my tongue
> Useless, could find about its roofed home
> No syllable of a fit majesty
> To make rejoinder to Moneta's mourn.
> There was a silence . . .
>
> (I, 228 32)

As these attempts at sympathy fail, the characters are pushed back into muteness and inertia.

By fixing the Titans in this way, the poet counterposes a stabilizing, collecting gesture to the inaccessible shattering of the ego in pain and to its "mutilated subjectivity."[21] The most private of states, pain goes public in both *Hyperion* fragments as the poet represents, at various points, subjective dissolution in seizure-like states: Apollo's "wild commotions" (III, 124), Saturn "[shaking] and [oozing] with sweat" (I, 137), the poet's struggle against the "cloudy swoon" (*FH* I, 55), and the "electral changing misery" of Moneta's brain (I, 246). Given Keats's emphasis on seeing and responding, one might ask whether it is sympathy that he seeks to elicit with these extreme displays? The display of pain, as David Hume and others make perfectly clear, more frequently unleashes a disturbingly antisympathetic response.[22] By virtue of the accumulation of these gothic moments, Keats can be said to evoke distaste, even aversion: affective responses that check sympathy. As early as "Sleep and Poetry," he identifies the gothic as a mode of power, not one of sympathy: "But strength alone though of the Muses born / Is like a fallen angel: trees uptorn, / Darkness, and worms, and shrouds, and sepulchres / Delight it; for it feeds upon the burrs, / And thorns of life; forgetting the great end / Of poesy, that it should be a friend" (241–46). The poet's Miltonic conceit that he cannot find words adequate to mourn Moneta's pain suggests rather his rhetorical inability to traverse the psychic *distance* necessary for a transformative sympathy. It is too close, and because of this, it is immeasurably alienating.

The Titans Oceanus and Clymene distance themselves from their family's pain when they become mouthpieces for Olympian glorification. Because they seem to concede that they should be enslaved because they are or remain powerless because they do not have any power, they end up collaborating with the Olympians at the least and idolizing them at the worst. They underwrite the Olympian claim to superior knowledge and power with the argument of their own visible inferiority. At the point where the subject of violence internalizes his abuse, the danger is that he will no longer be able to designate or identify his perpetrator. If, as Edward Peters writes in his book on torture, it is primarily the victim that torture seeks to win or reduce to powerlessness, then the Olympian victory is won by the Titans "self-hid or prison bound" (*FH*, II, 10).[23] The Titans' self-negation, in other words, signifies their opposite. Against a reading that would oppose the Titans to the Olympians as the different truths of two historical ages, Keats has them register the dialectical antagonism of disembodied power and embodied powerlessness.

In the first two books of *Hyperion* the poet stages a fantasy where the Titans' gigantic bodies are restrained and immobilized as a sign of their supersession; in Book Three and in *The Fall of Hyperion* he reduces the dimensions to a more life-size human body whose passivity brings rewards. The subjection of Apollo and the poet of *The Fall of Hyperion* carries not the burden of failure, paradoxically, but constitutes the mark of legitimation. Hesiod may halt the repetitive violence of the genealogical myth (after Zeus), but Keats rejects resolution and inscribes instead a continuing legacy of violence. In Keats's revision, the Olympian order installs one of its own—Apollo—as the embodiment of a discursive culture that punishes its heirs. With Book Three of *Hyperion*, however, what changes is the nature and the consequences of the painful experience.

When he introduces Apollo, the narrator ostensibly redirects the narrative away from the suffering bodies of the gothic scenes with the pastoral mode: "O, leave them Muse! Leave them to their woes / . . . . / Meantime touch piously the Delphic harp" (III, 3, 10). If he hopes to depart from that impious woe with a major shift in character, tone, and scene, his attempt fails. The pain of Books One and Two resurfaces. Newly awake in his bower, Apollo waits in impotence and ignorance as he anticipates the experience of Jupiter's/Olympian power on his body, just as the Titans did. Unlike their ineffectual resistance, however, Apollo longs for it. He eagerly awaits the physicalized intoxication of poetic power: "deify me, as if some blithe wine / Or bright elixir peerless I had drunk" (III, 118–99). When that power expresses itself through him, Keats scripts it as painful pleasure and pleasurable pain:

> Soon wild commotions shook him, and made flush
> All the immortal fairness of his limbs;
> Most like the struggle at the gate of death;
> Or liker still to one who should take leave
> Of pale immortal death, and with a pang
> As hot as death's is chill, with fierce convulse
> Die into life: so young Apollo anguish'd:
> His very hair, his golden tresses famed,
> Kept undulation round his eager neck.
> During the pain Mnemosyne upheld
> Her arms as one who prophesied. — At length
> Apollo shriek'd; — and lo, from all his limbs
> Celestial
>
> (III, 124–36)

Apollo's election turns strangely Dionysian. It is not unlike the shift registered in Keats's Elgin Marbles sonnet, where the poet's resistance to submissive weakness gives way and becomes overlaid with sensual pleasure. There, the reader follows the poet from his claim that "my spirit is too weak — mortality / Weighs upon me like unwilling sleep" to the startling reversal "Yet 'tis a gentle luxury to weep" (1–2, 6).

Whereas Olympian dominance in *Hyperion*, Books I and II, is understood by the Titans only as inflicted pain and as the distance from power and poetic agency, Apollo's participation in that Olympian order now enfolds distinctly eroticized pleasures. Not only do his "golden tresses," the "fairness of his limbs" and "flush" effeminize his male body, but the "wild commotions," the hot "pang," the "fierce convulse," the "undulation," and final shriek read overtly as a sexual climax. As described earlier by Clymene, Apollo's song also ties his poetic ascension to erotic transports. Her language of "living death" and "rapture" prefigure the final images of the fragment:

> A living death was in each gush of sounds,
> Each family of rapturous hurried notes,
> That fell, one after one, yet all at once,
> Like pearl beads dropping sudden from their string:
> And then another, then another strain . . .
>
> (II, 281–85)

Apollo's bodily coherence shatters under the pressure of a masculine-identified force: Jupiter's knowledge/power. The birth of the poet is the moment when Apollo finds himself in the sexual position of a man identifying with a woman's pleasures.[24]

The transgressive energies of this coupling, however, prior to this display, are subjected to certain strategies which efface their nature.[25] First and foremost, the narrator obscures the object of Apollo's desire: "where is power? / *Whose* hand, *what* essence, *what* divinity / Makes this alarum in the elements, / While I here idle listen on the shores / In fearless yet in aching ignorance?" (III, 103–7, my italics). Keats does not so much repress as *neutralize* the illicit drive by dematerializing or disembodying the object.[26] In these lines we slide from Apollo's desire to feel or see the power of Jupiter's hand, then to Jupiter's essence, and finally to Apollo's desire to know what he knows. Further, the infusion with Jupiter's disembodied power is mediated by a woman, the goddess Mnemosyne. Keats engages in these various strategies to push an implicitly homoerotic desire back into an acceptable homosocial sublimation. Given the climactic finale of the fragment, however, we could say that Keats's effacements fail to contain the intensities of Apollo's desire and his associations with a blurred gender.[27]

With the Titans, Keats explores the cancellation of (poetic) agency within a hierarchical relationship of power and powerlessness. Here, Apollo's subjectivity emerges within a sexualized hierarchy between men. In the classical encyclopedias known to Keats, Apollo, the god of poetry, has an ambiguous sexuality: he pursues the young men Hyacinth and Cypress as well as women.[28] Inheriting literary power amounts to the filling of an emptiness. The fantasy of sexual penetrabil-

ity includes the imagination of psychic penetrability (Apollo is penetrated through his ear). In his work on discursive constructions of the
homosexual, Lee Edelman argues that the perceived threat of sodomy
in eighteenth- and nineteenth-century England accrues precisely
around the bourgeois male's fears of being invaded and dispossessed of
an inalienable masculine identity. Deprived of what Locke calls "property in the person," a man filled with another man relinquishes both
autonomy and interiority, tantamount to the loss of a self-signifying potential.[29] With his lack of subjective interiority — an *alienable* discursive
identity — Apollo is effeminized by being receptive to and penetrated by
a dominant masculine subject.

By virtue of the narrator's returns, his investment in displays of male
submission and ego-loss emerges. Beyond expressing his complicity
with a dynamic or impulse that he wants to mythologize as poetry's and
the poet's origins; beyond his use of masochism to establish the subjective basis of culture's seemingly objective authority and its internalization, in Book Three the narrator depicts an enjoyment in the scenario
for the first time. His marginal position allows him to regard Apollo's
pleasure without having to represent himself, the would-be poet, in that
same position. With Apollo's deification, however, the impulse to narrate or to return to that fantasy site disappears.

In one crucial sense, the narrative of election is resolved. If narrative
is the playing out of desire, then *Hyperion* concludes, not with its desire
frustrated, but *fulfilled*.[30] The shift to Apollo's bower language (and to a
discourse of homoerotic desire) marks *Hyperion* as a *poet's* success story,
not the sign of his failure. The narrative orients itself around the desire
for acknowledgment by a cultural order that installs effeminate men.
Written neither as an oppositional or as a nostalgic mode, this desire is
Hyperion's mode of acknowledging and attaining a share in patriarchal
power. It designates and affirms a powerful, masculine other who rewards Apollo with enjoyment *and* with the status of poet. In Keats's
scenario, Apollo's bower poetry and the dominant sociosymbolic order
find themselves in bed together. These are the terms he writes for his
contract of succession.

When Keats returns to the election epic after several months, it is to
the interiorized dreamspace of *The Fall of Hyperion*. The bower returns
in a revised form and only briefly, as the pastoral meal with its awaken-
ing of hunger and promise of nourishment. And similar to *Hyperion*, *The
Fall of Hyperion* appears to reject the intrusion of the gothic mode, even

as it tropes the poet's experience as such. The transporting "draught"
the poet drinks is "No Asian poppy, nor elixir fine . . . no poison gender'd in close monkish cell" (47, 49; cf. with *Hyperion*'s "Not at dog's
howl, or gloom-bird's hated screech"). Traces of Apollo's deification re-
materialize as the poet swoons, overcome by the effects of the paternal
drink:

> That full draught is parent of my theme.
> No Asian poppy, nor elixir fine
> Of the soon fading jealous caliphat;
> No poison gender'd in close monkish cell
> To thin the scarlet conclave of old men,
> Could so have rapt unwilling life away.
> Among the fragrant husks and berries crush'd,
> Upon the grass I struggled hard against
> The domineering potion; but in vain:
> The cloudy swoon came on, and down I sunk. . . .
>
> (I, 46–55)

This partial restaging of *Hyperion*, Book III—the disempowering power
to speak, the swoon, the domination by the father-figure—is overlaid,
however, with threats not present there. Jupiter, the father idealized
and longed for by Apollo, is supplanted by a host of treacherous figures,
the fathers common to gothic and gothic-oriental tales, the "jealous Ca-
liphat" and the "scarlet enclave of old men."[31]

The poet submits unwillingly to the poisonous potion of these gothic
fathers, an ingestion which subjectively dispossesses him: being overcome by their will and desire ("I struggled hard against the domineering potion"), what he stands to lose and does in this instance is himself.
Now marked by his ineffectual resistance, the paternal domination
Apollo longed for feels like a violation or rape. The pleasures of the
bower now read as its gothicized, sodomitical terrors, as the word
"rapt" overtly implies. Yet disturbing as this scene is, the narrator reduces it to a prefatory stage, an incomplete introductory nightmare superseded by *The Fall of Hyperion*'s more extensive dream-vision.

The poet's new dream*work* will earn him his discursive inheritance
from Moneta, the retainer of patriarchal knowledge and authority. As
a figure for Memory, she suggests the ordering of time, its sequence,
and thus at least the potential for a developmental narrative. With the
poet no longer relying on seduction or passivity as Apollo did, he labors
to meet Moneta's demands with his ongoing physical and mental humiliation. He restrains his desire whenever it surfaces:

> To count with toil the innumerable degrees
> Towards the altar *sober-pac'd I went,*
> *Repressing haste, as too unholy there. . . .*
>
> (I, 92–94, my italics)

> . . . that lofty sacrificial fire,
> Sending forth Maian incense, spread around
> *Forgetfulness of everything but bliss,*
> And clouded all the altar with soft smoke,
> From whose white fragrant curtains thus I heard
> *Language pronounc'd. "If thou canst not ascend*
> *These steps, die on that marble where thou art. . . ."*
>
> (I, 102–8, my italics)

The embodied pleasures in *Hyperion* succumb in *The Fall of Hyperion* to corporeal, measured punishments—the "innumerable degrees," the sober pacing, the ascension of steps, the succession of questions and answers that suggest progress but make it impossible to gauge. When Apollo's shriek is voiced by the poet in *The Fall of Hyperion*, it no longer expresses the release of attained desire, but the perpetual self-excoriation and self-violation that now characterizes the poet-narrator's legitimation process:

> I shriek'd; and the sharp anguish of my shriek
> Stung my own ears—I strove hard to escape
> The numbness; strove to gain the lowest step . . .
> One minute before death, my iced foot touch'd
> The lowest stair. . . .
>
> (I, 126–28; 132–33)

Revising this constitutive fantasy, the narrator of *The Fall of Hyperion* penalizes Apollo and the narrator of *Hyperion*: not for their submissive strategy to gain empowerment, but for their open enjoyment of it. In *The Fall of Hyperion*, the would-be poet's ambitions surface instead as the privileging and enforcement of a need for discipline.

Incorporated into the election ritual are specific gender expectations: namely, if the poet acknowledge an originary moment rife with homoerotic pleasures, he must also invoke their subsequent refusal. By way of suffering, the poet proves that his worth is no longer affixed to discursive cruising but to discursive discipline.[32] Intellectual empowerment aligns itself with suppressing the transgressive weakness of the effeminized male body. Performing cruel, intimidating, or arbitrary

tasks ("If thou canst not ascend / These steps, die on that marble where
thou art," I, 107–8), the poet mythologizes ritualized violence against
the male body as systemic to a high culture insistent on suppressing the
(homoerotic) desire organizing it.[33] The poet now "directs [his] energies towards 'passing' within the system that oppresses [him]. [His]
strategy is not simply that of a survivor. [He] fully incorporates and
perpetuate[s] the split that enables hierarchy."[34] His unapologetic in-
vective against lesser poets testifies to his overt identification with the
cultural authority, a sadistic position that the poet now has Apollo assume as well:

> Apollo . . .
> Where is thy misty pestilence to creep
> Into the dwellings, through the door crannies,
> Of all mock lyricists, large self worshipers,
> And careless hectorers in proud bad verse.
> Though I breathe death with them it will be life
> To see them sprawl before me into graves.
>
> (I, 204–10)

Keats does not fail to imagine his possible inclusion into this group, intent as he is on justifying the conditions for success.

The domed temple, by virtue of being a public monument and bearing a resemblance to the skull's interior, is the point where externalized
and internalized pressures meet, where the social and the sexual con-
verge in the constitution of the Romantic poet. By calling his dreamspace eternal, the narrator authorizes and rationalizes the conditions
underlying poetic mastery. Pierre Bourdieu writes of the physical
body's complicity—at its own expense, something very like masochism—with the violence that culture's institutions wield against it:

> All groups entrust *the body, treated like a kind of memory*, with their most pre-
> cious possessions. . . . The use made of suffering inflicted on the body by
> rites of initiation . . . is understandable if one realizes . . . that people's adher-
> ence to an institution is directly proportional to the severity and painfulness
> of the rites of initiation.[35]

If the poet-narrator's body engaged with its own initiation reflects a
kind of cultural memory, then Keats places a bodily memory directly
beside, and makes it subject to, Moneta, the figure of culture's discursive memory. As the container of legitimating knowledge, or as the embodiment of cultural capital, Moneta subjects his body to pain, while

the poet imagines that she converts that loss into his symbolic gain. As the figure of Memory suggests, such violence is unforgettable. The poet-narrator finds himself in a compromising position: his vulnerable, hypersensitive body remembers itself by its denigration; its self-betrayal is allied with the sensationless, gigantic body of Moneta. The desires the poet seems intent on chastising paradoxically become constitutive of the very thing they supposedly stand in the way of: the legitimation he seeks, what he is proving himself capable of in *The Fall of Hyperion*.

This same contradiction inheres in the substantive inheritance, the things he imagines come with poetic election. In noticeable contradiction to the physical sensuality and transformative pleasures of the deification act, what Apollo receives is memory, not as a lived experience, but as already written history: the "names, deeds, gray legends, dire events, rebellions, / Majesties, sovran voices, agonies, / Creations and destroyings" (III, 114–16). The impersonal content of Apollo's inheritance, the undifferentiated list, betrays desire's specific pleasures in obtaining it. Similarly, in *The Fall of Hyperion*, when the poet-narrator stands before the monument's antique paraphernalia, he cannot find any stirring of desire in his inheritance: it is immobilized into things. As he confronts a baffling collection of objects, the universal or collective nature of its ritual content and function overwhelms and excludes him: "All in a mingled heap confus'd . . . / Robes, golden tongs, censer, and chafing dish, / Girdles, and chains, and holy jewelries" (I, 78–80). Whether it is Apollo or the poet-initiate, inheritance entails the cultural effacement of the subject of desire. Like cultural representations of the aristocratic sodomite who collects *objets d'art* and antiquities, the poet appears infertile, incapable of reproducing his image.[36]

Borrowing from Marx, we could say that when the poet imagines his election, he imagines the heritage inheriting him.[37] He will be appropriated by the things which he desires to appropriate. Legitimation will efface his particular experience of desire, yet he will accrue the wealth of culture's most valued signifiers (the robes, golden tongs, censer, etc.). In Romantic texts such as the *Hyperion* fragments, a particular western European discourse of male homosexual identity appears. That identity is one severely punished for a "desire that dare not speak its name" but rewarded by being entrusted the guardianship of all that it designates most valuable: its art, music, learning, taste and refinement, i.e., its symbolic memory.[38] His undesiring response to the contents of inheritance, however, express the narrator's ambivalence about the legitimation ritual he stages and the identity he is to assume. Culture's "sodomitical" inheritance is deemed unpossessable by Keats, since it is not his own.

The narrator remains uncommitted, prior to inheritance, in the position where his own illegitimacy may still be willed. As a not-yet poet, he places himself in the position of the immature boy so as to avoid affiliation; in Bourdieu's words, he is a "symbolic warder," since he does not yet possess or have any symbolic capital of his own.[39]

The figures of Mnemosyne and Moneta project an initiated poet as their sterile inheritor: the non-generative repository of their capital. Some critics have emphasized Moneta's maternal nature: the poet-narrator's efforts to see what her brain "enwombs," her voice's approximation at one point to a "mother's," and his child-like positioning beneath her knees (FH, I, 277, 250, 181).[40] In these moments, the poet-narrator suggests a mother figure (and even the longing for a pact between mother and son, one capable of resisting paternal power).[41] Yet this fantasy is barely sustained. Moneta (or Mnemosyne) rarely suggests female sexuality—she is oddly disembodied, referred to repeatedly as a voice, shade, and shadow; her physicality is denied, being immobile, unfeeling statuary; and the maternal gaze is replaced by eyes which blankly refuse to recognize the poet. Like Minerva, the virgin goddess born out of father Jupiter's forehead, whom she most closely resembles, Moneta/Mnemosyne's "reproductive" capacity is abstract or metaphorical as her allegorical status suggests: contained in her brain, aligned with the existing cultural order, and closer to conventional metaphors of male (poetic) generation.[42] If the poet-narrator seeks to identify with a mother in order to refuse the paternal legacy, Moneta (or Mnemosyne) does not answer that need. His act of seeing into her brain puts him in the position of being able to survey and internalize a history that does not rewrite the patriarchal order, but reinscribes it as collective memory and the source of poetry.[43]

What these figures finally do, however, is project the poet beyond the faultline of patriarchal humiliation. These asexualized feminine figures emerge as Apollo's and the poet-narrator's future. They ultimately gesture past the sadomasochistic fantasy of male intersubjectivity and homoerotic/homosocial bonding to a state of affective purity, where physicality and sexuality no longer feel out the issue of election. These depersonalized women who refrain from physical contact with the poet become a kind of alter-ego for the effeminate man forced to give up the particularity and mobility of his desire. If elected, he lands in their place: temporally marginal, affectively distant, with a subjectivity whose qualities signal an affinity with the museum. The sensory, painful staging leads to or implies this other place, yet the poet-narrator, breaking off the narrative, declines to inhabit it.

What he has claimed, however ambivalently, is an engagement with the dynamic that leads to this impasse, a dynamic which becomes the matter of repetition. Poetry's genealogy is subject to a compulsion to reproduce itself substantively; its contents are the plurals of Mnemosyne's lesson or the antiquarian objects of the temple, making history look like sheer, indifferent accumulation. This *material* repetition gives way to a *formal* drive for repetition: to the structuration of its fantasy. The uncanniness of the spectator's experience lies not only in the subject matter to be inherited, but in his awareness of the "again and again" of that process: in other words, with an awareness of its compulsive nature.[44] The Titans' reemergence at the end of *The Fall of Hyperion* propels a conclusive breaking off. The fragment does not resolve, but symbolically rejects Apollo's and the poet-narrator's gothic legacy.

In opposition to a transhistorical epic of mastery, of the transmission of an inheritance, the narrative impulse in the *Hyperion*s blocks succession and conclusion. Whether as homoerotic desire or its sublimation into a disciplinary regimen, Keats offers a mythologized cultural contract whose non-linear, repetitive energies align it closely with the gothic. And just as that contract invariably injures an effeminized male body, it invariably calls it forth. The poet-narrator's possibilities for identification fail to lead to mastery: the accession to a self-contained, stabilized masculinity able to transform the cultural contract. The spectre of homoeroticism returns as the offer and refusal of the masculinizing epic of inheritance and succession, preserving the pleasures and punishments of effeminacy. At the expense of a possible and legitimate conclusion, the gothic's interminable fictions intrude as Keats's incomplete manuscript of election.

3

Sharing Gothic Secrets:
Byron's *The Giaour* and *Lara*

. . . whatever effect this infamous passion had in other ages, and other coun-
tries, it seem'd a peculiar blessing on our air and climate, that there was a
plague-spot visibly imprinted on all that are tainted with it, in this nation
at least.

— John Cleland, *Memoirs of a Woman of Pleasure*

Unless like wise Tiresias we had proved,
By turns the difference of the several sexes

—*Don Juan,* 14.73

IN KEATS'S *HYPERION* FRAGMENTS, THE GOTHIC IS ALIGNED WITH THE effeminization of the male protagonist insofar as it unleashes, and occasions the need to discipline, the masochistic pleasures allied with the poet's election into a select all-male community. In *The Giaour* and *Lara*, the first and last of Byron's *Oriental Tales*, the gothic once again liberates homoeroticized energies between men, in individual and collective fantasy, only to demand their repudiation or punishment. With the exception of his drama *Manfred*, Byron's *Oriental Tales* count as his most extensive exploration of the gothic mode. Supernatural figures such as the vampire and the Gorgon, settings of imprisonment and exile, and allusions to William Beckford's *Vathek*, Matthew Lewis's *The Monk*, and Robert Southey's *Thalaba* signal a gothic provenance. More important to their thematics of dispossession, however, are the tales' expressly cultivated gothic rhetoric of the secret, unintelligible language, and the mysterious.

Because of their indeterminacy or "negativity," secrets attract and contain both the fear of, and desire for, knowledge. Andrew Elfenbein has noted the significance of the secret in the construction of late eighteenth-century selfhood: it is less the secret's content than the "secrecy effect" that anticipates nineteenth-century "deep selfhood" and contributes to that construction.[1] The *Oriental Tales*, however, shift the emphasis from the secret's relation to the formation of an interior or depth psychology to a questioning of the *audience*'s fantasies about secrets — from which they produce the hero's identity for their communal consumption.[2] Writing about the formal fragmentation of *The Giaour*, David Seed describes its strategic purpose in ways that resonate compellingly for this chapter's predominant focus on the secret, that specifically gothic mode of designating, and disrupting, the continuity or unity of the self. The tale's "use of fragments [or, as I would emphasize, secrets] . . . exploits a tactic of alternately whetting the reader's desire for information and actually withholding that information, so that even at the end of the poem there are significant areas of uncertainty left open."[3] While Byron provokes uncertainty in the audience, he does something more than acknowledge "the capacity of texts to stimulate inference."[4] As a curiosity-evoking object that mediates private and public knowledge, the gothic secret stands as a communal emblem for the hero's psyche, an emblem that necessarily reflects back on the communal psyche as well. The secrets of this neither solely individualized, nor wholly communalized, psyche are aligned with acts of gender-crossing and indirect implications of same-sex desire.

Byron's narrators and communities of readers within the *Oriental Tales* dwell on their protagonists' secrets, anticipating Eve Sedgwick's assertion that by the end of the nineteenth century "knowledge meant sexual knowledge, and secrets sexual secrets."[5] Given an oppressive social context, the tales' formal strategy of preserving ambiguity is obviously necessary. Excessively punitive social strictures and criminalization of male effeminacy and same-sex desire made it impossible to speak about directly, in terms other than vilifying — for which a gothic rhetoric of the unspeakable serves well. Gary Dyer has argued that sodomy was the age's "exemplary secret, infamous, unmentionable, and deadly"; because it was too dangerous to be chosen as an example of a secret, "other secrets had to stand in for sodomy."[6] The displaced reference in the *Oriental Tales* occurs as insinuations surrounding the Giaour's and Lara's "past," but it is increasingly around the gender ambiguous page figures, with whom the Giaour and Lara are identified, that the density of the secret accrues.

In Keats's gothic, the poet first dramatizes his dispossession through the Titans, those spectralized figures who somehow "mean" him. The audience and male protagonists of Byron's *The Giaour* and *Lara* have their own, less ghostly doubles: the effeminate page figures who, with their unmanly masculinity and unintelligible language, repudiate phallic power, patriarchy's symbolic estate. These page figures are particularly important because the attention of the audience visually and psychologically shifts from the Byronic hero to them.[7] They are the figures through whom the male protagonist—and the community, via their fascination with him—can project and measure the extent of his dispossession from a masculine estate. Yet for the imagined community within these narratives (and for the external one the narrator imagines reading them), it is not some revealed content that, binding the page figures to the protagonists, carries the aura of the uncanny, but rather the gothic rhetoric of the mysterious, extending to implication and rumor, that enfolds them. Jerome McGann has suggested that the reader's task is not to unlock the "truth" behind Byron's often encrypted texts but to note the process by which he enciphers meanings. In *The Giaour* and *Lara*, the represented encryption is itself equivalent to the production of homosexuality as a kind of "open secret," in effect collapsing the two things McGann would like to keep separate.[8]

Discourses about homoerotic desire have often been gothicized (see the introduction), which suggests the attractiveness of an idiom of the secret to mediate individual and cultural responses to imagined gender-crossing and sexual transgression in the *Tales*, precisely because the idiom announces that there is something to be concealed. Indeed, there are precedents in Byron's life for the use of a gothic vocabulary to denote or imply gender or sexual otherness. In a number of letters written between 1809 and 1811, Byron and his Cambridge friend Charles Skinner Matthews refer to same-sex desire through a coded vocabulary of "the mysterious," whose indirect, knowing tone prefigures that of the narrators and speakers in the *Tales*.[9] On receipt of a letter where Byron outlines his sexual activities with Greek boys, Matthews's response exposes the implicative character of Byron's writing: "I . . . congratulate you on the splendid success of your first efforts in *the mysterious*, that style in which more is meant than meets the Eye."[10] In the suppressed stanza on Beckford in *Childe Harold, Book I*, Byron refers to Beckford's pederasty as a "nameless crime," an "unhallowed thirst" leading to exile, a "solitude unsought" and the "worst of woes," a rhetoric that anticipates his portrayal of both the Giaour and Lara.[11] Byron indicates that the ostensibly feminine apostrophe of the love poem, "The Cornelian," accepted as the Cambridge choirboy John Edleston, will remain a "secret."[12] "*Why*" he cannot live in England, Byron writes to John Hanson, "must remain a secret"; the "why," both Louis Crompton and Leslie Marchand agree, refers to his homoerotic feelings. Even Augusta and Lady Byron indicate a familiarity with the secret's identification with prohibited desires. Referring to Byron's allusions to his past, Lady Byron hints that it "[involves] some fearful mysteries," while Augusta finds the rumors of Byron's homosexuality are "of a nature *too horrible to repeat*," beside which "every other [imputation] sinks into nothing besides [this] MOST *horrid* one."[13] In *The Giaour* and *Lara*, Byron continues to employ this gothic rhetoric of the secret or unintelligible language and introduces supernaturalized figures (such as the Medusa and the vampire) to show how society encrypts same-sex desire.

The protagonists of these narratives are not secluded in a prison, waiting for a sympathetic listener in order to confess, nor are their secrets concealed in old manuscripts. Far from being hidden or invisible, the fact that there is something to hide is ostensibly stamped on their bodies and their faces for audience and narrators to read. In terms of the critical agenda Byron attempts in the *Tales*, Sedgwick's discussion of character in the gothic novel resonates compellingly. Sedgwick calls attention to the predominance of the "marked countenance" in gothic fiction, whereby character is inscribed or impressed from the outside, displayed outwardly, thereby foregrounding the potentially social or relational nature of identity.[14] While the gothic genre characteristically emphasizes visible exteriors as markers of identity, the face as a half-language or code, it is Byron's contribution to do two critical things with this well-established gothic trope. First, he connects the emphasis on visual signifiers of identity to a broader cultural obsession (one lasting up to the present, one might add), with being visually able to distinguish — to see the secret of — the difference of other sexual and gender identities. If John Addington Symonds could affirm that the homosexual male is one whose "lusts [are] written on his face," it was an affirmation generated out of a cultural need to see the "plague spot" of homosexuality (as Mrs. Cole describes it in John Cleland's *Memoirs of a Woman of Pleasure*) and, by virtue of that seeing, to know and control it.[15] In *The Giaour* and *Lara*, the narrator and community compulsively read the body and face of the protagonist and the cross-dressed page. Their fixation implies that the "truth" of identity is both visual and sexual and, for this audience, a sexually "other" one. Writing in *The Quarterly Review* on *Lara*, George Ellis attempts to use those surfaces to penetrate the hero's psyche: poetry should reveal the "effects" of the "secret sensibility which lurks within our bosoms" — "its visible symptoms" are legible on "the whole animated frame" of the body.[16] Yet when the "ground" of identity is strictly seen as surface, it resists readings that emphasize depth or content.[17] The face of the Byronic hero and the body of the page figure as signifiers of identity never reveal any "thing" that the voyeur might be satisfied with. These faces and forms, however marked, seem impervious to definitive readings, and Byron, in this way, challenges what such literal or ocular signifiers say.

Secondly, representing the communal responses to the protagonist and the page figures, Byron maps a socially constituted discursive terrain of prohibited gender and sexual identities, one that allows the reader to see how heterosexuality produces homosexuality as its other. When he writes narratives about secrets and points to a private book of "incomprehensible" desires withheld from view, Byron, however ironically, may be as direct about his audience as he can be. He displays the fact that he is exposing a fascinated *and* complicitous audience to the secret, which, significantly, is not the same as revealing it. In doing so, however, Bryon critically "outs" his audience to itself, a complicated move to say the least:

> virtually from the beginning of modern consciousness of "homosexuality" . . . its cultural and literary expressions posed a fundamental problem for those whom it addressed. To accept being addressed by such productions is to be made uncomfortable at best, perhaps compromised, and at worst, infected.[18]

As Byron shifts the emphasis from these visual signifiers to the fascinated readers of that code, he foregrounds the uses and abuses of their reading practices. These gothic tales dramatize not only how the Byronic protagonist looks, but how the audience sees. The secrets of the cross-dressed pages Leila and Kaled reveal a communal fascination with a potentially limitless variety of genders and sexualities. One of Byron's favorite and recurrent rhetorical strategies, as Jerome McGann notes, is to present "the audience's character to itself . . . so that it can 'reflect' upon that reflection in a critical and illuminating way."[19] In other words, the audience sees itself seeing. Whatever "truth" appears will remain ambiguous, able to cover itself with alibis, if necessary.[20] In doing so, Byron plays with the audience's uneasiness that the codes they rely upon to identify and know otherness might not say anything at all, except, perhaps, about them. The final heterosexual solution Byron imposes on them becomes, ironically, his way of having the last laugh: what the reader thinks he knows, namely, that these figures are "deviant," is not "it." Take off their veils—and they are just "like" the reader. Through his use of this gothic code of visibly inscribed identity, Byron sets its limits.

Byron's decision to write and publish a series of gothic-oriental romances must be seen in light of their popularity, then riding a crest; they offered an engaged audience and an established market, invaluable for Byron or any young writer.[21] Yet by addressing an audience familiar with the genre's conventions, Byron also taps into the possibilities of critique, both of the genre and the audience, something Charlotte Smith had done in *The Old Manor House* and Jane Austen in *Northanger Abbey*.[22] Taking into account the point-of-view of the one looking serves to productively complicate visibility paradigms, as does Byron's use of another code, that "style," to quote Matthews, "in which more is meant than meets the eye"—here, the rhetoric of the mysterious and insinuation, in which the speaker's tone precedes and signifies more than the statement's revealed content. Lady Byron claimed that "Lord Byron has never *expressly* declared himself guilty of any *specific* crime—but his insinuations to that effect have been much more convincing than the most direct assertion."[23] The "more than" takes its meaning from the deferral it performs. This subtext, I contend, exists for those open to reading it—even if the outcome, as represented within *The Giaour* and *Lara*, is not the audience's critical self-assessment but further discrimination.

Insofar as they resist easy interpretation, the protagonists, the cross-dressed page figures, and their secrets disrupt symbolization. Like Hegel's negative, the "empty" spaces around the epistemologically indeterminate secret generate the fascination that drives or impels the making of meaning. We could say that these page figures, on the margins of legibility and legitimacy, generate or produce symbolic wealth. More importantly, Byron's exposure of the audience's project of reading surfaces for identities and sharing open secrets also suggests what critical reading means for Byron. In the failed attempts to "read" identity as a strategy of coercive knowledge, Byron points to the idea of something always necessarily missed and unpossessed. *The Giaour* and *Lara*, the first and last of *The Oriental Tales*, respectively, represent how society adopts (and the narrators purvey) a gothic discourse, and especially the secret, as the social and discursive limits within which other gender and sexual identities emerge. Through his own critical reading of the gothic, however, Byron also imagines the secret as the desire for something that one has not yet said—the idea, or promise, of an unrepresented significance or consciousness as the unrecuperated differences of other gender and sexual identities.[24]

Punning on a figure for disclosure, "to let the cat out of the bag," *The Giaour*'s narrative morbidly literalizes it. Early on, a secret is revealed to the reader: the bag holds Leila, a slave murdered by the harem master Hassan for her infidelity to him and her love of the Giaour. This divulgence, however, resolves little. Secrets spring up around this event, ones that bear explicitly upon the history and identity of the unnamed Giaour, and other mysteries that "dare not" be mentioned: "And all its hidden secrets sleep, / Known but to Genii of the deep, / Which, trembling in their coral caves, / They *dare not whisper* to the waves" (384–87, italics mine).[25] These secrets and their reflection in *The Giaour*'s formal fragmentation produce an indeterminacy that elicits the reader's involvement.[26] Locating the poem's weakness in Byron's idealizing mystifications and obscuratist discourses about the protagonist's fate, Daniel Watson ascribes this to Byron's lack of control of the material. This chapter will argue that it is precisely such mystifying discourses that necessarily and concomitantly arise as a response to excluded, uncertain sociosexual identities. Thus, instead of seeing mystification as the author's unconscious effacement of a social context, as Watkins does, it can be understood as Byron's conscious reproduction of social, including discursive, forms of effacement.[27]

That Leila's love, and not her murder, should be the crime deserving punishment, points to an oppressive, orientalized patriarchy where women's sexuality is reduced to men's property. If Leila's passion for the Giaour makes her unfaithful to Hassan, Hassan's prior assumption of the right to possess her identifies him as a slave owner and marks Leila's murder as the ultimate objectification. The narrator of *The Giaour* expresses sympathy for Leila's situation: "Oh! who young Leila's glance could read / And keep that portion of his creed / Which saith, that woman is but dust, / A soulless toy for tyrant's lust?" (487–90).[28] When Hassan's point of view is represented, the repetitive insistence on her status as slave reveals that his will to dominate outweighs other impulses: "Too well he [Hassan] trusted to the slave / Whose treachery deserved a grave" (461–62); "The faithless slave that broke her bower / And, worse than faithless, for a Giaour!" (535–36). While Hassan demands Leila's complicity with her own slavery, her "infidelity" signals her refusal to be reduced to a material possession. Transgressing the law of the harem for the racially and religiously "other" Giaour, her "crime" unleashes the direst consequences—first, her literal death, and second, a sociosymbolic death through the subsequent silencing and suppression of her murder.[29] Within this scenario, Byron does not depict the Giaour, the avenging murderer of Hassan, as a liberatory figure. Significantly, the Giaour admits that he would have acted as Hassan had done (1062–63); further, as Hassan's was, the Giaour's own murder is motivated by vengeance. This psychological parallelism marks Byron's ironic distance from the Giaour and casts *The Giaour's* orientalism in broader terms, namely, as a penetrating critique of racial and heterosexual gender relations in the Christian occident as well. Through the narrative of Leila's sexual repression, Byron dramatizes gendered divisions of power, property, and law.

The erotic implications, however, extend beyond the heterosexuality of the Giaour-slave-harem-master configuration. Violence is also directed at Leila's gender "deviance." Her escape and murder occur while she is dressed, with a punning nod to Georgian England, "in likeness of a *Georgian* page" (456, my italics). While partially a plot device, a disguise to avoid detection, the practice of cross-dressing at (and as) the narrative's critical moment succinctly aligns gender ambiguity with the flight from patriarchal sexual norms. Leila's "crime" occurs while she appears to be a boy, and, more exactly, a boy running off to be with a man. There are several codes shaping this figure, and this moment reads as the first in a number of "winks" addressed to the reader. According to James Creech, the wink is complicitous with the taboo against speech and yet transgresses that taboo: "The wink, then, is operationally tied to the literary closet and its paradox: it has to be published in order to function at all and to find its communicants, but in a guise that magically can conceal and cover its sexual secret with straight alibis if need be."[30] The page figure in *The Giaour* implicitly introduces cultural discourses of male effeminacy and homosexuality into the narrative.[31] By focusing on this figures in *The Giaour* and in *Lara*, Byron represents different models of desiring and longing, objects of eroticism prohibited in England, ones that may have recalled the adolescent boys and young men Byron encountered in the Levant, or even the desired young man of Georgian England that Byron himself was during those travels. While the Giaour's and Lara's psyches will be organized around an unnamed conflict that produces inexpiable guilt and social exclusion, the page figures, Leila and Kaled, resist the coercion inherent in the social demands for sexual or gender normalcy. In *The Giaour*, Byron articulates transgressive experiences in and through the "equivocal being," Leila. At the same time, he offers a compromise to the sexual status quo by punishing her.[32]

The extreme nature of Leila's punishment mirrors the opprobrium directed at gender deviance in Byron's England. If Leila "[flees] her master's rage, / In likeness of a Georgian page," in Georgian England, male cross-dressing, if it could be linked to sodomy, incurred the death penalty at the worst and provoked extreme rage at the very least (Leila's actions inspire both rage and murder).[33] Heterosexual infidelity and violence could and did unleash horror in Byron's time, but it was not subject to extreme censorship or codified as a nameless crime or the unspeakable, as was the sexually transgressive act of sodomy. Leila is the catalyst or "trigger for an act with *unspeakable* consequences," David Seed notes, without pursuing why her murder, as the central event of the narrative (or the Giaour's gaze, which, as he says, "encapsulates the whole poem's equivocation between utterance and silence, a tale never made completely manifest"), should be codified as unspeakable.[34] The punishment for Leila's "deviance" does not end with her death. It is transferred to the Giaour by the narrator and the community of interpreters within the tale. After her murder, those who look at the Giaour project onto his gaze "that nameless spell / Which speaks—itself unspeakable" (838–39).[35]

Leila's ambiguous gender identification allows the reader to see certain forms of erotic desire *as an activity and a discursive style* whose liberatory significance are implied by their use for escape. Evoking her beauty in a lyrical mode, the narrator slides from descriptions of gazelles to rubies to swans to pomegranates. By dissolving the attractions of Leila into incommensurable differences—is she animal? mineral? young man? young woman? the narrator taps into the seemingly endless, fragmentary nature of desire. By employing the attributes common to Levantine and Middle Eastern lyric to limn Leila's eroticism, Byron relativizes, at the very least, the discursive nature of desire. He illustrates that unconventional attributes in England can be the height of convention elsewhere. Potentially more disturbing for a British readership increasingly exposed to travel narratives and literary works from the Middle East and the Levant were Byron's orientalized metaphors for Leila's beauty, since they referred indiscriminately to young women *and* men as poetic apostrophes. Knowledge of seraglios of adolescent boys, who heightened their effeminacy through dress, cosmetics, and submissive behavior, further destabilizes Byron's signifiers, and consequently, the reliability of language to enforce the illusion of two genders and one sexuality in the representation of erotic desire.[36] By destabilizing Leila's identity, Byron multiplies the discursive imagination of erotic otherness.[37] Leila materializes the unfixed, transformative nature of erotic desire whereby gender-crossing can make women boys and boys women and whereby desire remains variously nameable.

It may not be so easy for some readers to assume Leila's feminized body is a female (heterosexualized) one, as Anthony Vital does: "[Leila's] powers of expression are made over to her body, [and] her body is there simply to be made over to the language of the feminine for any male to read."[38] After all, Byron's male body had been "made over" into a feminine one by the Ali Pacha and praised for his "little white hands," "small ears," and "curling hair." Of the Albanian princes, Byron had condescendingly remarked that they have "painted complexions . . . large black eyes and features perfectly regular . . . the prettiest little animals I ever saw." The "hyacinthine flow" of Leila's hair resembles the "ambrosial curls hanging down his [Eustathios Georgiou's] amiable back," described in Byron's letters, where "hyacinth" serves as a code word for boys with whom he has had sexual relations.[39] In his "Thyrza" lyrics, Byron uses a cross-gendered language to express his love and his grief for Edleston, to whom he referred with feminine pronouns and attributes.[40] In light of these examples, it is clear that Byron's poetic vocabularies could easily reflect a transgender encoding.[41]

This implicative mode in the lyric presentation of Leila's identity stands in sharp contrast to the *indirect diffusion* of Hassan's power over what can and cannot be publicly declared. Talk of Leila's murder does not circulate openly: "Doth Leila there [in the harem] no longer dwell? / That tale can *only* Hassan tell" (445–46). Instead, secretive forms of communication circulate—"strange rumors" (447), suspicions, fragmentary forms of knowledge: "Such is the tale his Nubians tell, / Who did not watch their charge too well; / But others say, that on that night . . ." (465–67). In the epistemologically discredited mode of rumors and speculation, the *talk* of secrets directs attention away from some thing or person, such as Leila or Hassan, and translates it into the shared pleasures of illicit knowledge, whose categories partake of the power that determines them. Facilitating suspicions and rumors and proving himself a fascinated voyeur, the narrator is complicitous in this translation. As oppositional acts, Leila's cross-dressing and escape become effaced in the safer indeterminacy of the socius's rumors and speculations: those secrets which do not oppose Hassan's dominance but are in fact constituted by it. Gossip serves conservative ends; it focuses communal attention on the *effects* of Leila's deviation from Hassan's values, reaffirming and ensuring conformity.

The narrative's patriarchal order draws on other gothic discourses besides the secret when it designates its arenas of punishment. According to a Muslim fisherman, in paradise Hassan will reign over a harem, enjoying the pleasures of the Houris, heavenly equivalents of his earthly slaves. Conversely, the Giaour will suffer the curse of the vampire, eternally roaming the earth as a solitary, unable to die:

> But first, on earth as Vampire sent,
> Thy corse shall from its tomb be rent;
> Then ghastly haunt thy native place,
> And suck the blood from all thy race . . .
> Thy victims ere they yet expire
> Shall know the daemon for their sire . . .
> Wet with thine own best blood shall drip,
> Thy gnashing tooth and haggard lip;
> Then stalking to thy sullen grave—
> Go—and with Gouls and Afrits rave;
> Till these in horror shrink away
> From spectre more accursed than they!
>
> (755–58; 763–64; 781–86)

Just emerging in Western literature, the vampire—here the Giaour—
blocks the family's generational or reproductive dynamics.[42] In
Southey's *Thalaba* (1803), the female Oneiza after her death metamor-
phoses into a vampire—presumably a punishment for using sexual
temptations to divert her lover Thalaba from his familial and national
quest. Her punishment mirrors her crime against the patriarchal
order—an excessive, unproductive female sexuality which drains the
masculine energies necessary for family- and nation-building. With a
lance provided by her own father, Thalaba must drive it through Oneiza's heart before he can resume his quest. In *The Giaour*, the fisherman's
curse amounts to a projection of his own fears, not those of the Giaour
(since the Giaour is not known to be a father or have a family, but only
a single surviving friend). For the fisherman, the vampire embodies a
destructive desire incompatible with the procreative order, one which
must be punished. With his curse, he suggests that if the Giaour's infamous existence which preys upon the social order cannot be eradicated,
it can be driven into exile, at the expense of those whom he loves.[43] The
myth of the vampire's destiny emerges as a communal fantasy that
serves two socially significant purposes: it externalizes collective fears,
while it interiorizes within the vampire the nature of the punishment.

The Giaour, however, already exists in a living exile: "his faith and
race alike unknown" (807), he possesses neither "name or emblem" to
those who consider him (1326). His identity and past cannot be defined
independently from the responses of those who look on him, including
the narrator's:

> On—on he hastened—and he drew
> My gaze of wonder as he flew:

> Though like a demon of the night
> He passed and vanished from my sight;
> His aspect and his air impressed
> A troubled memory on my breast;
> And long upon my startled ear
> Rung his dark courser's hoofs of fear.
>
> (200–207)

When the Giaour is compared to a "demon of the night," whose so-called "evil eye" (612) repulses Hassan, the poem exhibits horror first and foremost as a social act of mystification with the aim of exclusion. Byron's comments elsewhere on the "evil eye" emphasize the viewer's response, not the possessor's vaunted power. He writes of the Levantine superstition of the "'evil eye,' . . . of which the imaginary effects are yet very singular *on those who conceive themselves affected*."[44] *The Giaour*, in turn, leads not to the discovery of real monsters but to the social projection of sublime fixations and prohibitions.

Another monster aligned with the Giaour is the Gorgon (896). Associated in antiquity with the unspeakable, the Gorgon becomes affiliated with forbidden forms of eroticism in nineteenth-century literature: in particular, in a source Byron would have been familiar with, Matthew Lewis's *The Monk*.[45] Satan, whose desire for Ambrosio impels the plot of *The Monk*, has hair "supplied by living snakes, which twined themselves around his brows."[46] In Byron's tale, the Giaour is depicted as Gorgon-like: "*See*—by the half-illumin'd wall / His hood fly back—his dark hair fall—/ That pale brow wildly wreathing round, / As if the Gorgon there had bound / The sablest of the serpent-braid" (893–97). Similarly, the narrator's voyeuristic fantasy of being seen or pinned by the Giaour's gaze, equivalent to possession by some unspeakable knowledge, is dramatized through the Gorgon-like metaphor of a snake mesmerizing a bird:[47]

> Oft will his glance the gazer rue—
> For in it lurks that nameless spell
> Which speaks—itself unspeakable
> . . . .
> And like the bird whose pinions quake—
> But cannot fly the gazing snake—
> Will others quail beneath his look
> Nor 'scape the glance they scarce can brook. . . .
>
> (837–39; 842–45)

Otto Fenichal, writing on the Gorgon-Medusa figure, points to the connection between the rigid glance and fascination, an intimacy between looking and identification:

> To be turned into stone is, like losing [one's] sight, a frequent punishment for scoptophilia. . . . "To be turned into stone" by the sight of something means to be fascinated by it. . . . The rigidity of a person turned into stone stands for the fixed gaze and the rigidity of the whole muscular system of a person fascinated by something he sees. . . . In this train of thought the essential point is that looking is conceived of as a means of identification.[48]

Byron suggests that the quasi-supernatural power by which the snake/Gorgon fixes the viewer's attention results from those fascinated gazers who displace the intensity of their feelings onto the Gorgon/Giaour.

For his own punishment, the Giaour self-elects exile and brands himself with Cain's "mark." The Christian monk of the tale seeks a confession, if only to absolve the Giaour on the grounds that the murder of *an infidel* does not count as murder. The Giaour disdains such hypocrisy and acknowledges his guilt for Leila's and Hassan's deaths: "She died—I dare not tell thee how, / But look—'tis written on my brow! / There read of Cain the curse and crime, / In characters unworn by time" (1056–59). The apostate Giaour ironically appropriates the monk's religious discourse in order to reject his pardon. The Giaour insists on a private value, inaccessible and socially undetermined, not only for his punishment but for his love. Thus, the spectral Leila returns to him in a vision:

> I saw her—yes—she lived again . . .
> . . . .
> I saw her, friar! and I rose . . .
> . . . .
> And [clasped] her to my desperate heart;
> I clasp—what is it that I clasp?
> . . . .
> Alas! around a shadow prest,
> [My arms] shrink upon my lonely breast;
> Yet still—'tis there—in silence stands,
> And beckons with beseeching hands!
>   (1272, 1283, 1286–87; 1296–99)

This phantasmatic figure mediates between the Giaour's abiding desire for Leila and the social conditions in which that desire is compelled to assume a shadowy existence. Leila stands "in silence": unspeakable in the socius that engenders such a phantom, beyond its discursive reach.[49] Sequestered into his private fantasy space, the Giaour finds "consolation" in Leila's enduring—and sexless—claim.[50]

The Giaour's insistence on private meanings beyond social determination reflects, however, an internalization of its values. He imagines his self-imposed exile and oath of fidelity to the dead Leila make all the difference. Into this scenario where public norms governing gender and sexuality give rise to such "individual" truths, the supernatural intrudes as the mode both sides adopt to express their antagonism—as an imagined difference, or freedom, from one another. The vampire, the gorgon, and the secret expose the social will to exclude what it defines as the terrifying and fascinating forces or knowledges that threaten it, thereby establishing its own internal, if illusory, coherence. Conversely, with Leila's phantom, the Giaour wills something beyond the public's purview; in effect, however, he reproduces socially prohibited forms of eroticism as disembodied and unreal.[51]

The narrator speaks from both sides of this gothicized divide. A supposed eyewitness of the crime, he indulges rumors and withholds knowledge; he neither deciphers nor imposes a meaning on the secrets he hears. If he evinces sympathy for the Giaour, he is also not above flagrantly marketing the story to an imagined audience. His fascinated tracking of the Giaour mocks the desire for scandal, even as it reflects his own investment in it. His insinuating, conjectural tone dramatizes the explicit connection between illicit content and narrative suspense, and he exposes the dependence of his own narrative on proscribed identities as its condition of possibility.

One voice the narrator adopts to transmit the Giaour's story is the monk, the recipient of secrets who shuttles between the supposed privacy of the confessional and his role as an agent of socioreligious conformity. When the Giaour claims that the penitents' "secret sins and sorrows rest / Within [the monk's] pure and pitying breast" (980–81), he directs his irony at the monk's hypocritical service to "two masters." Yet the Giaour entrusts him with his story, encouraging him to guess his "soul's estate in secret" (1208), as if tacitly acknowledging that no dealer in secrets could be pure. The narrator, similarly compromised, peddles the identity of the Giaour *as a secret*, a valuable public commodity. Yet he says "nothing" about the Giaour that does not say more about the socius from which the Giaour finds himself excluded. In doing so, the narrator's speaking of secrets might also be said to constitute an act of sympathy or affiliation.

The Giaour, A Fragment of a Turkish Tale advertises itself as incomplete. According to the preface, it is composed of "disjointed fragments." The narrator concludes with the line "this broken tale was all we knew" (1333). Asterisks punctuate the narrative between sections, both those without transitions, implying missing material, and even those with them. These markers visually disrupt the text with signs of exclusion, like the text's frequent coupling of references to secrets with a dash. Beyond the visibility of absent presence, the graphic fragmentation posits the narrative's failure. The maintenance of secrets surrounding the cross-dressed Leila and the Giaour preserves their incoherent representation.[52] Eric Meyer reads Byron's fragmentation as a means of signifying the ongoing, and hence, always incomplete "social practice of meaning production."[53] In *The Giaour*, fragmentation alludes to what could be called a concomitant practice of linking the "meaningless" to the production of socially "unacceptable" identities.[54] A coherent representation of something other than heterosexuality is impossible within a cultural context where such coherence is neither given nor natural, and difficult to imagine. The narrator's refusal to bring together the pieces, to clarify the enigmatic events and inconsistencies reflects the more than constructed—and excluded—nature of certain sexual identities. Strict sociosexual divisions produce those that are spoken fragmentarily, in gothic terms, along with the critical promise of their difference.

Same-sex desire and gender fluidity, concerns indirectly suggested in *The Giaour*, are revisited when Byron writes *Lara*. There they find their most overt and compelling representation in the page Kaled, who recalls the page in *Childe Harold*, the "dark-eyed boy who loved his master well" (II, 10–11).[55] With Kaled at his side, Lara, long "absent from the . . . Gothic pile" (I, 41–42), returns home a stranger. The community scrutinizes his glances, gestures, moods, from which they try to read the secrets of his past. Their attention does not remain on Lara, however, but shifts to Kaled, who openly asserts what had been only nascent in the earlier tale, *The Giaour*: the identity of this "equivocal" persona supplants the Byronic hero as the primary nexus of narrative conflict and psychological interest. Reading the successive subject(s) of secrecy in *The Giaour* and *Lara*, Jerome Christensen sees only exhausted serialized production. These protagonists, however, point to significant, revised stagings of unresolved sociopsychological conflicts about sexual differences that Byron began in *The Giaour*.[56] While there is a return to similar concerns in *Lara*, the focus of attention shifts markedly. In *The Giaour*, for example, Leila as the cross-dressed page figure occupies a marginal role in relation to the narrative's primary point of interest, i.e., the social responses to the Giaour's identity. By the time of *Lara*, the male protagonist recedes in importance, and Byron progressively moves Kaled to the center of the narrative. *Lara* explores the social responses directed at and elicited by a cross-dressed figure, the effeminate male Kaled, something not only new to *Tales* but to the literature of the time.

The narrative begins with a communal feast for Lara, now the feudal lord. To the serfs, the son's return suggests a rejuvenation of the crumbling patriarchal order, a reinvestment in its values: "the Serfs are glad through Lara's wide domain, / And Slavery half forgets her feudal chain; / He, their unhop'd, but unforgotten lord, / The long self-exiled chieftain is restored" (I, 1–4). Yet the community's questions about Lara's past signal their anxieties about his transition from wayward son to *paterfamilias*, whether "his name / Might yet uphold his patrimonial fame" (I, 59–60). Fatherless, and for years without a "father-land" (I, 25), this "Lord of himself" may not be man enough to assume or inherit the father's real and symbolic estate. Lara's self-exile and return unleash doubts about his legitimacy.

The narrator whets the reader's appetite by offering and withholding events from Lara's obscure past. He refers to unnamed "faults" and "sins," points to his possession of "something more beneath, / Than glance could well reveal, or accent breathe" (I, 77–78), but decides that "it skills not, boots not step by step to trace / His youth through all the mazes of its race" (I, 21–22). These secrets, however, become the "food" the community feasts on:

> Opinion varying o'er his hidden lot,
> In praise or railing ne'er his name forgot;
> His silence formed a theme for others' prate —
> They guess'd—they gaz'd—they fain would know his fate.
> What had he been? what was he, thus unknown,
> Who walked their world, his lineage only known?
>
> (I, 291–96)

Lara's audience fantasizes about experiences unavailable for possession within a patriarchal narrative of succession: "was it a dream? / . . . / Or did his silence prove his memory fix'd / Too deep for words, indelible, unmix'd [?]" (I, 275; 281–82). Directing their activity toward bringing a hidden truth to light, the tale's community of readers reveals a growing cultural investment in the existence of secret truths. In struggling to pinpoint definitive physical characteristics that unveil the secret's contents, they imagine Lara's body will uncover "a 'difference' that threatens to remain 'secreted but inaccessible inside.' "[57] The question of whether Lara does indeed have a core identity is never ascertained, and the only available discourse remains one of supposition.[58]

Lara's effort to discourage the community's interest perversely heightens it into obsession. While they cannot forget him, Lara's own "seeming forgetfulness . . . [makes] / His vassals more amaz'ed nor less afraid" (I, 269–70). The more he is silent, the more they speculate. Because it is not available to them as common property, the content—the secret of Lara's past, his identity—cannot, according to the narrator, be "named" or accounted for in the language of "patrimonial fame" (I, 59–60). This is also to say, paradoxically, that the community invests it with the highest value, essential to the preservation of Lara's mystical authority. His power increases the more he appears resistant to their purview, and soon the serfs endow him with quasi-supernatural powers, imagining a "mysterious circle thrown" around him (I, 107). This projection of a privately cultivated mystery serves the public's conferring of power and privilege. Byron was highly attuned to how his own symbolic capital increased through allusion to a half-hidden, more dangerous, subversive self.[59] Lara's dispersal through the socius—he has collectively "stamped" their minds—reflects the communal desire to install him as their powerful other:

> None knew, nor how, nor why, but he entwined
> Himself perforce around the hearer's mind;
> There he was stamp'd, in liking, or in hate,
> If greeted once; however brief the date
> That friendship, pity, or aversion knew,
> Still there within the inmost thought he grew.
> You could not penetrate his soul, but found,
> Despite your wonder, to your own he wound;
> His presence haunted still; and from the breast
> He forced an all unwilling interest;
> Vain was the struggle in that mental net,
> His spirit seemed to dare you to forget!
>
> (I, 371–82)

To a greater extent than in *The Giaour*, the secret emblematizes that quasi-hypnotic bond, or, to use Byron's gothic term, the "haunting" through which the community struggles to constitute its identity.

In *Lara*, the preservation of the secret also guarantees peace within the social realm. When Ezzelin, for example, threatens to reveal the secret of Lara's past and then mysteriously disappears, the patriarchal order of feudal lords accuses Lara of crimes; Lara's serfs, siding with him, rise up in revolt. Social anarchy and bloodshed ensue. With the entrance of Ezzelin, Byron seems to flirt with the possibility of a paranoid gothic narrative, one in which the secret, as Eve Sedgwick points out, expresses cultural fears concerning homosexual blackmail.[60] Interestingly, Byron drops this possibility and imagines instead the use of the secret to establish communal cohesiveness. The tacit hoarding of the secret operates as a "safe" middle ground, mediating between two extremes: the conservative identification with the patriarchal order (and its claims to know and control, as represented in the figure of Ezzelin) and full-scale revolution. Having the secret function in this way to preserve social stability (don't ask, don't tell) is the obverse side of Byron's other common strategy, noted by Jonathan Gross, whereby erotic dissatisfaction gets played out or disguised as political protest.[61]

If Lara is secure in the serfs' eyes, he is denied insertion in the patriarchal line and history. In a gothicized scenario of gender inversion, Lara passes at night through a gallery of portraits that eye him with displeasure: "Through night's long hours would sound his hurried tread / O'er the dark gallery, where his fathers frown'd / In rude but antique portraiture round. / They [his attendants] heard, but whisper'd—'*that* must not be known'— / The sound of words less earthly than his own" (I, 136–40). Lara's estate, both familiar and strange, asserts its ancestral claims upon him, the demand to act as these (dead) fathers want. Among the "painted forms of other times," Lara fades to ghostliness, a shadowy figure among the forms of patriarchal history who disinherit him:

> He turned . . . ,
> And his high shadow shot along the wall;
> . . . .
> He wandering mused, and as the moonbeam shone
> Through the dim lattice o'er the floor of stone,
> And the high fretted roof, and saints, that there
> O'er Gothic windows knelt in pictured prayer,
> Reflected in fantastic figures grew,
> Like life, but not like mortal life, to view;
> His bristling locks of sable, brow of gloom,
> And the wide waving of his shaken plume

Glanced like a spectre's attributes, and gave
His aspect all that terror gives the grave.

(I, 181–82; 191–200)

The "wide waving of his shaken plume" alludes to Walpole's *Otranto*, in which a fluttering plume images the novel's crisis, the faulty transmission of the paternal estate. Lara's conflict with the dead fathers, overheard by attendants as a conversation in an unintelligible language, ends with a "long, loud shriek." He is discovered "senseless" and prostrate, with a "half-drawn sabre near." With "half" a sabre, he is "half" a man, and the loss of his masculine self-possession and his adoption of a foreign tongue dramatize Lara's alienation from the name and discursive legacy he is to assume as son and heir. Like the dispossessed, "swooning" young men in Walpole, Lara is unable to bear the father's legacy into the present.

Not coincidentally, it is at this moment of dispossession that Kaled steps forward: "His page approach'd, and he alone appeared / To know the import of the words they heard" (I, 235–36). Now assuming the foreground as the narrative's central figure, Kaled's secrets are tied to his androgynous markers (for example, the "hectic tint of secret care" on his visage, I, 534). Like the lines inscribed on the Giaour's face that confound image with history or narrative, Kaled's foreign language, his outlandish costume, and the indistinguishable gender of his name or alias mark him as "untranslateably other" (whether in the tale's Spanish locale or in the reader's Regency England).[62] Kaled knows the foreign tongue Lara speaks, and Lara's secrets pass almost imperceptibly to Kaled. From now on, the community turns to Kaled in order to read Lara. Unlike Leila, who has an identity distinguishable from the male protagonist, Kaled is physically and symbolically inseparable from Lara.[63]

The wavering between Kaled's integrity as a character and as a projection of Lara's own psyche is one way Byron can explore the risks of identifying with male effeminacy. Kaled's gaze, for example, suggests the dual identity they share: "For hours on Lara he would fix his glance, / As all forgotten in that watchful trance" (I, 544–45). His very name apparently an alias, Kaled thereby defers the disclosure of his identity—a deferral heightened by his failure to recognize even that alias: "For sometimes he [Kaled] would hear, however nigh, / That name repeated loud without reply, / As unfamiliar, or, if roused again, / Start to the sound, as but remembered then; / Unless 'twas Lara's wonted voice that spake" (I, 586–90). Lara provides the name with subjective identity, but one "subjected" to Lara's recognition. His act of naming brings Kaled into being.

Their mirroring intensifies through the private language they share. When Lara speaks "in terms that seem not of his native tongue, / Distinct but strange," Kaled "alone [appears] / To know the import of the words" others hear but do not understand (I, 230, 235–36). The community assumes these foreign words signify something illicit: "they [the words] were not such as Lara *should* avow, / Nor he [Kaled] interpret" (I, 238–39, my italics). To the community, what can be avowed "must" necessarily coincide with one's native tongue (Lara's and Kaled's words "*seem not* of his native tongue"): e.g., be equivalent to a recognizable ("native") identity. In *Lara*'s social universe, the "non-native" signifies prohibited knowledge—as well as the prohibited identity such knowledge would seem to establish.

In terms of the gothic, the idea of a private language, or the alignment between an unintelligible language and homoeroticism had been forcefully represented in Lewis's *The Monk*.[64] As the embodiment of gender instability and "demonic" desires, Matilda (a devil passing as a young male novice on behalf of Satan, who himself desires the monk Ambrosio) possesses a private language which she shares with Satan. During a ritual of black magic, Matilda calls on Satan "in a language unintelligible . . . and [is] answered in the same." In turn, Ambrosio reads from Matilda's book to summon Satan, in this same unknown language: "He contrived to finish the four first lines on the page. They were in a language, whose import was totally unknown to him."[65] Ambrosio's contract with Satan entails being pierced by his pen, presumably the initial and initiatory lesson in that language. In *The Monk*, this "foreign" tongue carries overtly homoerotic dimensions, since it both mediates and tropes Satan's desire for, and bond with, Ambrosio. Lara's and Kaled's private language, foreign to others, also refers to their emotionally and erotically charged bond.

Lara's and Kaled's dual identity is stressed by both the narrator and by the community. Experiencing Lara's impending death as his own, Kaled "strove to stand and gaze, but reel'd and fell, / Scarce breathing more than that he lov'd so well," II, 510–11). He chooses "like him he served, to live apart" (I, 550); like Lara, he exhibits "secret care" (I, 534), "a grief that none should share" (I, 541). Rejecting the absolution the priest offers an unconscious Lara with a Lara-like disdain, Kaled's words are accepted as the equivalent of Lara's own. Kaled often preempts Lara's need for language by anticipating his thoughts and wishes (I, 556–57; 605; 612–13). As the community transfers their interest in

Lara's secret to Kaled's, the crime is reconfigured too. Never firmly established, Ezzelin's murderer is rumored to be Kaled, not Lara. Tied once again to the cross-dressing page, the crime (as in *The Giaour*) is aligned with the infraction of gender norms. Unlike the punitive murder by drowning that Leila suffers, however, Kaled is spared; Ezzelin, who comes to expose Lara's secrets (which will presumably deny Lara social legitimacy) and to punish him, drowns.

Lara's dying words, which the community await, elude their comprehension:

> . . . each remaining word,
> They understood not, if distinctly heard;
> His dying tones are *in that other tongue,*
> To which some *strange remembrance* wildly clung.
> They spake of other scenes, but what—is known
> To Kaled, whom their meaning reach'd alone
>
> . . . .
>
> They seem'd even then—that twain—unto the last
> To half forget the present in the past;
> To share between themselves some separate fate,
> Whose darkness none beside should penetrate.
>
> (II, 442–47; 450–53)

Instead of illuminating their "separate fate [of] darkness," Kaled's silence reinforces the exclusive nature of their bond.[66] The scars on Lara's body, illegible to the audience eager to read them, reinscribe his "absolute" difference. This depiction of fetishized reading exposes how the conditions for social belonging depend upon the extent to which a body is "recognizable." Although they are determined by visibility paradigms, at times they manage to elude them. The survivors bury Lara separate from his family "line," excluding him from the legibility and continuity conferred by paternal names and histories. In a repetition of earlier transferences of identity, Kaled acts out and suffers what properly belongs to Lara, obsessively staunching a phantasmatic wound that does not heal, in a hystericized scenario.[67] The final object of the narrator's and audience's gaze, Kaled is associated with the secret's increasing density, not its disclosure.

What the narrator offers to the reader is the revelation of Kaled's gender crossing: Kaled, who has passed as a young man, is a woman. The sight of her breasts as she tears her shirt open in grief does not, however, amount to a heterosexual solution. Despite the alibi ultimately proposed, the reader's experience of Kaled's otherness cannot be effaced.[68] Calling attention to Romantic representations of same-sex friendship, Claudia Johnson argues that while they grant visibility to homoerotic relations, they divest them of real import. Heterosexual privilege may be challenged by such friendships, but they are less "gay" than they are beyond available discourses.[69] Yet this "friendship" between Kaled and Lara, sustained for the duration of the narrative, is a love ostensibly between men, and, as George Haggerty suggests, that is finally more threatening to heterosexist culture that two men having sex.[70] The narrator emphasizes this with his alternating, but equal, stress on the masculine pronoun oscillating between reference to a male love object *and* a male subject who loves: Kaled "scarce [breathes] more than that *he* lov'd so well / Than that *he* lov'd!" (II, 511–12, my italics).[71]

Kaled's feminine features have been read by critics as "winks" to the audience, meant to establish early on that Kaled is a woman. Byron, too, keeps his readers uncertain whether to invoke the literary convention of the female page. That interpretive gesture, however, runs contrary to the narrative's efforts to confound any norm through its sustained assertions of kinds of "half"-knowledge, those connections of supposedly irreconcilable or oppositional qualities of femininity and masculinity.[72] Prolonging the disguise, Byron ironically plays out his own and his audience's fears about other genders, as well as the failure of self-evident, visible evidence of sexual identity. Here, in a witty inversion, heterosexuality easily "passes" for homosexuality, and everyone, in such a world, is potentially prey to a "hermeneutics of suspicion."[73]

Like Gulnare in Byron's *The Corsair*, who is at once "above" and "beneath" her sex, Kaled perplexes by being something "more than" man or woman:

> [No] mark of vulgar toil that hand betrays,
> So femininely white it might bespeak
> Another sex, when matched with that smooth cheek,
> But for his garb, and something in his gaze,
> More wild and high than woman's eye betrays;
> A latent fierceness that far more became
> His fiery climate than his tender frame:
> True, in his words it broke not from his breast,
> But from his aspect might be more than guessed.
>
> (I, 575–83)

Kaled's body, which "should" reveal the "true" gender of her feminine psyche, gives ambiguous evidence: her femininely white hand is contradicted by her masculine "wild eye," which in turn bespeaks her psyche's masculine "fierceness." Neither body nor psyche are unitary or consistent, to say nothing of their supposedly "natural" relation.

The discovery that Kaled is a woman in the end resolves very little:

> That trying moment had at once reveal'd
> The secret long and yet but half-concealed;
> In baring to revive that lifeless breast,
> Its grief seem'd ended, but the sex confest;
> And life return'd, and Kaled felt no shame —
> What now to her was Womanhood or Fame?
>
> (II, 514–19)

If the narrative substitutes a cross-dressed woman for an effeminate boy attached to another man, one whose willingness to murder and absence of remorse situate her in no woman's land, it is an identity scarcely reassuring for its audience. The very indeterminacy of Lara's and Kaled's exteriors has compulsively generated the communal need to identify and expose difference, and Byron intuitively grasps and represents this subconscious response. He offers the audience the transparently cheap solution they seek in Kaled's baring of her breast, while ironically undermining the security of that solution. Kaled reveals, if anything, that all "truths" about gender wind up "half concealed" and only "seeming truths." Because Byron's "experiments with codes of gender are radical in their implications," as Susan Wolfson writes of *Lara*, so too are its "social and psychological consequences."[74] The audience's desire for such otherness motivates their engagement, while Regency England would demand that those equivocal subjects be punished. *Lara*, however, manages to walk the line to the end between preserving and recuperating otherness: the heterosexual solution inserted at the end comes too late to save anything.[75]

4

"This Dream It Would not Pass Away": *Christabel* and Mimetic Enchantment

I am there where no news of myself reaches me.

—Persian aphorism

Love transforms the souls into a conformity with the object loved
—Coleridge, Notebooks, entry 189

DURING THE WRITING OF *CHRISTABEL*, COLERIDGE THE CRITIC LAMbasts the gothic's broken charms: "I have just read *The Castle Spectre*—a flat unimaginative Bombast. . . . Passion-Horror! agonizing pangs of conscience! Dreams full of hell, serpents. . . . Its situations are all borrowed. . . . The whole plot, machinery, and incidents are borrowed. The play is a mere patchwork of plagiarisms."[1] Coleridge's most intense criticisms of the gothic as a "debased" genre, due to its imitative proclivities, or reliance on borrowing, happen to be directed at a male author suspected of a "debased" sexuality: Matthew Lewis, author of *The Monk* and *The Castle Spectre*, openly reputed to be homosexual.[2] According to Coleridge, since Lewis never explains away the magic of the demonic, he cancels individual moral agency by insisting on a supernatural one. To suspend natural laws is to suspend human agency.[3] Further, Coleridge derides Lewis's "lewd tales" and "voluptuous images" that "deeply deprave" the mind of the reader.[4] Interestingly, however, the description of Lewis's *The Castle Spectre* reads almost exactly like a description of *Christabel*, since it too features the suspension of individual agency, as well as passions, horrors, a serpent, hellish dreams, and the torments of guilt. Coleridge employs the same terms of moral depravity critics would apply to Geraldine's prolonged embrace of Christabel with "joyous look" and "heaving breasts." The accusations of Lewis, then, boomerang to implicate Coleridge, whose attack on Lewis's drama will fail to disguise or contain the literal and figurative homoerotics of

91

his own poem. His representations of a supernaturalized, irrational agency and transgressive sexuality make him morally suspect in the same ways he considers Lewis to be, and *Christabel*, in accordance with Coleridge's own evaluative categories, presents itself as a weak imitation.[5]

For Coleridge the critic, imitation is an aesthetic problem that records an effacement of interpersonal discursive boundaries, particularly troubling when it threatens the uniqueness and autonomy of the male author's voice. With the conventionally elitist rhetoric common to the detractors of gothic fiction, he chastises the borrowing and plagiarism he sees underlying the gothic as "unimaginative." Yet Coleridge, not just a reviewer but a reader and writer of the gothic, also identifies therein the imitative or mimetic tendencies permeating the pleasures and terrors of *Christabel*'s imaginative universe—a desire for sameness that also fueled the popularity of the gothic novel. Does the vehemence of Coleridge's language in this review reflect his anxiety that others might see what he has: that the *same*-sex desire which impels Geraldine and Christabel to share a couch arises from a particular form of mirroring or repetition compulsion that informs all telling, even the "unspeakable" moment in *Christabel*, that cliché of withheld revelation? With *Christabel*, as we will see, it becomes difficult to differentiate the identificatory exchanges underlying erotic and imaginative activity from the mimesis that governs aesthetic form. This, in turn, raises questions about the autonomy of Coleridge's masculine voice.

By writing the gothic, Coleridge distances himself from "authentic" and "contained" masculine speech and aligns himself with the "utterly conventional" and "licentiously imaginative" female readers, writers, and characters, as Karen Swann suggests. (For "utterly conventional" and "licentiously imaginative," we can substitute the critic Coleridge's terms, "borrowed" and "morally depraved").[6] Geraldine's and Christabel's homoerotic desire and transitive identities prove to be the means through which Coleridge resists their placement within an oedipal narrative. Through their contagious desire, Coleridge the writer finds a mode of identification that, according to the literary culture of the time, effeminizes him, just as Byron has staged alternative versions of masculinity through the cross-dressed page figures. Coleridge is enthralled by—and participates in—the fantasied loss of individuated self, the dispossession of singular or discrete identity, that Geraldine's union with Christabel exemplifies.

Coleridge, then, connects questions of aesthetic creation indirectly, if pointedly, to those of masculinity in his gothic verse narrative and its preface. He explores those connections not through representations of the submissive male body, as Keats does in the *Hyperion* fragments, but through Geraldine's and Christabel's erotic encounter and its uncanny effects on voice.[7] To underscore the links between male effeminization and symbolic dispossession, *Christabel* ties homoeroticism, as do *The Giaour* and *Lara*, to what cannot be signified. For Coleridge, it is not the mysterious, however, but another gothic cliché of unsymbolizable content—the unspeakable—that comes into play in this verse narrative at its most heightened moment of homoerotic revelation: "A sight to dream of, not to tell!" Christabel's desire for Geraldine becomes a metaphor for both the possibility *and* the prohibition of imaginative activity and certain sexual acts. The bedchamber scene dramatizes Christabel's—and the narrator's—ability to present the affective and libidinal energies of a homoerotic experience *and* the subsequent inability to represent it autonomously (Geraldine emerges as the malevolent usurper of Christabel's speech). "Rapt" by an enchantment, Christabel is dispossessed of her own voice and ventriloquizes Geraldine's. When, according to Tillotama Rajan, "the poet in *Christabel* is scarcely present as an identifiable masculine voice, submerging in his female character," it is because the fantasied scenario between Christabel and Geraldine affords Coleridge a vehicle for self-projection as a double negation: he is "rapt" of his masculinity and of authorial agency.[8]

By virtue of the poem's conflation of same-sex desire with imaginative plenitude, dissolving identities, demonic possession, doubling, and ventriloquism, one could say that the poet flirts deliberately with the destruction of his male authorial voice. That a fantasy of unspeakable content—in *Christabel*, same-sex desire between women—disrupts the process of signification does not, however, deflect from its paradoxical relation to culture's symbolic functioning. Represented in part as a willing relinquishment of autonomy indistinguishable from love, the suppressed homoerotic moment in *Christabel* comes to read as a figure for certain pleasures of aesthetic creation and reception. And instead of containing the supernaturalized impulses exemplified by Geraldine's power over Christabel as ones that relate solely to their sexual union, in Part Two Coleridge enchants everyone with a similar spell. "Being spoken by an other" is an uncanny effect, or relationship, that extends throughout the tale's represented social realm. The relinquishment of self and transgression of the symbolic order troped as same-sex desire in Part One is retroped in Part Two as a proclivity to mimicry that makes possible that same symbolic order. As Coleridge recognizes, the power of patriarchal discourse and custom depends upon a logic of repetition. Writing of patriarchal law, Judith Butler argues that it is constructed "by reiteration of a *norm* or set of *norms*" that enable the law to repress its own contingent basis.[9] The "lawlike" norms of culture would elide their indebtedness to citation and relegate certain forms of repetition—such as that underlying Geraldine's and Christabel's homoeroticism—to bad, degraded imitations. Coleridge, however, universalizes this "deviant" dynamic. A rhetorical repetition compulsion speaks through all the subjects of the poem, including the narrator, and Coleridge thereby converts a strategy of stigmatization into a condition of belonging within the imagined sociosymbolic community.

Thus, the parodic tone of *Christabel*'s narrator implies something other than a simple satiric condemnation of the gothic's excesses. Along with the poem's heightened consciousness of style, literariness, and penchant for quotation and allusion, his tone represents a formally conscious act of identification whereby Coleridge exposes his authorial—and his readers'—affinity for imitation.[10] Coleridge exposes the ruse of originality grounding patriarchal discourse, in effect, dispossessing himself of its authoritarian prerogatives. Troped through homoeroticism in the poem and preface, such a stance dovetails with contemporary cultural discourses that portray the sodomite as possessing a striking propensity for imitation. To read the mimetic energies within *Christabel* is to address how a gendering and (homo)eroticizing of formal questions is used to mediate literary relations between men, what their import might be for a male artist who identifies with such feminized forms, and looking beyond the category of gender, what cultural fantasies Coleridge taps into by framing a consideration of aesthetic creation and reception through a specifically sexualized rhetoric—the erotics of same-sex desire.

The plot of *Christabel* can be briefly summarized as follows: outside her father's, the Baron Leoline's, castle at midnight, the motherless Christabel meets a mysterious and beautiful woman Geraldine—abandoned, she claims, after an abduction and rape.[11] Christabel carries the fainting Geraldine into the castle and invites her to share her "couch" for the night.[12] As Geraldine undresses, Christabel sees a "sight to dream of, not to tell," identified by Geraldine as her "mark of shame" and "seal . . . of sorrow." Geraldine casts a spell over Christabel's speech, which, she asserts, follows from Christabel's "touch of [her] bosom." Christabel's "most shocking dreams" of the night alternate with blissful and soothing ones in Geraldine's arms. The morning after,

Christabel finds she cannot say what has happened to her. In Part Two, her father receives Geraldine warmly as the daughter of his estranged friend, Sir Roland, and vows vengeance against Geraldine's violators, imagining a reconciliation with Sir Roland. Mimicking Geraldine's covert glances, Christabel's demeanor appears increasingly sinister and reptilian. At the end of the fragment, Geraldine has displaced Christabel in her father's affections, and Geraldine and Baron Leoline depart arm-in-arm while Christabel watches.

From the poem's opening lines, erotic concerns are consistently troped as aesthetic ones. Like those *"strange"* and *"sweet"* carvings in Christabel's private space, her bedchamber (I, 179), Christabel's first glimpse of Geraldine in the woods falls upon a "lady *strange*" with a voice "faint and *sweet*" (I, 71–72). "Frightful" and "beautiful exceedingly" (I, 66, 68), Geraldine's image is like the marvelous, obscure figures of art in Christabel's chamber which excite the viewer's curiosity. Exoticized, "like a lady of a far countree" (I, 225), she captures Christabel's wandering gaze, and her disrobing provokes a "movement," or active fantasizing, within Christabel's mind:

> Her gentle limbs did she [Christabel] undress,
> And lay down in her loveliness.
> But through her brain of weal and woe,
> So many thoughts moved to and fro,
> That vain it were her lids to close;
> So half-way from the bed she rose,
> And on her elbow did recline
> To look at lady Geraldine.
>
> (I, 237–44)

The sensuous perception of a beautiful image, coupled with thoughts that scarcely know themselves, underlies sexual desire *and* the aesthetic impulse. Geraldine binds Christabel's gaze, so that Christabel is "filled with" Geraldine, taking her in as Geraldine "takes it off." In *Mimesis and Alterity*, Michael Taussig describes how, in mimetic magic, "appearance itself is power. . . . this is a function of the fact that appearance itself can acquire density and substance. It is this property that brings spirit, soul, and image, into one constellation."[13] Coleridge uses gothicized language in the *Notebooks* to describe a similar mimetic experience triggered by a visual image: "Ghost of a mountain—the forms seizing my Body as I passed & became realities—I, a Ghost, till I had reconquered my Substance." Coleridge describes the subject's loss of his own substantial reality—in favor of an other's, here the mountain's—as part of the perceptive act, a loss that requires an act of will to recover ("till I had *reconquered* my Substance").[14] When Geraldine is revealed "full in view," an image that presumably should determine who and what Geraldine is, Christabel cannot speak. Her speechlessness marks her inability to master or possess the image: "she [Geraldine] unbound / The cincture from beneath her breast: / Her silken robe, and inner vest, / Dropt to her feet, and full in view, / Behold! her bosom and half her side— / A sight to dream of, not to tell!" (I, 252–53). The narrator's exclamatory "Behold!" and "O shield her!" do not disclose the significance of the "unbound" image, but only the excessive affect that "undoes" Christabel (and the narrator) as an autonomous viewer.

In the conclusion to Part One, the culmination of the aesthetic-erotic mirroring occurs when the narrator assembles Christabel's features into a conventionalized Magdalen portrait from those Christabel herself has noted while watching Geraldine undress: the hands clasped in prayer, the heaving breast, a face lined with "bliss and bale," and the glittering eyes. With those eyes, Coleridge alludes not only to the visual nature of erotic engagements, but of aesthetic vision as a power *to bind the beholder or reader to see as the artist does (or as his characters do)*, in this case, doubling and redoubling the "homoerotic" spell (first of the narrator, then of the audience).[15] Subjective identity evaporates with the assumption of another's vision. This dispossessing power of the aesthetic is experienced in *Kubla Khan, The Rime of the Ancient Mariner*, and *The Nightingale*, as beauty, holy dread, and enthusiasm, respectively, or, in *Christabel*, as bliss and shame.

Because a *shared* vision can exist between creator and beholder, the image in *Christabel* recasts aesthetic and erotic experience as one that challenges the possibility of discrete identity.[16] When Christabel first starts at the sight of a "lady so richly clad as she" (I, 67), she registers the shock of the double: the referent of "she" keeps slipping between Geraldine and Christabel, suggesting their transitive identity. Christabel's rising "half-way" to watch Geraldine undress and Geraldine's revelation of "half her side" points to their complementary relationship, or dual identity. And in fact it seems fitting to describe, as Coleridge does, Christabel's and Geraldine's bond as a trance-like lack of awareness of difference. Another name for this semi- or unconscious emotional identification is mimesis. The subject of mimesis no longer exists as a subject, but is somewhere between waking and sleeping. Different cultures have understood such states of *depersonalization* differently: as spirit communication (as shamans would), as demonic possession, sacred transport or ecstasy (as theologians or mystics would), as suggestive rapport or transference (as hypnotists or psychoanalysts would), or as inspired speech (as poets might). Mikkel Borch-Jacobsen describes the *lived experience* of mimesis as incommunicable, since "one can not simultaneously be other while distinguishing oneself from that alterity" in order to represent it. Since mimesis is unaware of difference or opposition, it transgresses the symbolic order: "Every discourse on the trance . . . can do nothing but miss its object, precisely because it makes an object of it."[17]

This experience of mimetic alterity or dispossession saturates the phenomenological world of *Christabel*. It is also contemplated repeatedly in Coleridge's lyrics and notebook entries in the mid- and late-1790s. Activities central to *Christabel*—same-sex desire, aesthetic perception or imagination, dreaming, the mother-child bond, sympathy—are engendered by this dynamic. In its idealized form, Coleridge equates such self-loss with "fancy" or "faith," the self dispersed and assimilated by the Other, as in the poem "Religious Musings": "When he by sacred sympathy might make / The whole ONE SELF! SELF, that no alien knows! / Self, far diffus'd as Fancy's wing can travel! / Self, spreading still! *Oblivious of its own,* / Yet all of all possessing! This is FAITH!" (167–71; my italics). Speaking of prayer in the *Notebooks*, Coleridge calls it a "self-annihilation—the soul enters the Holy of Holies." Conflating erotic and religious language even further in the same entry, Coleridge describes the ultimate stages of prayer as "celestial delectation that follows ardent prayer" (*Notebooks* 1:entry 257).[18] (Coleridge also alludes to the significance of Richard Crashaw's "Hymn to Sainte Teresa" for *Christabel*: the figure Teresa embodies religious ecstasy as sexual ecstasy, with both understood as the relinquishment of the ego). Years later, in a lecture he delivers in 1818, Coleridge defines the sublimity of Gothic art by reference to its spiritual power to negate the self: "But the Gothic art is sublime. On entering a cathedral, I am filled with devotion and with awe; I am lost to the actualities that surround me, and my whole being expands into the infinite; earth and air, nature and art, all swell up into eternity, and the only sensible impression left is, 'that I am nothing!'"[19] The conversation poem, *The Nightingale*, displays an ambivalence to such mimetic otherness. The poet is passively receptive to Nature, "to the influxes / Of shapes and sounds and shifting elements / Surrendering his whole spirit" (27–29). Yet by virtue of the poet's identification with the nightingale and the Philomela myth, his imaginative transports oscillate between the desire for ecstatic immersion and the terrors of a sinister rape fantasy. The effect of such transports is the suppression of an autonomous voice, since to speak as a bird, purely affectively, without words, is to be truly other, an impossible speech act.[20]

More importantly for *Christabel*, the sacrifice of a discrete self also constitutes love, for, as Coleridge writes, love "transforms the souls into a conformity with the object loved."[21] The deep sympathy and desire to apprehend, imaginatively, another identity motivates Christabel's and Geraldine's connection and leads each to assume the shape of the other. The effect of her social exclusion and shaming, Geraldine's silence enfolds the psychic burden she wishes to share, but finds impossible to relate. The sight of Geraldine's "stigma," or mark of violation, precipitates Christabel's ongoing identification with her "weal and woe," her "bale or bliss." In turn, Geraldine responds to the orphaned Christabel's "woe." Wanting "in [her] degree to requite [Christabel] well" (I, 231–32) for her kindness, Geraldine adopts a maternal persona as she drinks the dead mother's wildflower wine and takes Christabel in her arms "as a mother with her child" (I, 301). Christabel's relationship with Geraldine is punctuated with moments representative of a reconstituted mother-child dyad: Christabel "oft the while . . . seems to smile / As infants at a sudden light" (I, 317–18).

Christabel's conformity to Geraldine, and Geraldine's to Christabel should be seen in part as the expression of love. Geraldine, as she herself puts it, is forlorn, and Coleridge himself seems in love with Christabel's love of forlornness.[22] As a dream-like image, Geraldine's "wound" is that which will not be seen by the social subject and her daylight world. It is a moment of obscurity, when thoughts, whether they be Christabel's, the narrator's, or the reader's, to paraphrase Adorno, can no longer fathom themselves, a moment of mimesis as a kind of yielding that resists the compulsion to dominate the other.[23] The impulse to see as an impulse to know and master the object fails, and Christabel is "lost to" the object she would know, in a kind of not knowing, without mastery because it is without coercive change to the object. (Christabel calls her actions "a sin *unknown*"; my italics). The object is preserved as other; Christabel's possession by it alienates her from herself, but this also precludes its damage.

The wound thus becomes a metaphor for mimesis, the moment when identity alters. Whether the imagined context in *Christabel* be same-sex eroticism or rape (as it increasingly will be), such self-abandonment or the ego's breaching by the other elicits the fantastic mode of the gothic, a genre uniquely capable of foregrounding liminal, "asocial" experiences. Christabel's stealth outside and inside the castle, when she draws

Geraldine in, is her way of stealing away from and staving off her destined inheritance, e.g., the marriage plot as a woman's social contract: "Sweet Christabel her feet doth bare / And jealous of the listening air / They [Christabel and Geraldine] steal their way from stair to stair, / Now in glimmer, now in gloom, / And now they pass the Baron's room, / As still as death, with stifled breath" (I, 166–71). Christabel's pursuit of her desires leads her to insert her key into the gate "that was ironed without and within" (I, 127), carry the swooning Geraldine into the castle's interior, watch her with fascination as she undresses, and share her bed. While the gothic often dramatizes the dangers inside and outside the castle that threaten the passive heroine's virtue, Christabel reverses these positions and actively embraces and carries the threat to her virtue inside. Geraldine's banishment of the spectral mother's admonitory presence with her words, "Off wandering mother, peak and pine / I have power to make thee flee" (I, 205–6) and Christabel's words, "so let it be" (I, 235), as she reclines on the couch to wait for Geraldine, express their *willed* estrangement from the sexual roles they are expected to assume in the reproduction of the father's estate. Thus, not surprisingly, the specter of Christabel's mother materializes immediately in response to her daughter's deviation from convention.[24] According to the Friar, the guardian of her spiritual welfare, Christabel's mother has promised that she will hear the clock strike twelve upon her daughter's wedding day (199–201). Her appearance at twelve strokes of midnight overtly signals that Christabel's sociosexual destiny—the marriage narrative underwritten by the family and the spiritual guardians of the community—is in imminent danger from the mutual seduction taking place.

Christabel's desiring gaze upon Geraldine's (disfigured) body seems to be the single "inimitable" moment in a poem where virtually everything else finds a formal and symbolic echo.[25] During the period of their union, "by tairn and rill, / The night-birds all that hour were still" (I, 306–7). Even the echo of rhyme is discontinued at this crucial moment; "view" is without an end rhyme: ". . . she unbound, / The cincture from beneath her breast: / Her silken robe, and inner vest, / Dropt to her feet, and full in view, / A sight to dream of, not to tell / O shield her! shield sweet Christabel!" (I, 248–53). The "sight to dream of, not to tell" marks an overdetermined moment of undecidability (and so too the poem's fragmentary status, the image of an unfinished, or unrecognized, intention).[26] Yet this moment is, in many ways, of a piece with other mimetic "after-images," ones of unspeakable sexual encounters, that do characterize their bond: earlier, Geraldine could not speak of her rape, or the perpetrators, except through a narrative riven with memory lapses, a hysterical somatization (mimesis) of her experience with the warriors who "[have] choked [her] cries with force and fright" (I, 82). Christabel's earlier question of identity addressed to Geraldine, "and who art thou?" (I, 70), elicits the fragmented rape narrative, and thereby ties her failed attempts at self-definition to the annihilation of autonomy that is rape. Geraldine's loss of voice continues in the bedroom, so that when asked about what has befallen her, she can only re-*present* her "entranced" state (she describes her traumatized condition after the rape as "entranced," I, 92). Here the narrator seems as fully subject to the passional images as Christabel, since he cannot articulate that which possesses him. Discursive bondage follows a literal one: if Geraldine has been "tied . . . on a palfrey white" (I, 84), her arms in turn become Christabel's "prison" (I, 304). Christabel's own subsequent loss of voice points to a similar identificatory "entrancement" ("the lady Christabel / Gathers herself from out her trance," I, 311–12), since she, like Geraldine, cannot be "other" and also differentiate herself, through the use of language.

If a markedly conflictual one, this scene also dramatizes a productive moment. The poet sets the boundaries of what can be spoken or written as a figure for the experience of being sexually other—whether this otherness of "entrancement" stems from rape's violation or the liminal eroticism of same-sex desire (in *Christabel*, these kinds of "spells" are *not* clearly differentiated).[27] Coleridge writes it both ways: the symbolic contract stifles experiences of otherness, and the "unrecognizable" experiences prove themselves lost to the "universality" of culture's symbolic contract. The stigmatization of the "sight to dream of, not to tell" is the cultural prohibition of its representation. Geraldine cannot "be there" to speak her rape, and Christabel cannot "be there" to speak her seduction—nor can the male writer who inscribes this homoerotic moment between women as an allegory bearing upon the conditions for his possession of an original poetic voice.[28]

Same-sex desire, with its complicated relationship to mimesis, thus becomes a meaningful trope for the possessing *and* dispossessing force of poetry, the impulse whereby aesthetic inspiration and reception "mean" the inexpressible experience of holding and being held by a body/text that is, or becomes, in some way, "the same" as one's own. Coleridge's impulse to point to such realities implies his own capacity to be subject to self-loss or violation and to effect his own exclusion as an autonomous speaking subject. The refusal to "unveil" what Geraldine and Christabel share (an act that would signify their domination) suggests an authorial refusal to assume power over the narrative. Undifferentiated from what he stages, the narrator becomes immersed in the experiences, reflecting his intense, fetishistic desire.[29] As Karen Swann points out, both in his questioning and responding modes, the narrator (singular or plural?) mirrors Geraldine *and* Christabel:

> The poem's interlocutor and respondent mime the entanglement of Geraldine and Christabel—I call them 'they,' but it is not clear if we hear two voices or one. Like the women they describe, they are overmastered by "visions." Repeatedly, they abandon an authoritative point of view to fall into the story's present; or they engage in transferential exchanges with the characters whose plot they are narrating.[30]

Conflating homoerotic desires, sexualized violation, and the aesthetic, Coleridge imagines a male speaker who mimes, but does not speak his difference from, the unfolding dramatic enactment.

In *Christabel*, Part One, the imagination of Christabel's and Geraldine's transitive identity fluctuates between blissful immersion and a collapse into "indifference." Christabel's nightmares vary with her "visions sweet," and her perception of Geraldine oscillates between a "worker of harms" and a "guardian spirit" (I, 239, 288, 294, 326; II, 453, 464–65). Same-sex eroticism as a special form of sympathy is homophobically overshadowed by a guilt that rewrites that bond as narcissistic, tending toward a unitary sameness, and appropriative of subjective identity.[31] In Part Two, when Christabel sees Geraldine prolong her father's embrace with "joyous look," "a vision [*falls*] / Upon the soul of Christabel," beyond her will to resist or ability to translate into words (II, 451–52). Christabel's pleasure in voluntary and sympathetic self-loss increasingly registers as an uncanny fear of repetitive, involuntary self-annihilation. Coleridge aligns lesbian sexuality with a kind of repetition peculiar to somaticization, the act of telling something again and again with the body. The refusal to speak *for* the other of Part One mutates to the terror that one can only be spoken as the other dictates. Geraldine's spell on Christabel *embodies* the unchosen fixation of a "forced unconscious sympathy." Acting out her possession, Christabel cannot tell, but can only "image" Geraldine:

> The maid, alas! her thoughts are gone,
> She nothing sees—no sight but one!
> The maid, devoid of guile and sin,
> I know not how, in fearful wise
> So deeply had she drunken in

That look, those shrunken serpent eyes,
That all her features were resigned
To this sole image in her mind:
And passively did imitate
That look of dull and treacherous hate!
And thus she stood in dizzy trance,
Still picturing that look askance
With forced unconscious sympathy. . . .

(II, 597–609)

Christabel's active desire degenerates into imitative automatism, beyond her conscious control, while Geraldine plants her disavowed psychic states into Christabel as the effect of her mesmerizing powers. *Christabel* may be the first instance of a particular literary configuration in which same-sex desire is associated with social marginalization, cancellation of the will, repetition compulsion, and a progressive wasting and loss of identity.[32]

It is not simply that Geraldine, who, having no discrete identity of her own, insinuates herself into Christabel's place and installs likeness as the operative dynamic, nor Christabel, who, re-presenting Geraldine, loses her autonomy. A kind of mimetic contagion wreaking havoc with the idea of difference governs communal relationships and replaces sympathy with conformity. Part Two opens with Sir Leoline's ringing of the bell in remembrance of his dead wife, Christabel's mother, an act which reinflicts his grief each day on the community:

Each matin bell, the Baron saith,
Knells us back to a world of death.
These words Sir Leoline first said,
When he rose and found his lady dead:
These words Sir Leoline will say
Many a morn to his dying day!
And hence the custom and law began
That still at dawn the sacristan,
Who duly pulls the heavy bell,
Five and forty beads must tell
Between each stroke—a warning knell,
Which not a soul can choose but hear
From Bratha Head to Wyndermere.

(332–44)

Sir Leoline's ringing imposes a ritualized *"custom and law . . . which not a soul can choose but hear"* (my italics), an organized control of the mimetic whose law-like or powerful quality is established through reiteration. He breaks down intersubjective boundaries in his domain because each person no longer chooses but *must* assent to Sir Leoline's telling, in a perversion of the Rousseauian social will. (Geraldine's *spell* on Christ-*abel* "rings" as the omitted but nonetheless obvious rhyme of the *bell-tell-knell* sequence). His law is arbitrary, yet absolute: the village sacristan "five and forty beads *must* tell / Between each stroke—a warning knell" (II, 341–42, my italics), although forty-five bears no integral connection to the event or its memory. The triple rhyme, *saith-death, said-dead, say-dying day*, draws the reader inexorably out of the world of dreams, silence, and the dark of Part One, where desires have not been subjected to the father's/lord's mortifying habits, or his death-trauma, which, in Part Two, inaugurates and organizes the daily social life of the community.

Like the impoverished wretch in *The Nightingale*, Sir Leoline fills "all things with himself / And [makes] all gentle sounds tell back the tale / Of his own sorrow" (*The Nightingale*, 19–21). And, as in *The Nightingale*, where "many a poet echoes the conceit" of one who falsely projects his melancholic distress upon nature's image, the feudal poet Bard Bracy is complicitous with Sir Leoline's customs. Echoing Christabel's "let it be" to Geraldine in Part One, he gives his aesthetic consent to the repetitive effects unleashed by the ceremony each morning:

> Saith Bracy the bard, So let it knell!
> And let the drowsy sacristan
> Still count as slowly as he can!
> There is no lack of such, I ween,
> As well fill up the space between
>
> . . . .
>
> With ropes of rock and bells of air
> Three sinful sextons' ghosts are pent,
> Who all give back, one after t'other,
> The death-note to their living brother;
> And oft too, by the knell offended,
> Just as their one! two! three! is ended,
> The devil mocks the doleful tale
> With a merry peal from Borodale.
>
> (II, 345–49; 352–59)

As retold by the poet Bracy, Leoline's ritual forecloses interpretive openness—that unfilled "space between" the notes, to use his image. First in "sinful" imitation, then in "devilish" mockery, the supernatural sexton figures (a sexton maintains graves as a profession) expose Leoline's fixation on repetitive, "dead" forms to impose upon, or dominate, others.

Elsewhere, Sir Leoline sounds a similar "death-note" to others' feelings through repetition. When he greets Geraldine, he passes quickly from what is painful in her history to that of her father's. In this way, he is able to return to his own: "But when he heard the lady's tale, / And when she told her father's name, / Why waxed Sir Leoline so pale, / Murmuring o'er the name again, / Lord Roland de Vaux of Tryermaine?" (II, 403–7). Twice more this substitution occurs: "Sir Leoline, a moment's space, / Stood gazing on the damsel's face: / And the youthful Lord of Tryermaine / Came back upon his heart again" (II, 427–30); and later, vowing revenge for Geraldine's violation, he does so because "the lady was ruthlessly seized; and he kenned / In the beautiful lady the child of his friend!" (II, 445–46). The tale of Geraldine's violation is narcissistically seized upon to re-present *his* suffering, replaying his rift with Roland, his "heart's best brother." Although the erotic relations between Christabel and Geraldine afford a context for the reader in which the love between these two men becomes visible, for Leoline Geraldine's identity is secondary, at best (as Christabel's has become). Just as the matins replay and diffuse his grief through the community, here others reflect his losses. He can neither see Christabel's growing distress, nor hear Bard Bracy's alternative plan to flush the evil out immediately, except to dismiss it "half-listening" (II, 565). The coercion that can make Geraldine "lord of [Christabel's] utterance" (I, 268) is overshadowed by Sir Leoline's affective fixations which determine his mode of governing.

The contagion of forced identification that "enchants" *Christabel's* characters is troped through the image of the snake. Sir Leoline introduces the serpent as a metaphor for the deceptive evil that endangers the realm, referring to Geraldine's abductors: he vows to "dislodge [the] reptile souls / From the bodies and forms of men" (II, 442–43). With mimetic facility, Christabel internalizes her father's image and converts its meaning from Geraldine's shameful violation to an experience of her inseparability from, and subjection to, that same shame: ". . . a vision fell / Upon the soul of Christabel, / The vision of fear, the touch and the pain! / She shrunk and shuddered, and saw again— / . . . / And drew in her breath with a hissing sound" (II, 451–54; 459). In turn, Geraldine casts a serpent-like gaze upon Christabel, an image of her mesmeric, appropriative force, while Christabel automatically returns that reptilian look full-circle, "those shrunken serpent eyes . . . full before her father's view" (II, 602, 610).

Bard Bracy, too, is receptive to these influences as a poet, who, in creating metaphors, possesses the capacity to see resemblances. "Such a gift" for metaphor, according to Walter Benjamin, "is nothing other than a rudiment of the powerful compulsion in former times of persons to 'become and behave like someone else.'"[33] Bard Bracy's dream (which occurs at the midnight hour, simultaneous with the seduction scene) condenses the operative confusion of identity. The interlocking embrace of the snake and the dove renders them inseparable: "And with the dove it [the snake] heaves and stirs, / Swelling its neck as she swelled hers!" (II, 553–54). As captivated by his dream as Christabel has been by hers, he claims that "it [will] not pass away / It seems to live *upon my eye*" (II, 558–59). He assumes the "perplexity of mind" that Christabel attributes to the confusion which "dreams too lively leave behind" (II, 385–86). Unleashed by the transitive serpent, a figure for the magical power of replication, the poet's perplexity mirrors the characters' spiraling inability to differentiate between the real and the imaginary, self and other, the true from the false, and essential selves from performed ones. It points to a dynamic no longer unleashed by or contained within a single subject, but one which subsumes multiple relationships within *Christabel's* imagined social world. Given such continual displacements of origin through the mimetic suturing of "the real to the really made up," Sir Leoline's misunderstanding of Bard Bracy's account of his dream befits the social dynamics of this poem (he interprets his daughter Christabel as the snake—not Geraldine, as Bard Bracy does).[34] If the serpent image appears to originate nowhere, it is adopted everywhere, passing from one character to the other.

Put differently, *Christabel's* second half jettisons plot in favor of dispersing these mimetic proclivities. Coleridge avoids substantiating whatever suspicions may lurk around Geraldine and, instead, universalizes the effects of psychosomatic and symbolic mimicry. In Part Two, ventriloquism emerges as the negative slope of the sympathetic or imaginative impulses figured in Part One. The conflation of desire and identification, where "to want to have" is no different from "to want to be" (which allows for the "unspeakable" lesbian desires of Part One), transmutes in Part Two into seemingly unconscious or passive imitation as the basis for social identity. Geraldine's prohibition upon Christabel's speech inaugurates the lesbian subject as social subject. The persons of the day-light world are similarly enchanted, similarly dispossessed of their autonomous voices. *Christabel* makes singular selfhood unimaginable, not because Geraldine and Christabel no longer relate as different subjects, but because *Christabel's* horizontal, proliferating replications of identity establish the existence of an odd collective bond—one that produces a non-narrative, mimetic unity of experience.[35] We might say that, for Coleridge, this projected mirroring becomes the imagined *status quo* of a subject who is informed by, or immersed in, repetitive rituals and kinds of knowledge—such as Sir Leoline's—that coerce other tellings.

For Coleridge, language rituals neither substitute, compensate, nor atone for the visionary and affective power of imaginative plenitude he associates with the homoerotic bedchamber scene or with the passionate bond that once existed between Sir Leoline and Sir Roland: "But never either found another / To free the hollow heart from paining—" (II, 419–20).[36] Underlying Christabel's and Sir Leoline's failed efforts at symbolic displacement in Part Two is a lost bond of same-sex love as identification—Christabel's for the blissful aspects of union with Geraldine, Leoline for Roland's friendship. As they speak or attempt to do so, the reader measures a return to mirroring rather than the achievement of difference. Caught between the symbol and the nonsymbol, their language is spellbound, and ritually acted out by the culture at large.[37] What language finally turns out to be identical with, or imitative of, is itself—which is to say that it possesses and stages its own formal affinity for repetition. For the reader, it is not only grief for Roland/ his wife that Sir Leoline expresses but the power of the symbolic to be experienced as a law that seems, uncannily, to perform itself. Instead of standing for something other, it stands for the indifference of custom. (Similarly, Christabel can choose to be different from herself in Part One, but cannot choose to be different from Geraldine in Part Two.) As the conclusion of *Christabel* announces, the "giddiness" of heart and brain, that vivid movement of thought that effaces boundaries in Part One, submits, in Part Two, to the paralysis of discursive habits. The poet-narrator in Part Two makes a social ritual of that sameness, replacing the chosen otherness of sympathy with the "[forcing] together / Thoughts so all unlike each other" (II, 666–67). Concluding the tale, the narrator "mocks and mutters a broken charm," broken, as he says, because it "talks as it's most used to do" (II, 666, 677).

While writing *Christabel*, Coleridge was engaged on the collaborative venture of the *Lyrical Ballads*. As the story goes in his *Biographia Literaria*, the question of the inclusion of *Christabel* and other poems by Coleridge in the second edition of the *Lyrical Ballads* becomes a determining

moment, at which point Coleridge agreed that their heterogeneous nature conflicted with what he (wrongly) deemed Wordsworth's unitary
voice.[38] Minimizing the collaborative nature of the *Lyrical Ballads* project and emphasizing Wordsworth's greater genius, he willingly surren-
ders his voice. For his part, Wordsworth claimed that *Christabel* could
not be printed "with any propriety," due to the poem's "extraordinary
incidents," among them, presumably, the most extraordinary, its representation of same-sex desire.[39] The desire to be spoken by the other
(and fear of it) that dominates *Christabel* reads in this context as a blurring of identity occasioned by their collaborative effort that would lead,
eventually, to Coleridge's exclusion from the project.[40] In a poet known
for his recurring desire to "mingle identities with other men," as both
Wayne Koestenbaum and Richard Matlak describe Coleridge, and in a
poem where same-sex desire is cast as an affinity for imitation (with a
narrative voice echoing Wordsworth's narrators in "The Idiot Boy" and
"The Thorn"), Coleridge, intentionally or not, inserts himself into discourses of ventriloquism that carry larger cultural resonances. The effacing of difference figured as a manner or style behind which, it was
thought, lay a proclivity for sodomy. One writer, speaking of a "frater-
nity of pretty men," asserts that

> as no associated body can possibly subsist, unless they are cemented by a
> union of hearts, the grand principle of this fellowship is mutual love, which,
> it must be confessed, they carry to the highest pitch. . . . Such an harmony
> of temper is preserved among them, such a sameness is there in all their
> words and actions, that the spirit of *one* seems to have passed into the *other*;
> or rather, they *all* breathe the *same* soul.[41]

The author's italicized words, where "*one* passes into the *other*," and "*all*
breathe the *same* soul," suggests how a threat to the fantasy of impermeable interpersonal boundaries between men can read as a threat to masculinity. Going further, the author describes how such an interchange
of sentiment reflects an incapacity to assert and maintain a consistency
of "manly" judgment—an inconsistency that translates into an unstable
identity.[42] Such hybridity of identity (the ongoing alterity in the adoption of an other's feelings and thoughts) easily slips into another common trope in the discourses on male effeminacy, namely, a collapsing of
language within these fraternities into a "great undifferentiated."[43] As
mentioned in the chapter on Keats, a recurring homophobic image of
the sodomist in pamphlet and trial literature of the eighteenth and nineteenth centuries was of a man who thrusts his tongue in another man's

mouth. This literal image of an invasive sexuality finds a figurative recasting as discursive trespass. The fears about sodomy extend to anxieties about authentic and original speech acts, dovetailing with the
stereotype of the sodomist's supposed gift or affinity for mimicry.[44] The
usurped and alienated speech acts in *Christabel* enact this same discursive constellation: the affinity for mimetic replication of "sameness,"
whether psychological, sexual, or discursive. If, by the end of the eighteenth century, as the historian Randolph Trumbach has argued, a man
is defined as masculine, not by what he does with women, but *by virtue
of what he avoids doing with other men*, then Coleridge's attempts at collaboration and his literary borrowings, not to mention the lifelong accusations of plagiarism he leveled and which would be leveled against him,
become the displaced arena where definitions of masculinity are repeatedly contested and defended by himself and other men, because of his
failure "to avoid" such behavior with them.[45]

A man speaking another man's words cannot be said to "possess"
himself.[46] In his 1816 preface to *Christabel*, Coleridge defends the poem
against charges of plagiarism—the unpublished poem had circulated
widely and given rise to imitations before Coleridge published it. It is
worth quoting the passage:

> The first part of the following poem was written in the year 1797, at Stowey,
> in the county of Somerset. The second part, after my return from Germany,
> in the year 1800, at Keswick, Cumberland. It is probable, that if the poem
> had been finished at either of the former periods, or if even the first and
> second part had been published in the year 1800, the impression of its origi-
> nality would have been much greater than I dare at present expect. But for
> this, I have only my own indolence to blame. The dates are mentioned for
> the exclusive purpose of precluding charges of plagiarism or servile imita-
> tion from myself. For there is amongst us a set of critics, who seem to hold,
> that every possible thought and image is traditional; who have no notion
> that there are such things as fountains in the world, small as well as great;
> and who would therefore charitably derive every rill they behold flowing,
> from a perforation made in some other man's tank. I am confident, however,
> that as far as the present poem is concerned, the celebrated poets whose
> writings I might be suspected of having imitated . . . would be among the
> first to vindicate me from the charge, and who, on any striking coincidence,
> would permit me to address them in this doggerel version of two monkish
> Latin hexameters.
>
> > 'Tis mine and it is likewise yours;
> > But an if this will not do;
> > Let it be mine, good friend! for I
> > Am the poorer of the two.

Coleridge's justified protestations of innocence—his listing of dates and self-reproach for laziness—bizarrely become interwoven with an admission of guilt. In the process of defending *Christabel*'s originality (ironically, in a poem about the impossibility of locating origins), he undermines himself by questioning the originality of *all poems*. After objecting to those critics who see permeable boundaries instead of singular origins and seek to "derive every rill they behold flowing, from a perforation made in some other man's tank," he declares the existence of original "fountains," or geniuses. Yet he then goes on to efface the difference between his own writing and those celebrated writers, Byron and Walter Scott, whose writings most resemble *Christabel*. Coleridge may be attempting to distinguish between a productive form of repetition, between great writers, and unnatural repetition, such Matthew "Monk" Lewis's gothic, with its homoeroticized suggestions of indiscrete borrowing (perforating another man's tank). Yet Coleridge falters when he identifies himself as a doggerel writer of "monkish" hexameters. Jokingly, he presents their individual works as a kind of communal property for which he hopes they will allow him the greater claim of originality, not because he has earned it, but because he is the "poorer," which implies a greater need for credibility concerning such matters: " 'Tis mine and it is likewise yours; / But an if this will not do; / Let it be mine, good friend! for I / Am the poorer of the two."[47]

This question of origins returns us to where we began, with the critical reception of *Christabel*. The early reviewers of *Christabel* were in fact more upset by Coleridge's *tone* than by Geraldine's and Christabel's "disgusting" and lewd" behavior. Concerned to establish whether the poem was serious or nothing but a joke, they argued to what degree such an aesthetic "failure"—which we might call, after Susan Sontag, the "failed seriousness" of camp or parody—was intentional.[48] By ultimately fixing their attention on the tone as the key to the poem's generic status, they indirectly noted how *Christabel*'s "deviant" content easily slipped into a question of the "deviance" of Coleridge's authorial voice, tainting him with Geraldine's femininity and degraded sexuality.[49] On two opposed fronts (and on neither of which Coleridge adopts a position whereby confidence in his masculinity could easily be restored), Coleridge's improper tone, according to critics, represents a violation of gender and generic norms: he fails to defend the boundaries of genre, since his joking plays with the authority such boundaries seek to instill, and further, given the cult of originality, he does not celebrate the new, but flagrantly exhibits the derivative nature of his narrative. Like other critical attacks on the gothic, two contradictory standards are employed: one which argues that the gothic's deficiency derives from its utter conventionality; and another which contends that the gothic is suspect because of its disregard for conventionality. The double prongs of this attack emphasize the gothic's "sameness" and "excess," a rhetoric whose supposed attributes equally apply to representations of same-sex desire.[50]

Parody wreaks havoc with the notion of generic rules. The copy, through performance, establishes the nature of the original it is said to imitate.[51] From the first lines, *Christabel*'s narrator establishes its generic "origin" with a wink—not its innocent quotation, but as a highly self-conscious nod at a jaded style: " 'Tis the middle of the night by the castle clock, / And the owls have awakened the crowing cock." The castle, the chimes at midnight, owls, and the narrator's pseudo-archaic vocabulary mimic the gothic genre as a way of disavowing aesthetic singularity. The linear repetition of "Is the night chilly and dark? / The night is chilly, but not dark" (14–15), is amplified by the represented doublings of sounds, the owls' hooting which is contagiously picked up by the rooster, who crows with the sound of the owl ("Tu-whit—Tu-whoo"), while the mastiff's barks re-play the chiming of the castle-clock with a facetious regularity.

In his adoption of a campy tone, Coleridge enacts the very loss of boundaries integral to the narrative's scene of desire and representation of the imagination in Part One, and its social dimension as the subjection to language rituals in Part Two. Thus, the thematics of homoerotic imitation and imagination and their threatening face, the destruction of the "self-containedness" of voice—not the least due to the "parasitic" repetition demanded by publishers and consumers in the literary marketplace—are formally and tonally reinflected. The narrator's mimicry of the gothic, however, affirms what we might call the pleasures of generic imitation, or dependent forms. As Sontag writes, "Camp taste is, above all, a mode of enjoyment. . . . Camp taste identifies with what it is enjoying. . . . Camp is a tender feeling."[52] The gothic's mockery of poetic form is a topic to which Coleridge, and later the reviewers of *Christabel*, frequently turned. The critics' outrage at *Christabel*'s impurity and their scrambling for generic order expose the category crisis of the masculine and authorial subject that Coleridge unleashes when *he* gives up on a fantasy of self-sufficiency. Imitating the gothic genre, but not passively, he accepts what his reviewers were unable to do: not simply the proximity of what one jokes about to what one finds desirable, but imitation itself as a mode of desiring. He disarms critics' potential attacks by exhibiting, parodically, the gothic's stylistic excesses and proclivity for dramatizing unstable sexual identities. By virtue of its humor, camp can invert standard pieties (e.g., mock Christabel's expressions of religious devotion) and tie that inversion to unleashed and dangerous sexual energies.[53] It can also, at least partially, protect Coleridge from a charge of effeminacy. He reassures his readers that he self-consciously imitates, and thereby projects a narrator "in control" of his material: one who writes its conventions too faithfully, not one who unconsciously identifies with them.[54] One could argue, following Taussig, that identity is strengthened by this mimetic play with "dangerous proclivities": "identity acquires its satisfying solidity because of the effervescence of the continuously sexualized border, because of the turbulent forces, sexual and spiritual, that the border not so much contains as emits."[55] In any event, Coleridge differentiates himself from Byron and Percy Shelley for whom the aesthetic success of *Christabel* lay in their own pleasure at being gripped and possessed by it.[56] If he fails to embody an "original" voice, Coleridge self-consciously, actively, dramatizes that failure.

With its obvious pleasure in borrowed modes, *Christabel* seeks to elicit the pleasures of borrowed responses. Coleridge challenges the reader (and critic) to see a bond established between them and the book as a kind of seduction: the "so let it be," or willing reception of known aesthetic forms. The tale satisfies, Coleridge insinuates, precisely because the readers' desire is, like Geraldine's and Christabel's, to dispossess themselves in identifying with what they find there.[57] Coleridge is aware of this impulse early on; in his review of Radcliffe's *Udolpho*, he notes that, after finishing the novel, "the reader looks in vain for the spell which had bound him so strongly to it," but then goes on to invoke that same kind of spell in *Christabel*.[58] From his opening lines, the narrator presumes and inscribes the reader as one "in the know" about forms of literariness; such knowledge, as his reviewers objected, can feel indecent and, if pushed too far toward the joke, like a forced complicity. The ostensibly safe, communal canniness of gothic generic norms, that bond of sameness, blurs with the more dangerous one he identifies with homoeroticism. *Christabel*'s self-conscious discourse about the performative, reiterative nature of writing and reading is also a performance of "deviant" sexuality. Same-sex desire, its "vices" and "pleasures," is aligned with a rhetorical repetition compulsion. The audience colludes in a communal act of voyeurism, one which alternates between the pleasure of "let it be" and the coercion of what they "cannot choose but hear." Challenged to reestablish the difference of their reading pleasures from the mode of desire they witness, they find, however, that their coherence is not so much established around an external enemy, such as Geraldine, but around their own collusive experience. In *Christabel*, innocent responses, whether by the narrator, the characters, or the reader, become impossible.

5

The Gothic Romance of Sigmund Freud
and Wilhelm Fliess

LOOKING AHEAD FROM COLERIDGE'S *CHRISTABEL* SOME SEVENTY
years, we find Sigmund Freud's correspondence with his friend and colleague, Wilhelm Fliess, uncannily preoccupied with identical concerns:
the attractions of mimetic desire and threats of subjective dispossession,
both emerging within a homoerotically-charged relationship and per-
mutating into disputes about (discursive or intellectual) originality and
property. This continuity within gothic discourse is in part attributable
to the enduring presence of the gothic in the popular consciousness.
Instead of waning in importance under the increasing pressures of literary realism, gothic forms, tropes, and themes saturate nineteenth-century literature in Great Britain and Germany, whether in the works of
the Brontës, Charles Dickens, Wilkie Collins, Margaret Oliphant, or
Oscar Wilde, or in the legacy of German Romanticism, in writers such
as Friedrich Schiller, E. T. A. Hoffman, Wilhelm Hauff, Achim von
Arnim, and Ludwig Tieck. It is not surprising that the fantasy material
and memories of Sigmund Freud, his friends, and his colleagues, as well
as his patients, intimately conversing with one another about the fears
associated with repressed desires, should assume gothic contours. What
is remarkable is how these terrors resurface, with theoretical power, in
his scientific writings.

Thus, when Freud describes his scientific method in his essay "On
the Psychotherapy of Hysteria," he compares the doctor's and the patient's work to the "unlocking of a locked door," behind which lies a
memory too frightening to be acknowledged consciously.[1] The end appears relatively simple: through his associations the patient confronts
that memory, or the doctor, guessing the secret, presents it at a time
when the patient is ready to face it. As if by magic, the closed door
opens, a catharsis begins, and "the picture vanishes, like a ghost that
has been laid [to rest]."[2] Freud's "ghost" behind the door, however, is

not singular. Reluctantly he concedes that this process has to be repeated over and over again, since the underlying causes of hysteria cannot be removed: there can only be a reduction in the severity of its
symptoms, the number and demands of its ghosts.

Freud's narrative of the history of psychoanalysis has its own closed
doors, equally well-guarded and as difficult to remember as those of its
most famous patients. Writing to Stefan Zweig in 1932, fifty years after
Anna O.'s therapy for hysteria with his colleague Josef Breuer, Freud
divulges a secret that he and Breuer shared about her treatment. Freud
refers then to his own amnesia and abrupt recall of this formative event:

> What really happened with Breuer's patient [Anna O.] I was able to guess
> later on, long after the break in our relations, when I suddenly remembered
> something Breuer had once told me in another context. . . . On the evening
> of the day when all her symptoms had been disposed of, he was summoned
> to the patient again, found her confused and writhing in abdominal cramps.
> Asked what was wrong with her, she replied: "Now Dr. B's child is
> coming!"
>
> At this moment he held in his hand the key . . . , but he let it drop. . . .
> Seized by conventional horror he took flight and abandoned the patient to
> a colleague.[3]

Freud talks about this event with Ernest Jones as well, who goes on to
explain the account in considerable detail:

> It would seem that Breuer had developed . . . a strong [attachment] . . . to
> his interesting patient. At all events he was so engrossed that his wife be-
> came . . . jealous. She did not display this openly, but became unhappy and
> morose. It was a long time before Breuer, with his thoughts elsewhere, di-
> vined the meaning of her state of mind. It provoked a violent reaction in
> him, perhaps compounded of love and guilt, and he decided to bring the
> treatment to an end. He announced this to Anna O., who was by now much
> better, and bade her good-[bye]. But that evening he was fetched back to
> find her in a greatly excited state, apparently as ill as ever. The patient, who
> according to him had appeared to be an asexual being and had never made
> any allusion to such a forbidden topic throughout the treatment, was now in
> the throes of a hysterical childbirth . . . the logical termination of a phantom
> pregnancy that had been invisibly developing in response to Breuer's minis-
> trations. Though profoundly shocked, he managed to calm her down by
> hypnotizing her, and then fled the house in a cold sweat. The next day he
> and his wife left for Venice to spend a second honeymoon, which resulted
> in the conception of a daughter.[4]

Jones is clear that the secret which causes Breuer to flee "in conventional horror" is Anna O's "phantom pregnancy," the unacknowledged effect of the erotic bond between the doctor and patient, something which Breuer, in hysteric fashion, could not face. Upon disclosure, it does not disappear obediently as did those compliant ghosts described earlier. For Breuer, the emergence of the secret does not provoke its fading but leads to a stiffer resistance, a more secure repression.

Given Freud's (and Jones's) condescension towards Breuer's conventional bourgeois shock, the reader might wonder what provokes Freud's own "forgetfulness" about the event. In fact, he is not above keeping secrets about his own patient's sexual lives in the interest of his audience's conventional morality, as the 1924 emendations to the *Studies on Hysteria* make clear. There he repeatedly confesses to narrative deformations (*Entstellung*) of the material. In one especially striking case, the trauma of paternal incest is represented as the young woman's virginal anxiety, an *Entstellung* he creates out of what could be deemed his own anxiously virginal discretion before the bourgeois men of science and society.[5] If Freud waits decades to present the secret of Anna O.'s phantom pregnancy—the key that Breuer lets drop—what motivates his own disingenuous silence?

At this point, there is another story that bears attending to, if only because its narrative shape surprisingly mirrors the crisis between Anna O. and Breuer. It pertains to Freud's closely guarded secret, his friendship with Wilhelm Fliess. Although it lasted from 1887 to 1904 (during the formative years of psychoanalysis) and was characterized by an intense intimacy (an "erotic, self-surrendering dimension," in the words of one critic), among Freud's autobiographical and scientific works, acknowledgements of its significance are so rare as to be nonexistent.[6] Given that Freud postulates the so-called "achievement" of the gendered and sexed subject during this same period, concomitant with his self-analysis, one could say that the representation and denial of this male friendship holds a kind of key to the narrative fashioning of the (masculine) psychoanalytic subject.[7] Within that narrative, a story emerges whose features resemble those of Anna O.'s. The estrangement and threatened termination of his friendship with Fliess, which Freud deeply fears, is attributed to Breuer's covert machinations.[8] Freud claims that Breuer has planted doubts in Wilhelm's wife's (Ida Fliess's) fertile mind where they "ripen" unconsciously into a "dark compulsion" (*dunklem Zwang*) (we might say that *Freud* is especially receptive to Breuer's suggestions). As with Anna O., a Breuer with a "supernaturalized" agency has fathered a phantom pregnancy: his powerful influence over Ida's mind threatens to bear an illicit progeny. This time, the off-spring is not a disclosed, then repressed, erotic attraction between the male doctor and female patient, but an improper intimacy between Freud and Fliess. This uncanny thing, displaced to Ida's mind and pe-culiarly reified in order to be expelled, emblematizes Freud's and Fliess's growing alienation from one another, the rupture of their bond—just as Anna O.'s phantom childbirth scene represents the rejec-tion of her tie to Breuer.

Freud constructs the Anna O. scenario after the fact, fifty years later. Whether he remembers correctly does not really matter. What is sig-nificant is the narrative doubling Freud engages in when he re-con-structs the hysterical contours of the Anna O. crisis and the crisis that ends his friendship with Fliess. Freud understands his relationship with Fliess along the lines of an erotic transference relationship between doc-tor and patient, *because he remembers and writes it that way*. The illicitly shared erotic thing/knowledge, called a dark compulsion or a phantom pregnancy, embodies for Freud the relationship between Freud and Fliess *and* the reason for its undoing. This thing, or stillborn offspring of one of psychoanalysis' early affairs, is forgotten, until the science es-tablishes its own legitimate dynasty.[9]

Using primarily the letters of Freud to Fliess, this chapter argues that a gothic narrative of dispossessed masculinity constitutes the subtext of Freud's reading of his relationship with Fliess. It situates their friend-ship, with its acknowledged and unacknowledged homoeroticism and homophobia, apposite to the emerging science of psychoanalysis with its stories of ghosts, dissolving identities, demonic possession, incorpo-rated foreign bodies, phobic formulas, and phantom agencies and preg-nancies. Intertwined as the writings on hysteria and the defense neuroses are during this period, it is not surprising to find homoerotic impulses hystericized and hysteria homoeroticized.[10] The effeminization of Freud turns upon his somaticization of female hysterical symptom-atology, but also upon a rapport between himself and Fliess, character-ized by powerfully submissive or passive impulses—the desire for, and fear of, self-annihilation, or, as Leo Bersani and Lee Edelman have the-orized anality, for the shattering of psychic (egoic) structures as the masculine subject adopts the feminine, receptive position in sex.[11] Like the gothic turn evident in the patients' narratives and the doctor's theo-rizing of the hypnotic and hysterical passions, Freud, in his letters to Fliess, supernaturalizes same-sex desire and then controls its occult passions by fixing it into a theoretical object, into intellectual property that can be owned, recognized, contested, or alienated. In Freud's construction of his relationship with Fliess, there are the outlines of a fantastically hysterical plot: one where Freud suffers the effects of a phantom pregnancy by Fliess, a pregnancy which is segregated as a foreign body and expelled in a perversion of childbirth—a repetition of Anna O.'s, and later, Emmy von N.'s, exorcism of Breuer and Freud, respectively.[12] This expelled offspring of Freud's hysterical pregnancy with Fliess is converted, through language, into an intellectual object, namely, the theories of the anal drives, paranoia, and their relationship to male homosexuality/bisexuality.[13] These theories become the sublimated arena where homoerotic desire, named as such, can be localized in the more safely passionate contestations of intellectual property and disputes about plagiarism. After that point, in 1904, the story ends: Freud never again communicates with Fliess directly, and only once more indirectly in 1906.[14] Although Freud designates homosexuality as a stage, a temporary blockage or impediment in the developmental telos of the heterosexual masculine subject, at the same time, he also refuses to complete that narrative, by granting homoeroticism a permanent presence as unanalyzable, incurable remnant. In terms of his theorizing of homosexuality, Freud's attempts to suppress the story of the friendship, even the name of Fliess, become the sign of its ongoing symptomatic role—as the repressed secret—in his version of psychoanalysis' development.[15]

> *It would be more to the point to explain being in love by means of hypnosis rather than the other way around.*
>
> —Freud, *Group Psychology and the Ego*

From the beginning of their correspondence in December 1887, Freud intimately confides in Fliess, investing him with an authoritative, even magical power of influence, similar to that he describes between hypnotist and patient. Fliess "has power over the spirits that cannot be transferred"; Freud looks to him "as the messiah" and hails him diversely as his "daimonie" and his "dear magician," who either cloaks himself in impenetrable silence or "[anticipates his] question." Like many of his hysterical patients, Freud claims not to know things about himself that Fliess does. Speaking of his heart ailment, Freud accuses Fliess of withholding information from him: "I secretly believe that you know precisely what it is."[16] These passages re-create Freud's descriptions of the hieratic aura with which the suggestible patient surrounds the hypnotizing doctor and reveal the underlying power imbalance implicit in hypnosis, where the doctor is said to know things about the patient that the patient neither knows nor remembers.[17]

The psychic conditions for and effects of suggestibility are a field
Freud traverses repeatedly in his writings, because he feels accountable
for his use and subsequent rejection of hypnosis by the mid-1890s.[18] In
one of his earliest essays, "Psychical (or Mental) Treatment" (1890),
written at a time when Freud is firmly committed to the therapeutic
potential of hypnosis and wants to normalize its image, he maintains
that the power of suggestion is nothing more than a simple harnessing
of the power of words over the psyche, something very ordinary that
only appears to be inexplicable and mystical:

> Foremost among such measures [of psychical treatment] is the use of words.
> . . . A layman will no doubt find it hard to understand how pathological
> disorders of the body and mind can be eliminated by "mere" words. He will
> feel he is being asked to believe in magic. And he will not be so very wrong,
> for the words we use in our everyday speech are nothing but watered-down
> [abgeblaßter, faded] magic. But we shall have to follow a roundabout path in
> order to explain how science sets about restoring to words a part at least of
> their former magical power.
> . . . . we begin to understand the "magic" of words. Words are the most
> important media by which one man seeks to bring his influence upon an-
> other; words are a good method of producing mental changes in the person
> to whom they are addressed. So that there is no longer anything puzzling in
> the assertion that the magic of words can remove the symptoms of illness,
> and especially such as are themselves founded on mental states.[19]

The magical effects of hypnotic treatment, however, even those disci-
plined by science, are anything but ordinary, since the hypnotist's
words determine the shape of the patient's mental world. By virtue of
them, the doctor becomes a human "miracle worker" whom the patient
regards with awe; he takes over where the ancient priests with their
"magical formulas and purificatory baths, or the elicitation of oracular
dreams" leave off.[20] The reward for the doctor who cures in this fashion
is actually greater than that enjoyed by ancient healers: whereas the
priests present themselves as mediums for external or transcendental
forces, in his patients' eyes, Freud possesses that quasi-supernatural
power within himself. The authority this confers upon him is enormous;
he has "an un-dreamt of influence on another person's psychic life."[21]
Freud recalls in his Autobiography that "there was something positively
seductive in working with hypnotism. . . . [It] was highly flattering to
enjoy the reputation of being a miracle-worker."[22]
    The tributes to Fliess's power as a "dear magician" attest as much, if
not more, to Freud's suggestibility and desire for intimacy. With Fliess,

Freud takes pleasure in having his "fantasies taken seriously," but more so, in sharing what he calls the "powerful mental processes which remain hidden from the consciousness of men."[23] From his inability to contradict Fliess to his admission that he, Freud, "really believes [him] in everything," we glimpse a Freud whose trust and susceptibility to Fliess's influence evoke the conditions he makes necessary for his own therapeutic technique.[24] The capacity to be influenced hypnotically, or a patient's suggestibility, depends upon a readiness to believe and submit to the doctor's psychic proximity and contact during hypnosis. The success depends almost entirely upon the patient's affinity for identification, a mode of transitivity or suspension that blurs the difference between self and other. The patient follows the doctor's commands as if they are his own, because he identifies with, or becomes undifferentiated from, the doctor. The efficacy of hypnotic treatment depends upon the doctor's charisma, his mastery of words, as well as the patient's willingness to submit, to relinquish control, and to receive the doctor's desires, wishes, and commands.[25] As Freud later writes, the patient adopts a "passive masochistic attitude under hypnosis."[26]

While the obvious attractions of hypnosis lie in the narcissistic gains for the doctor, for the suggestible patient the seduction lies elsewhere. According to Freud, the pleasures of suggestion are the pleasures of docility, obedience, and credulity, which, in a state of deepest hypnosis, can be experienced "to an almost unlimited extent."[27] For reasons of professionalism, however, and given the already contested status of hypnosis, Freud does not want to dwell on the erotic, submissive impulses contributing to the hypnotic rapport.[28] Yet at one point early on he draws a clear parallel between the patient's credulity and the devotion characteristic of love:

> It may be remarked, by the way, that outside hypnosis and in real life, credulity such as the subject has in relation to his hypnotist is shown only by a child towards his beloved parents, and that of an attitude of similar subjection on the part of one person towards another has only one parallel, though a complete one—namely in certain love relationships where there is extreme devotion. A combination of exclusive attachment and credulous obedience is in general among the characteristics of love.[29]

Without pursuing the implications, Freud nevertheless warns that some patients may become emotionally dependent on the doctor, a dependence that expresses itself as an addiction to hypnosis or as a resistance to getting well (foreshadowing his future understanding of the transference relationship as the most significant impediment to completing analysis).

In an oft-cited passage from the letters, Freud unreservedly admits to Fliess, "I can barely do without the other—and you are the only other, the *alter*."[30] Fliess plays the part of the other, necessary for the constitution of Freud as a subject; disappointed over a canceled meeting, Freud regrets the loss of the idealized version of himself that Fliess carries:

> . . . I do care that I cannot see you in Berlin. . . . Since I regard this trip in the sense of a singular treat that I am giving myself, I have been led to forego this pleasure. . . . I expected a great deal from my contact with you. . . . When I talked with you and saw that you thought well of me, I even used to think something of myself, and the picture of absolutely convincing energy that you offered was not without its effect on me.[31]

Beyond this, however, many of Freud's greatest pleasures with Fliess lie in the projection of their undifferentiated identity, much as hypnosis produces a kind of dual subject.[32] He speaks of their bodies as telepathically connected, registering the same sensations: "Your sleepiness now explains to me my own simultaneous state. Our protoplasm has worked its way through the same critical period. How nice it would be if this close harmony between us were a total one"; or, "as a consequence of the secret biological sympathy of which you have often spoken, both of us felt the surgeon's knife in our bodies at about the same time, and on precisely the same days moaned and groaned because of the pain."[33]

Freud's dependency on Fliess coincides with a fantasy of equality whose arena is their scientific work. Their meetings, designated "congresses," express his need for a full interchange and collaboration; he comes "[to slake] . . . hunger and thirst" with "two open ears and one temporal lobe lubricated for reception," to find the "burning desire once again to live fully, with head and heart simultaneously, to be a *zoon politikon*, and, moreover, to see you."[34] Although their work divides along different fields, psychology for Freud and biology and physiology for Fliess, Freud imagines them conquering "the empire of medicine" together. He writes of "*our* etiological formula," asserts that "the thought that both of us are occupied with the same kind of work is by far the most enjoyable [he] can conceive," pleads with Fliess to tear himself away from his family "to exchange ideas with [him]" and affirms that Fliess's concerns about his (Freud's) hypotheses on anxiety are the "echo" of his own. In a move to insure their future together, he envisions the pleasure of "cementing" Fliess's work to his own, while, in moments of generosity, he effaces himself in order to pass the mastery over to Fliess that he desires for himself:

> I will pay proper respects to your discovery. You will be the strongest of men, holding in your hands the reins of sexuality, which governs all mankind: you could do anything and prevent anything.[35]

After validating Fliess's theories with his own observations, Freud writes that "when the matter occurred to me, I had a happy day without really knowing why, a sort of blissful aftertaste like after a beautiful dream."[36] Freud "[hopes] it will go so far that [they] can jointly build something definitive . . . and thereby blend [their] contributions to the point where [their] individual property is no longer recognizable."[37] These passages suggest that Freud's impulse to share work is an extension of his affective impulse to share Fliess, the longing for a mutual incorporation wherein their differences are suspended through identification and symbiotic partnership.

Describing the hypnotic rapport between doctor and patient, "that group of two," Freud leads the reader in "Psychical (or Mental) Treatment" to a scenario of a mother nursing her child:

> While the subject behaves to the rest of the external world as though he were asleep, that is, as though all his senses were diverted from it, he is *awake* in his relation to the person who hypnotized him; he hears and sees him alone, and him he understands and answers. This phenomenon, which is described as *rapport* in the case of hypnosis, finds a parallel in the way in which some people sleep—for example, *a mother who is nursing her baby*. It is so striking that it may well lead us to an understanding of the relation between the hypnotic subject and the hypnotist.[38]

While we might assume that it is the doctor who gently holds the patient-child while feeding him with his thoughts, as the idea of influence as a kind of "feeding into" would suggest, here he inverts the relation. It is the patient who, like a blissful mother, falls into a sleep-like trance while holding and feeding her child—the doctor's psyche. If it is the patient who unconsciously introduces himself into the infantilized doctor, then the doctor is the receptive and powerless one, a vessel for what the patient produces and gives as "naturally and willingly" as a mother gives milk to her child: with so much trust in the safety and innocence of the scenario that it can be done while asleep. The doctor transforms this milk into words or suggestions in the hypnotic exchange. The tran-

sitivity of the exchange is foregrounded here, where both patient and
doctor allow themselves to find expression through the other, because
they are not yet differentiated.[39] Besides suggesting where Freud's pleasures might lie, this remarkable image works to defuse the hierarchical
implications of what were felt by many to be the main defect of hypnotism as a therapeutic tool, namely, the doctor's unethical intrusion into
the patient's unconscious mind. (In fact, it effaces the issue of authority
or control. The doctor-baby no more wants to control the mother than
the sleeping patient-mother unwillingly receives the baby's demands).
In this scene, the therapy of hypnosis embodies the "good feed" without
any threatening demands, appropriations, or unfulfilled needs. It is pure
pleasure.

Significant in this metaphor, it seems to me, and unlike the earlier
images of the hieratic doctor in which the imagined professional gains
seem uppermost, is Freud's refusal of masculine identification in favor
of a specifically female or feminized experience. Maternity, and specifically breast-feeding, organizes the dynamic relationship, here between the male doctor and male patient. In his letters to Fliess, as well,
Freud frequently describes their exchanges with metaphors of female
reproduction, including fertility, conception, gestation, pregnancy, delivery, and birth.[40] Fliess not only possesses the mental potency to
"solve the problem of conception," but, by way of Freud's curious somatization, Fliess's work on labor pains makes him more directly subject to them ("die Wehenschwäche stehen dir wohl voran," labor pains
certainly lie ahead of you). Freud's new ideas are like a "six-month old
fetus," and he promises to come to a congress "avid for all your *novis*
and laden with . . . germinating embryos." He playfully insists that
Fliess must bring two things to their meeting: evidence of a "23-day
period for sexual processes" and "evidence for the necessity of a period
not exceeding three months in matters of friendship," to attest to their
reciprocal capacity to fertilize and "incorporate" one another.[41]

I do not want to belabor this point since such metaphors are themselves, in part, common usage and further, imply a masculine desire to
appropriate and sublimate the specifically female capacity to reproduce.
They take on another significance, however, in the context of Freud's
and Fliess's respective scientific work on bisexuality. Fliess writes of
the existence of similar 23- and 28-day hormonal cycles or periods
which, he argues, are part of a biological foundation shared by both
men and women; evidence of these cycles supports his views of an innate bisexuality.[42] The relative strength and proportion of these cycles
determine the relative biological masculinity or femininity of the indi-

vidual. The male can experience displaced symptoms of ovulation and menstruation in the membranes of the nose which, Fliess believes, register the fluctuations or disturbances in these cycles. Fliess originates the term "male menopause," which he describes in similar terms to that experienced by women.[43] Madelon Sprengnether points to Freud's determination of his own vulnerable "periods" with calculations set by the female menstrual cycle.[44]

Significant too is Freud's adherence to "gender-neutral" aspects of Charcot's model of hysteria: Charcot ascribes the etiology of male and female hysteria to neural lesions. Further, he describes the somaticizations and symptomatology of the hysterical male in ways identical to those of the female, including the same genital hysterogenic zones and "pseudo-ovarian points." Both Fliess's and Charcot's works hypothesize a hysteria with an identical symptomatology in men and women.[45] By paving the way for a specifically male somaticization of the disease along what had been, traditionally, female lines, they bring masculinity and femininity in proximity and minimize the absoluteness of gender differences. Given Freud's familiarity with the female hysteric's "phantom pregnancies," his demonstrated affinity for metaphors of procreation in describing same-sex affection, and his theoretical considerations of male menstruation and male menopause, it is no giant leap to a male phantom pregnancy as well. Finally, underlying a number of the earliest hysterical case studies, all the way through to the case history of Dora, is the patient's gender confusion and its repression. When Freud talks of "much . . . germinating and, for the time being, thrashing around" in his head, it may reflect his unconscious desire to identify with active components of a female fertility cycle in men. Put simply, Freud's narrative of his and Fliess's theoretical work feminizes his role in their relationship; at the very least, it attests to his desire to substantiate Fliess's theories (for which he provided much data, observing himself and others), and thus to parent or carry Fliess's "brainchild."[46] Beyond that, it appears that an effeminization, for Freud at least, characterizes his affectionate and erotic feelings for Fliess.

Freud hints that the sexual nature of their work, their "dirty talk," necessitates that it be kept private, i.e., that Fliess's "young wife" be protected from its explicit nature: "I am writing the whole thing [the draft of the Etiology of the Neuroses] down a second time for you, dear friend, and for the sake of our common work. You will of course keep the manuscript away from your young wife."[47] If Ida plays the potential impediment to their "full interchange," it is because Freud imagines that their work, being so intimate, necessitates a secrecy, something shared only by them. Freud places his wife Martha in the same role: his friendship with Fliess becomes the impediment to fulfilling his conjugal responsibilities. Following him unexpectedly to the mountains to share vacation time with him, time that will interfere with a proposed congress with Fliess, Martha makes an unwelcome appearance and provokes his astonished resistance: "initially I stared at her as at an apparition and then had to recognize my wife."[48]

> *Our home is haunted by some kind of illness which refuses to show itself.*
> —Freud to Fliess

By virtue of its condensed form, the event which emerges as the complex crisis in their relationship has been designated by Masson and other critics as "the Emma Eckstein episode."[49] Although originally Freud's patient and treated for hysteria with very limited success, on Freud's referral Emma Eckstein becomes Fliess's patient. Freud supports Fliess's decision to perform nasal surgery on Emma during a visit where Fliess will operate on Freud's nose as well. In one sense, Emma Eckstein realizes Freud's dream of sharing work with Fliess; yet Freud also identifies with Emma.[50] That this compounding of wish and identification should coincide with a near fatal disaster for Emma provides Freud with a complex reference point for his emerging ambivalence toward Fliess, bearing on the possible marital, professional, and social repercussions of his deep attraction to him. In Freud's mind, as we shall see, what happens to Emma happens to him. Yet there is a difference: if the hysteric's body is vulnerable and exposed to the doctor's influence, then that openness signifies differently, depending on the body's gender. For hysterical women, resisting the doctor is to claim a privacy and ownership of what was, culturally speaking, male property, i.e., their bodies' reproductive capacities. For hysterical men, resisting the doctor is also to insist that their body is private property, but that assertion must be made in order to underscore their masculinity, i.e., prove that they are not effeminate or homosexual. As a feminine other onto whom Freud can safely project aspects of his erotic desires for Fliess and the intensity of their disavowal, Emma Eckstein can be said to mediate Freud's crisis of gender and sexuality. The episode catalyzes Freud's attempts to confirm his own masculine, heterosexual identity, by increasing the conflicts allied to his intimacy with Fliess.[51]

Freud calls on Fliess in hopes of finding an organic etiology for what he had assumed were Emma Eckstein's hysterical symptoms. That an operation on the nose could cure a disease with a psychosexual symptomatology appears bizarre, but in fact such an approach lies at the base of Fliess's work: the establishment of connections between the nose and the sexual organs. Two weeks after the operation on Emma's nose, however, and after Fliess had returned to Berlin, Freud writes to Fliess that Emma suffers from severe pain, swelling, hemorrhaging, and a putrid nasal discharge. Consulting other doctors, Freud records Dr. Rosanes's discovery:

I asked Rosanes to meet me. He did so at noon. There still was moderate bleeding from the nose and mouth; the fetid odor was very bad. Rosanes cleaned the area surrounding the opening, removed some sticky blood clots, and suddenly pulled at something like a thread, kept on pulling. Before either of us had time to think, at least half a meter of gauze had been removed from the cavity. The next moment came a flood of blood. The patient turned white, her eyes bulged, and she had no pulse. Immediately thereafter, however, he again packed the cavity with fresh idoform gauze and the hemorrhage stopped. . . . In the meantime—that is, afterward—something else happened. At the moment the foreign body came out and everything became clear to me—and I immediately afterward was confronted by the sight of the patient—I felt sick. After she had been packed, I fled to the next room, drank a bottle of water, and felt miserable. The brave Frau Doktor then brought me a small glass of cognac and I became myself again . . . Since then [yesterday] she has been out of danger, naturally very pale, and miserable with fresh pain and swelling. She had not lost consciousness during the massive hemorrhage; when I returned to the room somewhat shaky, she greeted me with the condescending remark, "So this is the strong sex."

I do not believe it was the blood that overwhelmed me—at that moment strong emotions were welling up in me. So we had done her an injustice; she was not at all abnormal, rather, a piece of iodoform gauze had gotten torn off as you were removing it and stayed in for fourteen days, preventing healing; at the end it tore off and provoked the bleeding. That this mishap should have happened to you; how you will react to it when you hear about it; what others could make of it; how wrong I was to urge you to operate in a foreign city where you could not follow through on the case; how my intention to do the best for this poor girl was insidiously thwarted and resulted in endangering her life—all this came over me simultaneously. . . . I was not sufficiently clear at that time to think of immediately reproaching Rosanes. It only occurred to me ten minutes later that he should immediately have thought, There is something inside; I shall not pull it out lest there be a hemorrhage. . . .

Now that I have thought it through, nothing remains but heartfelt compassion for my child of sorrows. I really should not have tormented you here, but I had every reason to entrust you with such a matter and more.

You did it as well as one can do it. The tearing of the iodoform gauze remains one of those accidents that happen to the most fortunate and circumspect of surgeons. . . . Of course, no one is blaming you, nor would I know why they should. . . .[52]

Freud's epistolary recapitulation of the event dramatizes its recasting as his gender crisis. Emma remains conscious *without the aid of anaesthesia*, while Freud nearly faints. She scornfully reproaches Freud by disputing his masculinity: "So this is the strong sex!" Her crisis turns into his, one that necessitates a "Frau Doktor" who reveals herself to be more in command than "Herr Doktor" and who serves cognac in order to restore him. Alcohol is in fact only a substitute for virility: worse, it is one offered by a woman.[53]

Second is the matter of the gauze that is left behind, which Freud refers to as a "foreign body." Reading the nose as a displacement for the female sexual organs, as it was in Fliess's theories, the gauze itself looks like another displacement, in this case, for a "child": a phantom pregnancy which Fliess leaves behind after having implanted it there. Instead of substantiating Emma's trust, its near-fatal presence puts Fliess in the role of a torturer rather than a salutory figure. Fliess's betrayal of Emma extends implicitly to Freud too, if only because he has allowed Fliess to operate on him at the same time. More significantly, however, Freud experiences Emma's psychosomatic health as an extension of his own: she is his "child of sorrows," so that Fliess's lodging of a foreign body in her leaves a foreign body in Freud, something, moreover, which "stinks" to high heaven.[54] Uncomfortable with reproaching Fliess, Freud tries to cloak and master his reproaches by distorting what is going on. He assumes the guilt. Fliess is not the tormenter of Emma Eckstein, but Freud: as he exclaims in his letter, "I should not torment you here." Yet his rapid recuperation of an idealized Fliess allows us to see something else as well. Through his imposed prohibition—"I should not torment you"—he suggests in fact that he wants to torment Fliess. He establishes their relationship as one that now houses a disavowed foreign body split off from consciousness: in this case, the "Emma Eckstein episode."[55] The foreign body is repressed, for both men a sign of guilt and failure, and for Freud alone, the trauma of having been so influenced by, and intimate with, Fliess that he has not been able to see him as he really is, i.e., as a tormenter and not a healer. In short, Freud hystericizes their relationship.

Beyond the already potent combination of a masculinity crisis coupled with the dispossessing presence of a foreign body, it is time to look at a more powerfully homosexualized element that Freud adds to the episode. This is revealed in the famous specimen dream recounted in *The Interpretation of Dreams*, the so-called Irma dream of the night of 23 July 1895, which Freud interprets in conjunction with the Emma Eckstein episode. The Irma dream runs as follows:

A large hall—numerous guests, whom we were receiving.—Among them was Irma. I at once took her on one side, as though to answer her letter and to reproach her for not having accepted my "solution" yet. I said to her: "If you still get pains, it's really only your fault." She replied: "If only you knew what pains I've got now in my throat and stomach and abdomen—it's choking me"—I was alarmed and looked at her. She looked pale and puffy. I thought to myself that after all I must be missing some organic trouble. I took her to the window and looked down her throat, and she showed signs of recalcitrance, like women with artificial dentures. I thought to myself that there was really no need for her to do that.—She then opened her mouth properly and on the right I found a big white patch; at another place I saw extensive whitish grey scabs upon some remarkably curly structures which were evidently modelled on the turbinal bones of the nose.—I at once called in Dr. M., and he repeated the examination and confirmed it. . . . Dr. M. looked quite different from usual; he was very pale, he walked with a limp and his chin was clean-shaven. . . . My friend Otto was now standing beside her as well, and my friend Leopold was percussing her through her bodice and saying: "She has a dull area low down on the left." He also indicated that a portion of skin on the left shoulder was infiltrated. (I noticed this, just as he did, in spite of the dress) . . . M. said: "There's no doubt it's an infection, but no matter; dysentery will supervene and the toxin will be eliminated." . . . We were directly aware, too, of the origin of the infection. Not long before, when she was feeling unwell, my friend Otto had given her an injection of a preparation of propyl, propyls . . . propionic acid . . . trimethylamin (and I saw before me the formula for this printed in heavy type). . . . Injections of that sort ought not to be made so thoughtlessly. . . . And probably the syringe had not been clean.[56]

Some four and a half months after the operation, Freud's Irma dream and subsequent explanatory notes supplement and confirm an already hystericized response to the event. As Freud reveals, Otto is Fliess, the doctor responsible for the origin of the infection because his *injection* has been made *thoughtlessly. . . . probably the syringe had not been clean.*

With his dirty syringe, Otto injects Irma with a preparation of *propyl . . . propyls . . . propionic acid . . . trimethylamin.* Freud elucidates the significance of the substance as follows:

During the previous evening, before I wrote out the case history and had the dream, my wife had opened a bottle of liqueur, on which the word "Ananas" appeared and which was a gift from our friend Otto . . . This liqueur gave off such a strong smell of fusel oil that I refused to touch it . . . to be poisoned . . . The smell of fusel oil (amyl . . .) evidently stirred up in my mind . . . propyl, methyl, and so on . . . I carried out a substitution in the process: I dreamt of propyl after having smelt amyl. *Trimethylamin.* . . . [It directed my attention] to a conversation with [a] friend who had for many years been familiar with all my writings during the period of their gestation, just as I had been with his [Fliess]. He had at that time confided some ideas to me on the subject of the chemistry of the sexual processes, and had mentioned among other things that he believed one of the products of sexual metabolism was trimethylamin. . . . Trimethylamin was an allusion not only to the immensely powerful factor of sexuality, but also to a person whose agreement I recalled with satisfaction. . . .[57]

Now I would like to set aside Freud's own interpretative use of the dream, that is, as a "specimen dream" of wish-fulfillment and specifically as his wish to blame others (Irma/Emma, Otto/Fliess) for what in fact is his own failure to cure Emma's hysteria. Instead, I would emphasize what it reveals about his relationship with Fliess: for "the immensely powerful factor of sexuality" allied "to a person whose agreement [he] recalled with satisfaction." Freud points to Otto as the "originator" of the injection/infection made *thoughtlessly*, i.e., through a mode of unconscious exchange very much like that of hypnosis or thought transference.[58] As the holder of the syringe, Otto becomes the hypermasculine figure whose injection is a by-product of sexual metabolism, a scarcely veiled displacement for a sexual act. To Freud, it smells disgusting. The alcohol suggests not only the "bad liqueur," Fliess's gift that Freud refuses to ingest, but the cognac served by the "Frau Doktor" at the time of Emma Eckstein's actual crisis, which reminds Freud that, even as a Herr Doktor, he does not live up to being one of the "strong sex." The rejection of Fliess's gift, and thus of Fliess, is Freud's rejection of his effeminizing, submissive position: the gift or "child" from Fliess's incursion, the "thoughtless," undifferentiated organization of their affective, homoeroticized bond. The sexual pricking with Otto's needle easily reads, as Freud's writings on hysteria at the time illuminate, as an anal rape that produces a toxin, an illness, not the fantasy child of their common work. To Freud's reassurance (and this dream's other wish-fulfillment), the toxin will be expelled through the effects of dysentery; in other words, the exorcism of Otto's/Fliess's intrusive activities into Irma/Freud will be through shitting.[59]

Before continuing with Freud's representation of the aftermath of the Emma Eckstein episode, I would like to turn back to certain narrative predecessors of the episode: Freud's early hysteria case studies and writings on hypnosis. Through the gothicized concept of the counter-will, these narratives foreground a psychosomatic, sexualized transgression of the patient by the doctor and allow us to see more clearly how Freud is engaged in constructing the unfolding epistolary narrative of his relationship with Fliess according to these already available gothic-hysterical models.

In the *Studies on Hysteria*, it is the case of Emmy von N. whose hysteria most dramatically takes the associative and affective path of a gothic performance peopled with uncanny presences and resistances.[60] Her hypnoid deliria and hallucinations include interiorized encounters with a puppet double, confinement within a madhouse, a startling nocturnal bedside visit by a madman, the sudden discoveries of corpses and the necessity of dressing one, and fears of being buried alive—what Freud calls her "horror stories" (*Schauergeschichten*). Perhaps the most bizarre and disturbing aspect of this narrative proves to be her revelation that the real events provoking these terrifying visions are every bit as gothic and unreal as the "pathological" responses they engender. She unveils a number of traumatic experiences: seeing her sister in her coffin; her brother, dressed as a ghost, terrorizing her as a small child; her dead aunt's jaw dropping open at the moment Emmy looks upon her; the commitment of her mother and cousin to an insane asylum; an intruder's visit to her bedside one night in her isolated castle; and her discovery of the bodies of both mother and brother, recently deceased. Emmy von N. makes it hard to differentiate between the "psychopathology of her everyday life" and that of her hysterical illness.[61] Experience is mimetically reconfigured into symptom, and further, into their fantastic representation in the patients' and doctor's narratives, as Freud's oft-quoted statement suggests: "It still strikes me as strange that the case histories I write should read like short stories."[62]

Emmy von N.'s symptoms include hand gestures that she defensively directs at some supernaturalized presence, attempting to banish it with her own talismanic signs:

What she told me was perfectly coherent and revealed an unusual degree of education and intelligence. This made it seem all the more strange when every two or three minutes she suddenly broke off, contorted her face into an expression of horror and disgust, stretched out her hand towards me, spreading and crooking her fingers, and exclaimed, in a changed voice, charged with anxiety: "Keep still!—Don't say anything!—Don't touch me!" She was probably under the influence of some recurrent hallucination of a horrifying kind and was keeping the intruding material [*die Einmengung des Fremden*, the intrusion of alien material] at bay with this formula.[63]

According to Freud, her formula protects her against a recurring traumatic hallucination, an alien agency she attempts to disengage through externalizing it. As an *intra*psychic struggle, Emmy von N. is defending herself against aspects of herself which she splits off from consciousness. It dramatizes one of Freud's major insights into hysterical mechanisms: the multiplication of the subject's psyche into parts dissociated from one another. Indeed, it is the fears surrounding the *alienable* autonomy, integrity and control of the body-mind that surface with a hysterical splitting of consciousness:

> Through the study of hypnotic phenomena, the conception, *strange* though it was at first, has become *familiar*, that in one and the same individual several mental groupings are possible, which may remain relatively independent of each other, "know nothing" of each other, and which may cause a splitting of consciousness along lines which they lay down. Cases of such a sort, known as "double personality" ("*double conscience*"), occasionally appear spontaneously. If in such a division of personality consciousness remains constantly bound up with one of the two states, this is called the *conscious* mental state, and the other the *unconscious*.[64]

Freud introduces the mind's capacity to contain several mental groups at once, a plurality of counterwills, as it were, before he calls up the gothic "double" of conscious and unconscious mind as a more manageable depiction of the disturbing multiplicity of who is knowing and what is not known.

Suffering from and resisting social norms, the hysteric's intense excitement, matched against the demanding pressures of conscience, unconsciously split off what Freud calls a "demonic impulse" (*dämonischen Zug*): the counterwill.[65] Unlike the daytime world of the conscious will, the counterwill is an outsider inside:

> The question of what becomes of inhibited intentions seems to be meaningless in regard to normal ideational life. We might be tempted to reply that they simply do not occur. The study of hysteria shows that nevertheless they *do* occur, that is to say that the physical alteration corresponding to them is retained, and that they are stored up and enjoy an unsuspected existence in a sort of shadow kingdom, till they emerge like bad spirits and take control of the body, which is as a rule under the orders of the predominant ego conciousness.[66]

For Freud, the counterwill is best articulated through a gothic discourse of uncontrolled dispossession. Disclaiming antisocial desires and unable to incorporate them, the psyche pays with the production of spectres whose contrary acts of willing and speaking constitute one of hysteria's symptoms. At times, Freud reifies the counterwill, altering it from a ghostly agency (*Spuk*) into a "foreign body" (*Fremdkörper*): the resilient kernel of a psychic trauma or disavowed desire that needs to be integrated, diffused, or expelled.

Freud assumes that Emmy's formula protects her against herself, her unassimilable memories and sexual longings. But Freud overlooks the significance of the fact that she stretches out her fingers "against [him]" (*gegen mich*).[67] With her *Schutzformel*, Emmy von N. enlarges the hysterical pathology from an *intra*psychic struggle to an *inter*psychic one, between the patient and doctor. What becomes increasingly troubling for Emmy is that a splitting of her psyche occurs *during hypnosis*, and the doctor's directives themselves occasion the split.[68] Without being known as the originator, the doctor inserts his directives; they cohabitate within the patient's mind, motivating actions, feelings, thoughts, and memories. These "alien" agents within the patient's psyche are not unconscious, though they are introduced and acquire their strength from being implanted while the patient is unconscious. Their strangeness arises after the fact, as the subject of hypnosis embodies the confusion between what one feels to be one's own and what one is incapable of examining or modifying:

> what distinguishes a suggestion from other kinds of mental influence, such as a command or the giving of a piece of information or instruction, is that in the case of a suggestion an idea is aroused in another person's brain which is not examined in regard to its origin but is accepted just as though it had arisen spontaneously in that brain.[69]

The therapeutic mechanism of hypnosis replicates the splitting of the disease itself, and there is no name to differentiate the subject's own production of phantom agency from the introduced phantom agency that bears the doctor's commands. Because it is beyond the patient's capacity to reflect upon, but not beyond the ability to act out, hypnosis registers the weird, unaccountable effects of doctor upon patient, those uninterpretable forms of exchange that elsewhere have been called "the unthought known."[70] Both hypnotic transfer and the hysteric's performances reveal a mind receptive to being self-alienating and alienated by an other.[71]

With her hands, Emmy von N. protects herself against Freud's possession of her psyche.[72] Acting out of defense, she raises serious questions about the implications of his cure: if health is predicated on the idea of the individual subject as unified or singular, how can it be created out of such submission, the relinquishment of difference between the patient and doctor? As written by Freud, Emmy von N. only reluctantly follows his commands, caught between obedience and mistrust, acquiescing to his directives with ambivalence: "since you insist" and "only because you say so."[73] Freud claims with dismay that Emmy does not accept his "lesson . . . any more than would an ascetic medieval monk, who sees the finger of God or a temptation of the Devil in every trivial event of his life."[74] In her psychomachia where Freud's omnipotence makes the salvation he offers equivalent to her damnation, she uses various strategies to refuse symbiosis or, more aptly, appropriation: "she was in open rebellion."[75] She dismisses him as a "foreigner" or "stranger" (*ein Fremder*) and treats the doctor's transplanted incubus as an intrusive, pathenogenic agency she must dispel.[76]

Freud adopts and revises Emmy's symbolic vocabulary to amplify his genealogy of hysteria some seven years later. He refers back to medieval accounts of demon possession in a letter to Fliess:

> What would you say, by the way, if I told you that all of my brand-new prehistory of hysteria is already known and was published a hundred times over, though several centuries ago? Do you remember that I always said that the medieval theory of possession held by the ecclesiastical courts was *identical* with our theory of a foreign body and the splitting of consciousness? But why did the devil who took possession of the poor things invariably abuse them sexually and in a loathsome manner? Why are their confessions under torture *so like* the communications made by my patients in psychic treatment?[77]

Once the judges' role in the medieval ecclesiastical courts, medical doctors now hear their patients' confessions of sexual abuse as if "under torture." Like Emmy von N.'s experience in which she cannot distinguish internally the torments of the disease from the doctor's cure, Freud describes how the judges' torture of the possessed coincides with the judges' self-inflicted suffering, the torment by their own memories: ". . . the diabolus sticks needles into her fingers . . . once more, the inquisitors prick with needles to discover the devil's stigmata . . . *not only the victims but also the executioners recalled in this their earliest youth.*"[78]

It is a very short step in Emmy's mind from demonizing the perpetrators or experiences underlying her own illness to resisting the doctor as a demon in another guise—the recurring trauma of an other who claims power and authority over her body and mind. In this letter, Freud justifies Emmy's conclusion by drawing the parallel himself between victimization by the demons and by the judges (yet he then goes on to exonerate the judges in part, when he makes them also victims of abuse). Identifying with the scene before their eyes, the medieval executioners hysterically suffer and act out the trauma of abuse they suffered as children; they reinflict abuse upon those whom they are supposedly there to assist or cure—the power of the law perpetuating what it has been given the power to expel. Although Freud does not directly say so, he suggests that medicine, like ecclesiastical law, succeeds in its fight with the demons of mental illness by simply being a more powerful demon, one whose superior strength lies in the ability to foster the illusion that the (violating) internalization of its norms somehow defines psychic health. Directed at Freud, Emmy's magical formula wards off the adjudicator of her terror (the doctor mastering hysteria) as just another one of the demons she must contend with.[79] She literally acts this out in the dramatic scene between the two of them. Returning to our metaphor of pregnancy, she refuses to carry his presence inside her. When she externalizes her demons, the doctor's introjected hypnotic imago falls victim to her exorcistic delivery.[80]

In addition to her gestures, Emmy von N. tries to talk her way out of the hypnotic transfer, by withholding information or revising her account in the face of Freud's claims to know the truth before she speaks it.[81] In other words, she learns to keep secrets from the doctor.[82] Conversion into language no longer functions as the medium that allows the obedient patient to trust and share her secret fears and desires and to rid herself of their potent influence by a "talking cure."[83] When Freud uses suggestive commands as a therapeutic shortcut, he obviates the need for the patient's discourse, since the doctor wills his language in the place of both memory and affect. Emmy resists his "gag-rule" by insisting on a different version of events, as Freud reveals: "She . . . said . . . that I was not to keep asking her where this and that came from, but to let her tell me what she had to say. . . . I had assumed that her narrative was finished and had interrupted it with my concluding suggestion. . . . She had probably wanted to reproach me."[84] According to Freud, she frequently makes "false" associations, false because they cathect the affect to an inappropriate idea and thus delay the cure (the fulfillment of the *doctor's* wishes and demands), and false because they deny the truth of his already written conclusion.[85] Her narration diverges from his, in what amounts to an ongoing refusal of their possible confusion of identity.

Emmy von N.'s false connections exemplify her *narrative counterwill*. If she acquiesces with his/society's narrative, she subjects herself to the effacement of her difference, to the incorporation of the doctor's foreign will/body. Thus, she speaks without the goal of shared revelation and confesses profusely while denying herself his absolution; her "demonic" accomplishment is a self on guard to the doctor's incursions and orderings of her story. By virtue of these narrative substitutions, the disappearance of the illness becomes impossible; she chooses to be haunted by her own ghosts rather than cured by the incorporation of his. While he cannot let the superiority of science be compromised by Emmy's inventive counterwill, Freud nevertheless concedes defeat by naming the stories her own property: "the pathogenic psychical material appears to be the property [*Eigentum*] of an intelligence which is not necessarily interior to that of the normal ego. The appearance of a second personality is often presented in the most deceptive manner."[86]

The impropriety of hypnosis (and Freud's ultimate rejection of it as a therapeutic tool) exemplifies a larger violation of psychosomatic boundaries, or psychic trespass, one all the more terrifying because the patient never knows the extent of the doctor's crossings. When it becomes clear that hypnosis disregards, or undermines, the liberal notion that individual identity is, to quote Locke, property in the person and that this identity is inalienable and private, exempt from outside intrusion, hypnosis' threat to the-self-as-property begins to register as more pathological than the hysteria itself. Hypnotic trepass is marked as a more egregious violation of the socius. Within this struggle, the hysteric's secret does a kind of double service in the relationship between patient and doctor. On the one hand, it emblematizes the erotically charged, socially inadmissible psychic exchange between the patient and the doctor, their transitive, undifferentiated being in hypnosis. It speaks of the ways Freud imagines we desire otherness, of a part of our affective-erotic life that is driven by the desire to dissolve notions of property in a communal exchange. In this narrative of healing, the patient phantasmagorically gives birth to an idea in the image of the doctor. On the other hand, subverting the enjoyment of hypnotic symbiosis and converting its experience into terror, the secret is the malignant foreign body as well, the fear of dispossession or alienation of one's own psychic property. We could say that when the erotic interchange between doctor and patient shifts to read like a gothic narrative, they are left with passionate disputes over property. Figuring out how to make subjective property private, or how to keep one's own desire to oneself, becomes the achievement in the subject's developmental narrative. As we shall see, by way of the Freud-Fliess relationship, when the subject is male, the achievement of such privacy is the achievement of heterosexuality. To be a man is, above all, to avoid doing, or holding, certain things in common with other men.

> *He that has eyes to see and ears to hear may convince himself that no mortal can keep a secret. If his lips are silent, he chatters with his finger-tips; betrayal oozes out of him at every pore.*
>
> —*Dora: An Analysis of a Case of Hysteria*

Just a few months after the Irma dream, Freud works out the so-called seduction theory, where he traces hysteria's origins back to a trauma of infantile sexual abuse by the father. In a case of male hysteria, he finds "what he expects," namely, "sexual shock"; or, as he also terms it, "fright hysteria," whose primary symptoms, like Emmy von N.'s, are fright accompanied by the introduction of a splitting, or *gap*, in the psyche due to an "overwhelming of the ego." The ongoing experience of fear and being overwhelmed are the affective remnants of the early trauma.[87] They also echo the patient's response to hypnosis mentioned earlier, the "fear and embarrassing sensation of being overwhelmed." In the case of boys, the sexual shock is anal penetration, the ego subsumed by the experience of a powerful male other. As he continues to work on the seduction theory, Freud transforms the hysteric's memory of real traumatic abuse to a fantasy construction imposed upon the past.[88] Such fantasy constructions, he suggests, allow for the gratification of a repressed pleasure at the same time that the fantasist pays for it. The fright of "fright hysteria" reflects less on the abusive nature of the imagined trauma than that it masks or repudiates the pleasure or libidinal investment of the hysterical subject. Hysteria, in other words, is not repudiated sexuality but repudiated perversion: the choice not to act it out in reality but instead, to "suffer" it in fantasy. Male hysteria, Freud concludes, is the repression of the enjoyment of the pederastic element.[89]

The same symptoms of "fright hysteria" surface within his relationship to Fliess. In the letter that accompanies the theoretical draft outlining fright hysteria, Freud writes: "Your letters, as again the last one, contain a wealth of scientific insights and intuitions, to which I unfortunately can say *no more than that they grip and overpower me. The thought that both of us are occupied with the same kind of work is by far the most enjoyable one I can conceive at present.*"[90] If work is the only arena in which Freud allows for such pleasurable and overwhelming feelings, he nevertheless "can say no more" than that: he finds himself in some kind of gap, subjective and discursive, a splitting of consciousness that signals the presence of a counterwill. Freud then vaguely intimates that his relationship with Fliess is at the bottom of his own self-diagnosed hysteria. Characterizing defense neuroses as "curious states . . . twilight thoughts, veiled doubts," he links similar neurotic states in himself to Fliess's communications:

> Something from the deepest depths of my own neurosis sets itself against any advance in the understanding of the neuroses, and *you have somehow been involved in it.* For my writing paralysis seems designed to inhibit our communication. I have no guarantees of this, just feelings of a highly obscure nature.[91]

Freud refers openly to his hysteria in his letters of 8.14.97 and 10.3.97, although he conceals from himself the "pederastic element," namely, that in his fantasy, as the Irma dream begins to suggest, Fliess is a father figure who has "overwhelmed" him.[92]

Freud recognizes that it is the judges and doctors who "prick with needles . . . whereby they remember their earliest youth," but in the next letter he notes a "characteristic vagueness concerning the evildoers, who are, of course, concealed through defense."[93] If Fliess is implicated in Freud's inability to understand the defenses, then, *pace* Freud, it is because he is an "evildoer," i.e., simultaneously a devil, judge, doctor, and father. In the figure of Fliess, Freud condenses the etiology first of his hysterical responses and subsequently, as we will see, of his paranoid ones: the male whom Freud desires and to whose influence he has submitted; the powerful male who overwhelms an effeminized Freud and leaves something behind (via hypnotic/hysteria identification); the male who will punish Freud's desire; and a reproaching agent who, compelling the repression and repudiation of homoerotic desire, in actuality exposes his own complicity (the persecution fantasies of the paranoiac).[94] By way of the fantasy described in this letter, he ends up making Fliess one of those doctors who likes anal penetration.

As he ties the hysteric's sexual fixation to what he soon designates the oral-anal phase, where the smell of urine, feces, blood, indeed, all the surfaces of the body have a sexually exciting effect, Freud notes the hysteric's particularly keen sense of smell.[95] Whether it is the odor of the gauze or the smell of a sexual by-product, it recalls Freud's own fainting, overwhelmed, when Otto/Fliess leaves something behind in Irma/Emma, something with a nasty smell. And like Irma, who is able to exorcise the pathogenic influence through dysenteric purging, in Freud's construction of hysteria as a modern form of demon possession, "the gold that the devil gives his victims regularly turns into excrement."[96] In other words, libido finds itself associatively linked to disgusting pleasures. If the devil's sexual seduction is a mischievous equivalence between something worth possessing—gold—with a piece of shit, Freud's permeation by Fliess allows him to find shit a priceless substitute for gold: "after frightful labor pains of the last few weeks, I gave birth to a new piece of knowledge." It yields theoretical gold, the theory of the anal instincts, instincts whose memory "stinks just as in the present the object stinks," even if they are the "base for a multitude of intellectual developments."[97] In spite of his claim that the abandoned zones can only yield unpleasure, Freud in fact barely contains his pleasure with his "smut," as he calls it:

> I can scarcely detail for you all the things that resolve themselves into—excrement for me (a new Midas!). It fits in completely with the theory of internal stinking. Above all, money itself. I believe this proceeds via the word "dirty" for "miserly." In the same way, everything related to birth, miscarriage, [menstrual] period goes back to the toilet via the word *Abort* [toilet] (*Abortus* [abortion]). This is really wild. . . .[98]

For the first two months of 1898, he sends Fliess his ideas in what he entitles *Dreckology* reports [*Dreck*, shit].[99]

By way of this "phantom anal pregnancy" Freud conceives a theory which, if it allows for the pleasure of anal instincts, also turns them into something infinitely more refined than excrement. The "new Midas" of sexuality sees extinct, virtual, or abandoned anal libidinal zones as the powerful affective base which he can harness and put in the service of "a multitude of intellectual developments." By the time he writes up *Dora* two years later (five years before its publication), the pleasures of *Dreck* are unrecognizably betrayed, sublimated into the unspecified—unimaginable? or unimaginative?—pleasures of "important social functions":

> We surely ought not to forget that the perversion which is the most repellent to us, the sensual love of a man for a man, was not only tolerated by a people *so far our superiors in cultivation* as were the Greeks, but was actually entrusted by them with important social functions.[100]

Designating it the "most repellent" perversion, Freud nonetheless applauds the Greeks by claiming that they elevate their perversion into cultural pursuits. Like these Greeks, the hysterical Freud proves himself to be also "far superior in cultivation" because he manages to convert his repellent "perversion" into a scientific theory. He writes to Fliess:

> I do not share your contempt for friendship between men, probably because I am in a high degree party to it. In my life, as you know, woman has never replaced the comrade, the friend. If Breuer's male inclination were not so odd, so timid, so contradictory—like everything else in his mental and emotional makeup—it would provide a nice *example of the accomplishments into which the androphilic current in men can be sublimated.*[101]

Underlying the historical and cultural origins of Western civilization, *and* the origins of Freud's own civilizing pursuits, namely his work with Breuer on hysteria and his work with Fliess on the biological and psychological etiology of sexuality, Freud acknowledges a homoerotic libidinal drive.

Perhaps the most overdetermined element in this gothic-hysteric story is that when Freud's own "androphilic" inclinations become the subject of their letters at the end of 1897, it is Fliess's proposed *needle* and thread test that Freud objects to as the substantiation of his (Freud's) feminine side or homoerotic tendencies. Left-handed people, according to Fliess, manifest a psychological affinity for the inherent gender attributes of one's biologically opposite sex. Presumably, Freud's ability to wield a needle in his left hand will establish his highly developed feminine nature.[102] The significance of the reappearing needle, that Fliessian signifier of gratification and punishment, is never directly acknowledged by Freud as his disavowed, effeminizing desires to submit to another man. Freud acknowledges his "androphilic" inclinations only as a neurotic remnant from his early childhood relations with his brother and nephew: "this nephew and this brother have determined, then, what is neurotic, but also what is intense, in all my friendships."[103] He confesses to homoerotic feelings in their sublimated guise, as the need for an intense friendship or intellectual partnership. If he is being averse and hysterical about Fliess's notion of left-handedness, it is, he claims, for other reasons than as proof of his own "feminine side."[104] His reservations about Fliess's theory concern its *permeation* (Fliess's quasi-hypnotic demand) which Freud feels he cannot consent to: "I object only to the permeation of sexuality and bilaterality tha you demand." Freud cloaks his need to exorcise Fliess's dangerously sexualized influence with an intellectual skepticism. He suggests that this scientific matter [the question of bisexuality-bilaterality] "is the first in a long time on which our hunches and inclinations have not taken the same path." Just two weeks later, however, he convinces himself, with a button test, of Fliess's bilaterality theory, and presumably, his own homosexual inclination.[105]

> *We are becoming estranged from each other with what is most our own.*
>   —Freud to Fliess, 1 February 1900

Whether it is called a foreign body, a phantom pregnancy, the injected toxin, gauze, gold, shit, what is psychically smuggled in via an improper influence becomes a thing that can be contained—and then owned, hoarded, exorcised (in the "Non-vixit" dream, Fliess returns as a "revenant" to be banished after Freud has killed him), disposed of, expelled, described, used, subjected.[106] He converts homoerotic fantasies—a "primitive form of sexual longing . . . the first sexual aim, analogous to the infantile one—a wish that does not extend beyond the inner world"—into symbolic power, a theory of anal drives which transforms the wishes of the past without necessitating their fulfillment.[107] When he names his bond with Fliess a hysterical one, his understanding of that bond alters from a reciprocal influencing into an unwanted or uncanny *thing*. Homosexual impulses are no longer characterized by a mutual trespass between self and other, similar to affective hypnoid and hysterical states, but reified into theoretical property ("I gave birth . . . to a new piece of knowledge"), defensively fixed into an early phase of a much larger developmental narrative. This reification reinscribes an existing cultural alignment: that of heterosexual marriage with the generational transmission and inheritance of property, i.e., a masculine, heterosexual control over property. This is an inscription in which homoeroticism can stake no claim of its own to reproduce, to transmit, or to own anything. Freud's abandonment of hypnosis, his developmental argument for sexuality, as well as this constructed gothic narrative of their relationship, become different versions of the same argument, an argument for private property (and therefore, implicitly, an argument for heterosexuality, as Freud writes it). Dangerously, Fliess appears to have been able to go and instill himself everywhere; this homoerotic threat jeopardizes Freud's increasing need to substantiate masculine identity as a form of internalized private property.

Freud turns his theoretical preoccupations to the neuroses of defense,

concentrating on those psychic impulses that repudiate the kind of symbiotic identification underlying hysteria and hypnosis—and homoeroticism. It is, above all, a concern with paranoia that surfaces as the
defensive response to (and signals the presence of) homoerotic impulses. Paranoia dissolves the longing and identification of hysteria and
represses anal desires by projecting those impulses and their punishment onto an other, whose inclinations represent the disavowed parts
of one's own ego.[108] Plagiarism, specifically, is the paranoic symptom
that erupts into the Freud-Fliess relationship. With this discursive trespassing and the erasure of intellectual origin and property, plagiarism
represents the next stage in a narrative of the undifferentiating terrors
of hypnotic transfer. The pleasures of identification now constitute an
intellectual crime, the violation and erasure of intellectual property. In
the sublimated vocabulary of a paranoid, to accuse someone of plagiarism is to call him a sodomite.

During the last phase of their relationship, Freud repeatedly traverses the ground where he tries to determine what is intellectually his
and what is Fliess's.[109] As he once called Emma Eckstein, he now calls
the dream book his "child of sorrow," whose seeds were sown, according to him, on the night of the Irma dream, and whose appellation, despite his disavowal of Fliess's participation and his desire for sole
paternity, nonetheless conjures up his partner. As his homoeroticized
merging with Fliess has been transmuted into a sodomitical trespass
whose pathological results must be expelled, the dream book expresses
Freud's stake in differentiating himself from Fliess. He demonizes and
segregates his influence, signaling his own refusal of love, just as Emmy
von N. and Anna O. had done earlier. The dream book carries the symbolic weight of being "his first-born," his "child," compared with which
"no other work has been so completely my own."[110] Its completion becomes its own complex act of dispossession; as Freud tells Fliess, letting
go of it is "distressing for me because I [have] to surrender not only my
intellectual but also my emotional property."[111]

In the final letters, Freud calls Fliess's attention to numerous authors
whose work overlaps with Fliess's unpublished work—imputing not
only that Fliess is unoriginal but that he takes his ideas from elsewhere.[112] Fliess, in Freud's words, has been promiscuous with the ideas
of other men, having none of his own. In turn, Fliess denigrates Freud's
analytic technique as "thought-reading," that is, reading his [Freud's]
thoughts into others, paranoically construing psychotherapy as another
suspect form of mental trespassing (and therefore not really different
from hypnosis).[113] In response to Fliess's insinuations, Freud defen

sively overcompensates by asking whether he can "borrow" an idea of
Fliess's. At the same time, he aggressively encroaches on Fliess's terrain
of bisexuality: "now, the main thing! As far as I can see, my next work
will be called 'Human Bisexuality.' It will go to the root of the problem
and say the last word it may be granted to say—the last and the most
profound." Even as he anticipates garnering the recognition for what is
Fliess's idea and the satisfaction of occluding his presence, Freud
admits that bisexuality is Fliess's brainchild. He then reluctantly backs
down from his threat of an intellectual trespass:

> . . . then I must have a long and serious discussion with you. The idea itself
> is yours . . . So *perhaps* I must borrow even more from you; *perhaps* my sense
> of honesty will force me to ask you to coauthor the work with me. . . . That,
> then, is the next project for the immediate future, which I hope will *quite*
> *properly* unite us again in scientific matters as well.[114]

In fact, Freud never writes this book, circumventing the desire to prove
his intellectual honesty in relation to Fliess and to install their proper
union "in scientific matters as well."

The handful of letters in 1904 return for the last time to the contestations of plagiarism after an interval of three years' silence. The only surviving letters of Fliess to Freud date from this time. At issue for Fliess
is a book by Hermann Swoboda, where Fliess's ideas about biological
periods appear without citations or the dates of the observations—
worse, Hermann Swoboda is Freud's pupil (in an earlier letter, Freud
had proudly taken credit for being the "intellectual originator" of the
work).[115] Three months later, Fliess writes once again, this time furious
about Otto Weininger's book *Sex and Character* where he finds "a description of my ideas on bisexuality and the nature of sexual attraction
consequent upon it." Further, he has learned that Swoboda and Weininger were "*intimi.*" Fliess's charge: Weininger learned about Fliess's
ideas indirectly through Freud (and directly by way of his, Weininger's,
"improper" sexual conduct with Swoboda) and thus Weininger/Freud
"misused someone else's [i.e., Fliess's] property."[116] At this point, Freud
backtracks (Swoboda wasn't really his pupil, and he exploited Freud),
corrects Fliess (Weininger could have gotten his ideas anywhere, i.e.,
Fliess's ideas are common property), incriminates Weininger (he is the
"burglar," the "robber," who uses a "stolen key" and allegedly kills
"himself out of fear of his criminal [homosexual] nature"), admits his
culpability ("in conjunction with my own attempt to rob you of your
originality, I better understand my behavior toward Weininger"), apol-

ogizes ("how much I have forgotten . . . I handed your idea of bisexuality to Swoboda" and "I reproach myself with my generosity or carelessness with your property"), and finally minimizes his responsibility (it is a "petty incident" that Fliess "can clear up with a good piece of work"). In conclusion, he imputes a pettiness of spirit and carelessness to Fliess for sharing ideas on which he "sets great store by [his] right of ownership."[117]

Freud's and Fliess's interpretation of a homoerotic impulse behind Swoboda's and Weininger's transitive exchange of ideas easily reads as a displacement for their own relationship. According to Freud, Fliess's ideas, since they are everywhere, belong therefore to no one (the homosexual only holds things in common). According to Fliess, Freud encroaches upon and indiscriminately shares others' ideas (the homosexual as burglar or trespasser, who uses a "stolen key"). Freud ends their correspondence by converting this "insult" into a victory of his masculinity: he, Freud, "freely scatter[s] [his] ideas without asking what will come of them."[118] In other words, he is hyperpotent, having begotten so many original ideas that his image is everywhere. That his ideas are common property signifies to him the opposite of Fliess's ideas being everywhere, since Fliess is only receptive to what is already there, while Freud dispenses. Fliess's petty haggling over the ownership of any single idea is made irrelevant by Freud's megalomaniacal dispersion. At the end, then, we return to the beginning: with Freud's fantasy of dissolving psychic boundaries. This time, however, it is not hypnosis that is the means, nor is it a homoerotic fantasy about sharing with Fliess; in his sublimated guise as common cultural property, Freud achieves a fantasy of inclusion in an all-male intellectual community that is also a fantasy of omnipotence.

This return to an undifferentiated state in sublimated, intellectual form is not a resolution but a compromise. There is something left over and something unsaid.[119] Despite his threats, Freud never writes about bisexuality. Like the erasure of Fliess's name from Freud's histories of psychoanalysis, this book is never written. As soon as the homoeroticism between Freud and Fliess becomes the "wish that does not [cannot] extend beyond the inner world," the "much that could be said [that] cannot be put into writing," he makes the formative (pregnant, we could add) influence of Fliess into an undivulged secret, one he keeps to himself. It exists as a hysterical remnant in the theoretical progression of psychoanalysis toward heterosexuality, its untranscended pleasures in identification and its recognition of the erotics of common psychic property without differentiation—between men. Alluding to an "unborn piece . . . attached to what has already been born," Freud keeps something in reserve from the dream book; so, too, from the *Psychopathology of Everyday Life*, of which Freud says that "only half will be born."[120] Buried alive, these unborn fetuses are the unshaped fantasies of the "unforgettable Other" Freud holds onto.[121] As late as "Analysis Terminable and Interminable," writing on the male's struggle against his passive, "feminine" attitude to other males, Freud concludes that this aspect is unanalyzable (and hence incurable), the undivulged part of the "great riddle," or secret, of sexuality.[122] Projecting the present of his relationship with Fliess onto a universalized past—the prehistory of every individual's sexuality—he creates a past whose interminable presence he is able to discover again and again in others' "perverse" or repressed desires: the "need to restore an earlier stage of things."[123] Freud creates an indissoluble, universal tie to Fliess, while the particular, specific attachment goes underground. His professional despair aside, the clinical and theoretical work on hysteria records the secret homoerotic promise Freud makes to himself: the hysterical patient— i.e., Freud—simply does not want to get better: "no one can replace for me the relationship with a friend which a special—possibly feminine— side demands."[124] Without the banishing light of knowledge or the sublimating benefit of words, he maintains the connection to the irreplaceable impulse which, despite punishment, uniquely embodies his gratification: "in the darkest core, glimpses of the contours of Luzifer-Amor."[125]

Notes

INTRODUCTION

1. Horace Walpole, *The Castle of Otranto*, ed. W. S. Lewis (New York: Oxford University Press, 1996), 65.

2. As telling is Conrad's situation. Representing an unconventional, effeminate masculinity encoded as his inappropriateness for marriage, his sickliness, and his incapacity to meet the expectations of an ambitious father, in the premier scene of the novel Conrad is crushed to death by Alfonso's gigantic helmet.

3. Eve K. Sedgwick's chapter on the gothic in *Between Men: English Literature and Male Homosocial Desire* was the first to consider the gothic's associations with male homosexuality, by force of its foremost writers—Horace Walpole, William Beckford, and Matthew Lewis—being openly or indirectly reputed to be homosexuals, and to the homophobic mechanisms in the gothic novel (New York: Columbia University Press, 1985). For further connections between the gothic and explorations of male homosexuality, see George Haggerty's "Literature and Homosexuality in the Late Eighteenth Century: Walpole, Beckford, Lewis," *Studies in the Novel* 18 (1986): 341–52. According to Andrew Elfenbein, the gothic is "one much-investigated genre in studies of gender and sexuality," yet full-length studies have been predominantly restricted to female gender roles and sexuality. See *Romantic Genius: The Prehistory of a Homosexual Role* (New York: Columbia University Press, 1999). In *Art of Darkness: A Poetics of the Gothic*, Anne Williams defines the "male gothic" as highly attuned to the dangers threatening patriarchal property and violations of class boundaries, and hence, as a conservative genre (Chicago: University of Chicago Press, 1995). Cyndy Hendershot's recent study of gothic masculinity is the most comprehensive to date, focusing on the nineteenth and twentieth centuries as well as film. Hendershot presents a theory of the gothic where a fluid or ambigious "one-sex body" emerges as a response to anxiety generated by the binary model of sexuality that arose in the eighteenth century. See *The Animal Within: Masculinity and the Gothic* (Ann Arbor: University of Michigan Press, 1998).

4. Henry Abelove points to the overarching social changes in male-female gender relations, a narrowing of acceptable sexual behaviors, an increased importance awarded to penetrative sex, domestic values, and the nuclear family, and an imperative to reproduce in "Some Speculations on the History of 'Sexual Intercourse' During the 'Long Eighteenth Century' in England," in *Nationalisms and Sexualities*, ed. Andrew Parker (New York: Routledge, 1992), 337.

5. George Haggerty argues in *Men in Love* that the eighteenth century offered a number of such tropes as melancholy and friendship, but he neglects to mention how the "fantastic" discourses of the gothic work against naturalizing and accommodating tendencies (123). Leo Bersani's work on both masochism and the repudiation of phallic masculinity (as it emerges in fantasies of assuming the receptive position in anal sex),

has been helpful to my thinking about the gothic's depictions of male masochism; see his study *Baudelaire and Freud* (Berkeley: University of California Press, 1977) and "Is the Rectum a Grave?" in *AIDS: Cultural Analysis/Cultural Activism*, ed. Douglas Crimp (Cambridge: MIT Press, 1988), 197–222.

6. Such alienability of identity represents a particular threat to notions of male subjectivity, for, as Cyndy Hendershot notes, the evacuated subject has been "adamantly troped as feminine" in Western culture, as has been the proclivity to be possessed by an "alien" body or nature. Cyndy Hendershot, "The Possession of the Male Body: Masculinity in *The Italian, Psycho*, and *Dressed to Kill*," *Readerly/Writerly Texts* 2.2 (Spring/Summer 1995): 75.

7. Anne K. Mellor and Marlon Ross both argue that the Romantic male poet's imaginative strength is based on a conquering, suppression, or silencing of the feminine; Mellor, *Romanticism and Gender* (New York: Routledge, 1993) and Ross, *The Contours of Masculine Desire: Romanticism and the Rise of Women's Poetry* (Oxford: Oxford University Press, 1989).

8. For Romantic incompletion as a form of insight, see Marjorie Levinson, *The Romantic Fragment Poem: A Critique of Form* (Chapel Hill: University of North Carolina Press, 1986); Thomas McFarland, *Romanticism and the Forms of Ruin: Wordsworth, Coleridge, and Modalities of Fragmentation* (Princeton: Princeton University Press, 1981); and Marlon B. Ross, "Beyond the Fragmented Word: Keats at the Limits of Patrilineal Language," in *Out of Bounds: Male Writers and Gender[ed] Criticism*, ed. Laura Claridge and Elizabeth Langland (Amherst: University of Massachusetts Press, 1990), 110–31.

9. Jerrold Hogle, "Introduction: Gothic Studies Past, Present, and Future," *Gothic Studies* 1.1 (August 1999): 1–3.

10. Hogle, "Introduction," 4.

11. Indeed, the gothic seems ideally suited to trouble cultural projects of sexual self-definition, with the genre's strong associations with sexuality and repressed desire, its ongoing linkage of the erotic and the taboo, and its understanding of subjectivity as fractured or fluid. For the gothic's alignment with the erotic/taboo, see *The Literature of Terror: A History of Gothic Fictions from 1765 to the Present Day*, 2nd ed., 2 vols. (New York: Longman, 1996). The gothic is "a coherent code for the representation of fragmented subjectivity"; Robert Miles, *Gothic Writing, 1750–1820: A Genealogy* (New York: Routledge, 1993). According to Hogle, the gothic arises "from an awareness of the difference between an identity shored up out of fragments and counterfeits and a definite ground of inherited selfhood"; "The Ghost of the Counterfeit in the Genesis of the Gothic," *Gothick Origins and Innovations*, ed. Allan Lloyd Smith and Victor Sage (Amsterdam: Rodolpi, 1994), 33; and David Punter, *Gothic Pathologies: The Text, the Body and the Law* (New York: St. Martin's Press, 1998).

12. Generically hybrid from the outset (think of Walpole's theatricality and Radcliffe's poetic sensibility), the gothic's "slipperiness," in which horror films, video games, popular fiction, visual art, and eighteenth-century "romances" all receive the designation "gothic," makes defining the gothic a vexed question to this day (see Hogle, "Introduction," 1). Even during the historical period of this study, as James Watt has recently shown, the designation "gothic" accommodates a tremendous variety of works and conflicting canons, from the conservative Loyalist gothic to the radical and sensationalist German gothic, with other varieties in between. See James Watt, *Contesting the Gothic: Fiction, Genre, and Cultural Conflict, 1764–1832* (New York: Cambridge University Press, 1999).

13. April Alliston, Ian Watt, and James Watt discuss the eighteenth-century gothic in terms of the dominant issues of legitimacy and property; April Alliston, *Virtue's Faults: Correspondences in Eighteenth-Century British and French Women's Fiction* (Stanford: Stanford University Press, 1996); Ian Watt, "Time and Family in the Gothic Novel: *The Castle of Otranto*," *Eighteenth-Century Life* 10.3 (October 1986): 159–71; and James Watt, *Contesting the Gothic*; Anne Williams and Maggie Kilgour read the gothic genre as a troubled version of the *Bildungsroman* (*The Art of Darkness*; Maggie Kilgour, *The Rise of the Gothic Novel* (New York: Routledge, 1995); and David Punter stresses the gothic as a genre representing psychic fragmentation in the face of a transgression of cultural taboos and prohibitions (*The Literature of Terror: A History of Gothic Fictions from 1765 to the Present Day*).

14. See E. J. Clery, "Introduction," *The Castle of Otranto: A Gothic Story*, xv.

15. Ian Watt, "Time and Family in the Gothic Novel," 161. Compare also Marx's gothic vocabulary in his *Eighteenth Brumaire of Louis Bonaparte* to represent the past's hold on the present: "Men make their own history, but they do not make it just as they please; they do not make it under circumstances chosen by themselves, but under circumstances directly encountered, given and transmitted from the past. The tradition of all the dead generations weighs like a nightmare on the brain of the living"; in Karl Marx and Friedrich Engels, *The Collected Works*, vol. 11 (New York: International Publishers, 1979), 103.

16. In her study of the gothic, Maggie Kilgour identifies a male and female gothic, both of which she characterizes as troubled *Bildungsromane*. While the male gothic stresses the psychic costs provoked by the demands on men to achieve individuation and autonomy, namely, extremes of alienation and isolation, the female gothic, by pointing to the pressures of identification between mothers and daughters, questions whether socialized women can maintain any individuality (*The Rise of the Gothic Novel*, 37–39, 92, and 94).

17. Ronald Paulson, "Gothic Fiction and the French Revolution," *ELH* 48 (1981): 532–54; Norman Brown, echoing this cultural association of the gothic as posing a challenge to patriarchal, or inherited authority, adopts the "supernaturalized" vocabulary of John Locke's attack of Sir Robert Filmer's *Patriarcha* in his *Treatise of Civil Government*: "Locke contradicts Filmer's primal fatherhood—a 'strange kind of domineering phantom, called the "fatherhood,"' he says, a 'gigantic form'—with the postulate of all men in the primal state of nature free and equal. To vindicate liberty is to vindicate the children, *liberi*, the sons, against paternal despotism. Locke kills Filmer's fatherhood, slays that phantom"; in *Love's Body* (New York: Random House, 1966), 3–4.

18. Charles Maturin, *Melmoth the Wanderer* (Oxford: Oxford University Press, 1989), 111.

19. The gothic of dispossession could be said to represent a radical response to the conservative Loyalist gothic mapped out by James Watt (*Contesting the Gothic*). Loyalist gothic is defined as the appeal to an exemplary medieval era and foregrounds the restoration of property to legitimate heirs. See also Ian Duncan's understanding of the genre as one that privileges legitimacy and succession (*Modern Romance and the Transformations of the Novel: The Gothic, Scott, Dickens* (New York: Cambridge University Press, 1992). *Gothic Masculinity* argues that there exists another narrative within the variety of concerns designated as gothic that privileges illegitimacy and the impediments to patrilineal succession.

20. Lauren Fitzgerald, "(In)alienable Rights: Property, Feminism, and the Female

Body from Ann Radcliffe to the *Alien* Films," *Romanticism on the Net* 21 (February 2001). <*http://users.ox.ac.uk/~scat0385/21fitzgerald.html*> .

21. See April London, *Women and Property in the Eighteenth-Century Novel* (New York: Cambridge University Press, 1999), 1–4 and, for the gendered implications for men, J. G. A. Pocock, *Virtue, Commerce, and History: Essays on Political Thought and History, Chiefly in the Eighteenth Century* (New York: Cambridge University Press, 1985), especially chapter 6 ("The Mobility of Property and the Rise of Eighteenth-Century Sociology").

22. Their forays into dreamscapes, altered states of consciousness, and self-alienating experiences dovetail with the canonical gothic's increasing affinity for the psychological during the nineteenth century, which infuses works such as Mary Shelley's *Frankenstein*, Thomas De Quincey's *Confessions of an English Opium Eater*, Emily Brontë's *Wuthering Heights*, and the works of Edgar Allan Poe.

23. According to Tosh, masculinity as interiority did not exist during the long eighteenth century. The molly (a molly was a man who adopted female attire and an effeminate manner), whose sexuality constituted a core identity, was the exception that proved the rule. Anthony Fletcher, *Gender, Sex, and Subordination in England 1500–1800* (New Haven: Yale University Press, 1995); John Tosh, "The Old Adam and the New Man: Emerging Themes in the History of English Masculinities, 1750–1850," in *English Masculinities, 1660–1800*, ed. Tim Hitchcock and Michele Cohen (New York: Longman, 1999), 232 (see also 231–36).

24. The term for the foundation of the egalitarian, companionate marriage, is "affective individualism," which stems from Lawrence Stone's *The Family, Sex, and Marriage in England, 1500–1800*. See also: Randolph Trumbach, *The Rise of the Egalitarian Family* (New York: Academic Press, 1978); Jeffrey Weeks, *Sex, Politics, & Society*, 2nd edition (London: Longman, 1989); and for the Western European context, Simon Schama, *The Embarrassment of Riches* (New York: Knopf, 1987). *English Masculinities* is particularly good at tracing the critical error of assuming a distinct demarcation of gendered spheres too early, as are the works of Hannah Barker and Elaine Chalus, George Shoemaker, and John Tosh. See the "Introduction" of *English Masculinities*, 1–22; Hannah Barker and Elaine Chalus, "Introduction," *Gender in Eighteenth-Century England: Roles, Representations and Responsibilities*, ed. Barker and Chalus (New York: Longman, 1997) 1–28; George Shoemaker, *Gender in English Society, 1650–1850: The Emergence of Separate Spheres* (1998) and John Tosh, "The Old Adam and the New Man," 217–38.

25. "Orgasm, Generation, and the Politics of Reproductive Biology," in *The Making of the Modern Body: Sexuality and Society in the Nineteenth Century*, ed. Catherine Gallagher and Thomas Laqueur (Berkeley: University of California Press, 1987), 1–41.

26. Randolph Trumbach concurs with Laqueur that the eighteenth century gave rise to "the argument that biologically there are only two sexes, that on these anatomical differences are founded two gender roles, but that both genders sexually desire only the opposite gender. No individual was able to perform the role of a gender which was not a reflection of the individual's sexual anatomy." See "London's Sapphists: From Three Sexes to Four Genders in the Making of Modern Culture," in *BodyGuards: The Cultural Politics of Gender Ambiguity*, ed. Julie Epstein and Kristina Straub (New York: Routledge, 1991), 120.

27. Abelove, "History of 'Sexual Intercourse,'" 339–40.

28. Trumbach, "Gender and the Homosexual Role," 153–54; Theo van der Meer, "Sodomy and the Pursuit of a Third Sex in the Early Modern Period," in *Third Sex*

Third Gender: Beyond Sexual Dimorphism in Culture and History, ed. Gilbert Herdt (New York: Zone Books, 1994), 149.

29. See the "Introduction" in *English Masculinities* and Anthony Fletcher, *Gender, Sex, and Subordination in England*, 411.

30. Sedgwick, *Between Men*, 88–90.

31. Elfenbein, *Romantic Genius*, 8.

32. Laurence Sterne, *A Sentimental Journey Through France and Italy* (London: Oxford University Press, 1968) and Henry Mackenzie, *The Man of Feeling* (New York: Harper, 1836). See Diane Long Hoeveler, *Romantic Androgyny: The Women Within* (University Park: Pennsylvania State University Press, 1990).

33. Terry Castle, *The Female Thermometer: Eighteenth-Century Culture and the Invention of the Uncanny* (New York: Oxford University Press, 1995), 34.

34. Claudia Johnson, *Equivocal Beings: Politics, Gender, and Sentimentality in the 1790s* (Chicago: University of Chicago Press, 1995), 14 and Michael McKeon, "Historicizing Patriarchy: The Emergence of Gender Difference in England, 1660–1760," *Eighteenth-Century Studies* 28 (1995): 314.

35. Elfenbein, *Romantic Genius*, 8.

36. In eighteenth-century writing, "the ideals of male friendship are described so as to make them indistinguishable from erotic love"—in effect, public expressions of love which can be dismissed as "simple" friendship or as "simple" same-sex erotic desire. More valuable, as Haggerty suggests, is to see how these complex relationships open a window onto the era's wide-ranging cultural interest in affectual bonds, including varieties of love between men. See George Haggerty, *Men in Love*, 5 and 19.

37. Lawrence Stone identifies the effeminate aristocrat stereotype, one recognizable from popular literature, in his *The Family, Sex, and Marriage in England*, 541–42; see also Sedgwick, *Between Men*, 91–92.

38. Elfenbein, *Romantic Genius*, 34.

39. G. S. Rousseau, "The Pursuit of Homosexuality in the Eighteenth Century: 'Utterly Confused Category' and/or Rich Repository?" in *'Tis Nature's Fault: Unauthorized Sexuality during the Enlightenment*, ed. Robert Purks Maccubbin (New York: Cambridge University Press, 1987), 132–68; and Weeks, *Sex, Politics, & Society*, 108–13.

40. This is the argument of Haggerty's *Men in Love*. See also Christopher Craft, *Another Kind of Love: Male Homosexual Desire in English Discourse, 1850–1920* (Berkeley: University of California Press, 1994); Richard Dellamora, *Masculine Desire: The Sexual Politics of Victorian Aestheticism* (Chapel Hill: University of North Carolina Press, 1990); Linda Dowling, *Hellenism and Homosexuality in Victorian Oxford* (Ithaca: Cornell University Press, 1994).

41. van der Meer, "Sodomy and the Pursuit of a Third Sex," 173.

42. Judith Butler points out how the heterosexualization of desire "institutes the production of discrete and asymmetrical oppositions between 'feminine' and 'masculine' . . . [and] requires that certain kinds of 'identities' cannot 'exist,'" appearing "only as developmental failures or logical impossibilities" (*Gender Trouble: Feminism and the Subversion of Identity* (New York: Routledge, 1990), 17).

43. Michael Hadley, *The Undiscovered Genre: A Search for the German Gothic Novel* (Bern, Switzerland: Peter Lang, 1978).

44. Some studies of the developing influence of German literature in England include Rosemary Ashton, *The German Idea* (Cambridge: Cambridge University Press, 1980); Richard Brantley, *Coordinates of Anglo-American Romanticism* (Gainesville: Uni-

versity of Florida Press, 1993); Robert Alan Charles, "French Mediation and Intermediaries, 1750–1815," in *Anglo-German and American-German Crosscurrents*, ed. Philip Shelley (Chapel Hill: University of North Carolina Press, 1957), 1–38; Manfred Eimer, "Einflüsse deutscher Räuber- und Schauerromantik auf Shelley, Byron," *Englische Studien* 48 (1915): 231–45; James Engell, *The Creative Imagination* (Cambridge: Harvard University Press, 1980); Lilian Fürst, "Mme de Staël's 'De l'Allemagne': A Misleading Intermediary," *Orbis Litterarum* 31 (1976): 43–58 and "Two Versions of Schiller's *Wallenstein*," in *The Contours of European Romanticism* (Lincoln: University of Nebraska Press, 1976); *German Literature in British Magazines, 1750–1860* (Madison: University of Wisconsin Press, 1949); Geoffrey Hartman, "Wordsworth and Goethe in Literary History" and "From the Sublime to the Hermeneutic" in *The Fate of Reading and Other Essays* (Chicago: University of Chicago Press, 1975); Emma Jaeck, *Madame de Staël and the Spread of German Literature* (London: Oxford University Press, 1915); Roxana Klapper, *German Literary Influence on Byron* (Salzburg: University of Salzburg Press, 1974); Gregory Maertz, "To Criticize the Critic: George Saintsbury on Goethe," *Papers on Language and Literature* 30.2 (Spring 1994): 115–31; V. Stockley, *German Literature as Known in England, 1750–1830* (London: George Routledge, 1929); and F. W. Stokoe, "The Appreciation of German Literature in England Before 1820," *Publications of the English Goethe Society*, NS, 3 (1926): 122–42 and *German Influence in the English Romantic Period, 1788–1818, with Special Reference to Scott, Coleridge, Shelley, and Byron* (Cambridge: Cambridge University Press, 1926).

45. Devendra Varma's study, *The Gothic Flame* (London: Arthur Barker, 1957) includes a chapter on "Chambers of Horror," a paradigm traceable to the *Schauerromantik* tradition. Among the English works reflective of this tradition Varma lists: Beckford's *Vathek*, Godwin's *St. Leon* and *Caleb Williams*, Lewis's *The Monk*; Mary Shelley's *Frankenstein*; Polidori's *Vampyre*; and Maturin's *Melmoth the Wanderer*. Karl Guthke's study explores the impact of Lewis's extended visit to Germany, and his knowledge of and indebtedness to German literature. Some of the German sources for *The Monk* include: Bürger's "Lenore"; Herder's *Volkslieder*; Hölty's "Die Nonne"; Müsaus's *Volksmärchen der Deutschen*; Naubert's *Elisabeth von Toggenburg* and *Neue Volksmärchen der Deutschen*; Schiller's *Der Geisterseher* and *Don Karlos*; Schubart's "Der ewige Jude"; Spiess's *Das Petermännchen*; and Weber's *Sagen der Vorzeit* (*Englische Vorromantik und deutscher Sturm und Drang: M. G. Lewis' Stellung in der Geschichte der deutsch-englischen Literaturbeziehungen* (Göttingen: Vandenhoeck & Ruprecht, 1958). Syndy M. Conger revises and complicates Guthke's account in her study *Matthew Lewis, Charles Robert Maturin and the Germans. An Interpretive Study of the Influence of German Literature on Two Gothic Novels* (Salzburg: University of Salzburg, 1977). See also Eino Railo's *The Haunted Castle: A Study of the Elements of English Romanticism* (New York: Dutton & Co., 1927) for a biography of Lewis which includes a treatment of the influence of contemporary German melodrama on his own dramas. For the German influences on Sir Walter Scott, his translations from the German, and his role in making German literature known to a larger British audience, see John Koch, "Sir Walter Scotts Beziehungen zu Deutschland," *Germanisch-romanische Monatsschrift* 15 (January-February 1927): 36–46 and P. M. Ochojski, "S. W. Scott's Continuous Interest in Germany," *Studies in Scottish Literature* 3 (1966): 164–73.

46. Two studies provide excellent material on the reception of German gothic literature and its relation to the composition of national character: David Simpson, *Romanticism, Nationalism, and the Revolt against Theory* (Chicago: University of Chicago Press, 1993) and James Watt, *Contesting the Gothic*, 68–101.

47. See Simpson, *Romanticism* and Watt, *Contesting the Gothic*, for a treatment of these associations of antipaternalism with gender deviance.

CHAPTER 1. HEGEL POSSESSED

1. M. H. Abrams, *Natural Supernaturalism: Tradition and Revolution in Romantic Literature* (New York: Norton, 1971), 225–37 and Judith Butler, *Subjects of Desire: Hegelian Reflections in Twentieth-Century France* (New York: Columbia University Press, 1987), 17. For a reading that emphasizes education in the *Phenomenology* as the acquisition of forms of rhetorical expression, see John H. Smith, *The Spirit and Its Letter: Traces of Rhetoric in Hegel's Philosophy of Bildung* (Ithaca: Cornell University Press, 1988).

2. Georg Wilhelm Friedrich Hegel, *Phänomenologie des Geistes* (Frankfurt am Main: Suhrkamp, 1970), 32. All German citations refer to this edition and will be cited by page number parenthetically in the text. The English translations are my own.

3. Here, in contrast to the contemporary casting of performativity and the constitution of the subject as a kind of subversive play, Hegel elevates it to the status of work or labor. As Karl Marx writes of Hegel: "Hegel erfasst die *Arbeit* als das *Wesen*, als das sich bewährende Wesen des Menschen" [Hegel conceives of *work* as the *essence*, as the perpetually proven essence of the human being]. Marx refers specifically here to Hegel's master-slave dialectic and the possibility of an unalienated relationship to one's own work; this essay considers whether the philosopher's memory-work, as the condition of its own possibility, can be anything other than self-alienating.

4. Grimm's dictionary lists, among the meanings of *ungeheuer*, a number that align it with the gothic, as a synonym for uncanny: horrific (*entsetzlich*); unfamiliar; without a concern for family, house, home, or homeland (*ohne Anteil an Familie, Haus, Heim, Heimat*); without protection or security (*ohne Schutz oder Sicherheit*); hostile (*feindlich*). The overlapping of the gothic tropes used in the preface and conclusion is a way of measuring their conceptual proximity. In his essay "Facing the Preface," Howard Adelman argues that the preface is in fact an epilogue, since it was written a few months after Hegel finished the *Phenomenology*; in *Idealistic Studies* 14 (May 1984): 159–70.

5. Sigmund Freud, "The Uncanny," in *The Standard Edition of the Complete Psychological Works of Sigmund Freud*, trans. and ed. James Strachey, vol. 17 (London: Hogarth Press, 1953–66): 241–42.

6. Pierre Bourdieu, *Language and Symbolic Power*, ed. John B. Thompson, trans. Gino Raymond and Matthew Adamson (Cambridge: Harvard University Press, 1991), 145.

7. Few critics have read Hegel through his tropes, and most English translations fail to capture the literal and figurative meanings attached to many of his most abstract terms. Donald Verene's study *Hegel's Recollection: A Study of Images in the Phenomenology of Spirit* (Albany: State University of New York Press, 1985) and Jacques Derrida's essays, most notably, "The Pit and the Pyramid" in *Margins of Philosophy*, trans. Alan Bass (Chicago: University of Chicago Press, 1982), 69–108 are the exceptions. Both of these writers, however, overlook the metaphorical field in *The Phenomenology* that supernaturalizes consciousness. Slavoj Žižek draws on the repertoire of popular culture, especially horror and suspense films as well as mysteries, to explore the political ideologies at work in philosophy, psychoanalysis, and current events. Although he does not specifically focus on a gothic subtext in Hegel, his writings inform my understand-

ing of the *Phenomenology*; especially, *For They Know Not What They Do* (London: Verso, 1991); *The Sublime Object of Ideology* (London: Verso, 1989); and *Tarrying with the Negative* (Durham: Duke University Press, 1993).

8. Immanuel Kant, *Träume eines Geistersehers, Erläutert durch Träume der Metaphysik*, in *Vorkritische Schriften bis 1768* (Darmstadt: Wissenschaftliche Buchgesellschaft, 1983), 923–93.

9. Friedrich Schiller, letter to Christian Gottfried Körner, 6 March 1788, quoted in *Schillers Werke*, ed. Hans Heinrich Borcherdt, vol. 16 (Weimar: Hermann Böhlaus Nachfolger, 1954), 415.

10. In contrast to the empirical schools of psychology and sensory physiology, Romantic psychology was nonmathematical, nonexperimental, and metaempirical: a speculative engagement with the representation of mental processes. It developed concepts and concerns central to the science of psychology as we know it today, including, especially, consciousness, the unconscious, the ego, the imagination, and the will, as well as the phenomenological study of consciousness. David Leary distinguishes the idealist project from nineteenth-century empirical psychology in detail in "German Idealism and the Development of Psychology in the Nineteenth Century," *Journal of the History of Philosophy* 18 (July 1980): 299–317 (see esp. 312–15).

11. John Russon, "'For Now We See Through a Glass Darkly': The Systematics of Hegel's Visual Imagery," in *Sites of Vision. The Discursive Construction of Sight in the History of Philosophy*, ed. David Michael Lewin (Cambridge: MIT Press, 1997), 198 and John Smith, "Sighting the Spirit: The Rhetorical Visions of *Geist* in Hegel's *Encyclopedia*," in *Sites of Vision*, 241–64. John Smith's argument about the *Encyclopedia* emphasizes Hegel's normalization and rhetorical exploitation of such "pathology": "The only way to come to see speculatively is to learn to see what is not there, to accept the possibility of visions. Those visions, however, are not yet, for Hegel, philosophy in its full form. They are products of the 'feeling psyche' and hence pathology. His speculative philosophy of Spirit thus cannot be reduced to a spooky sighting of spirits (*Geisterseherei*)," 259.

12. Terry Castle, "Phantasmagoria: Spectral Technology and the Metaphorics of Modern Reverie," *Critical Inquiry* 15.1 (1988): 52.

13. For a study of the modern's uncanny spaces, see Anthony Vidler, *The Architectural Uncanny: Essays in the Modern Unhomely* (Cambridge: MIT Press, 1992).

14. Freud, "The Uncanny," 224–25.

15. Mladen Dolar, "'I shall be with you on your wedding night': Lacan and the Uncanny," *October* 58 (1991): 6.

16. "... ihre Bewegung [die der Substanz] [scheint] ihr durch eine fremde Gewalt angetan zu werden; aber ... sie [hat] ihr Anderssein selbst an ihr" [substance's movement appears to be inflicted upon it by a foreign force; but its difference is to itself] (53).

17. Ellis, *The Contested Castle*, xiii.

18. Mikkel Borch-Jacobsen writes that the terror of the double is that "what had been one's own living identity (or identification) becomes, once represented, an expropriated, deadly resemblance"; in *Lacan: The Absolute Master*, trans. Douglas Brick (Stanford: Stanford University Press, 1991), 45. Commenting on the appearance of the double in different cultures (the Scottish wraith, for example, is "an apparition thought to be seen by a person in his exact image just before death"), Jorge Luis Borges concludes that the double embodies the idea that to meet oneself always turns ominous. See Jorge Luis Borges with Margarita Guerrero, *The Book of Imaginary Beings*, trans. Norman Thomas di Giovanni (New York: Dutton, 1969), 80.

19. "What we call 'subject' is ultimately a name for this . . . paradox or, more accurately, this short-circuit, whereby *the conditions of possibility coincide with the conditions of impossibility.*" Žižek, *Tarrying with the Negative: Kant, Hegel and the Critique of Ideology* (Durham: Duke University Press, 1993), 171.

20. Žižek points out that in literary works such as *Antigone* and *Hamlet*, and films such as *The Night of the Living Dead, Halloween,* and *Nosferatu,* the revenant's appearances reveal culture's "melancholic" fantasies: events that remain symbolically and psychically unresolved; in *Looking Awry: An Introduction to Jacques Lacan through Popular Culture* (Cambridge: MIT Press, 1992), 23.

21. Philosophically, Hegel's *Phenomenology* is an ontology; he is speaking of the nature of appearance and essence as they relate to being. In this essay, I am not reading the *Phenomenology* philosophically but narratively, by looking at the symbolic discourse of Hegel's *Geist.* By symbol, I mean the representational mode of mind whose determinations are sociocultural (which Hegel equates with phenomena).

22. In "The Imaginary and the Symbolic," Frederic Jameson writes: "This incommensurability between the particular and the universal, between the [lived] and language itself, is one in which we dwell all our lives, and it is from it that all works of literature and culture necessarily emerge"; in *Yale French Studies* 55/56 (1977): 339.

23. By virtue of its incorporation of the lost object (itself a kind of possession), Nicholas Abraham describes melancholy as the inability (or refusal) to symbolize, in other words, to displace or allow for a substitute of the object in words. In this way, the dead person or thing is not "put to rest," and the melancholic survivor refuses to let him die, preferring to keep him alive as part of himself. See Nicholas Abraham and Maria Torok, "Introjection-Incorporation: Mourning or Melancholia," in *Psychoanalysis in France,* ed. Serge Lebovici and Daniel Widlocher (New York: International Universities Press, 1980), 6.

24. My understanding of the psychological stakes of the phobic experience is drawn from Adam Phillips's essay, "First Hates: Phobias in Theory," in *On Kissing, Tickling, and Being Bored* (Cambridge: Harvard University Press, 1993), 12–26.

25. Phillips, "First Hates," 23.

26. Although this essay discusses the emergence of the Hegelian subject, it seems valuable to point to its Freudian successor. Phillips writes on the Freudian phobia: "In order to become what Freud thinks of as a person, one has to become phobic; and one can become phobic only by believing that there are an external and an internal world that are discrete. 'What is bad, what is alien to the ego and what is external are, to begin with, identical,' Freud writes in 'Negation'. . . . For the ego to sustain itself as good, which means in Freud's terms for the ego to sustain itself, depends upon expelling everything experienced as bad into the outside world. . . . The first world we find outside is, in part, a repository for the terror inside us . . . And the world we make outside is the world we need to get away from . . . To be at home in the world we need to keep it inhospitable" ("First Hates," 24). Anticipating Freud, we could say that Hegel offers a philosophy of the phobia.

27. " . . . das Bewußtsein als reine Einsicht ist nicht *einzelnes* Selbst, dem der Gegenstand ebenso als *eigenes* Selbst gegenüberstände, sondern es ist der reine Begriff, das Schauen des Selbsts in das Selbst, das absolute *sich selbst* doppelt Sehen; die Gewißheit seiner ist das allgemeine Subjekt und sein wissender Begriff das Wesen aller Wirklichkeit" [Consciousness as pure insight is not the singular self confronted by the object as a singular self; rather, it is the pure notion, the gazing of itself into itself, the absolute

seeing of itself doubled. Self-certainty is the universal subject, and his conscious notion is the essence of all reality] (432).

28. Phillips, "First Hates," 22.

29. Phillips, "First Hates," 22.

30. Interestingly, Hegel's letters succumbed to a fate similar to those gothic manuscripts. As his son Karl prepared the first edition after his father's death, he made a number of the originals illegible. Karl apparently did this to conceal any suggestion of political subversion on Hegel's part. H. S. Harris believes that some were simply destroyed. See his *Hegel's Development. Night Thoughts*, (note on p. lxviii), referred to in Jacques D'Hondt, *Hegel in His Time*, trans. John Burbidge (Peterborough, Ontario: broadview press, 1988), 216.

31. Friedrich Schiller, *Gedichte*, ed. Gerhard Fricke (Stuttgart: Reclam, 1978), 19 (my translation).

32. According to Freud (after Otto Rank), the double was originally an insurance against the destruction of the ego. The immortal soul was probably the first double of the body. Beyond this narcissistic fantasy, however, the double carries a reverse aspect: it becomes the uncanny harbinger of death (in "The Uncanny," 234–35). Hegel, with his collection of skulls, registers both aspects of the double: he insures against a destruction of the ego by insisting on the past's capacity to be reflected or remembered in a subject (its underdetermination), *and* he is at the place where he is reflected in dead things, or is sheer materiality. This ironic conjunction is further reinforced by the relation of Absolute Knowing to memory, since memory's topography is "die Schädelstätte des absoluten Geistes" (the place of the skulls of absolute mind)—that place where things hover between being lost and found.

33. In a section where Hegel anticipates critics rejecting the *Phenomenology*, he makes a similar metaphorical move: critics, the living dead who bury their dead (*Toten, wenn sie ihre Toten begraben*, 67), will be insuring the *Phenomenology's* conclusion by insuring it has no future narrative, i.e., no reception or viability, no after-life or posterity (*Nachwelt*).

34. While the affect of horror in the above passage is attributed to those who are ignorant of the nature of mediation (and hence truth), indirectly it refers to Mind as well, who, through negation, must learn to recognize himself in and as simple becoming.

35. In his *Hegel: Three Studies*, Theodor Adorno points to the significance of Hegel's Schwabian accent and use of Schwabian idioms in his lectures, years after completing the *Phenomenology*, as a successful professor in Berlin—the capital of Prussia and emerging cultural and national center of Germany. By refusing to alter his pronunciation to conform to the standard High German, Hegel refused a totalizing German national identity. In light of the discussion here, Hegel's "Schwäbisch," like the Latinate *perhorreszieren*, counts as the eruption of difference, the expression of the foreign brought into the familiar of standardized usage. The degree to which his Schwäbisch was remarkable (inspired shuddering) can be said to reflect the Prussian-German resistance to difference: and its idea of a singular national identity as a single standardized pronunciation. See Adorno, *Hegel: Three Studies*, trans. Shierry Weber Nicholsen (Cambridge: MIT Press, 1993), 120–22.

36. *Deutsches Fremdwörterbuch*, ed. Otto Basler und Hans Schulz (Berlin: Walter de Gruyter, 1942), 457.

37. See *Phänomenologie*, 24–25. Žižek points to the irony of this position: "at every given historical moment we speak from within a finite horizon that we perceive as abso-

lute—every epoch experiences itself as the 'end of history.' And 'absolute knowledge' is nothing other than the explication of this historically specified field that *absolutely limits our horizon*: as such, it is 'finite,' it can be contained in a book—in the works of the individual named Hegel"; in *For They Know Not What They Do* (London: Verso, 1991), 218.

38. "Das Selbstbewußtsein erfährt, was [die absolute Freiheit] *ist. An sich* ist sie eben dies *abstrakte Selbstbewußtsein*, welches allen Unterschied und alles Bestehen des Unterschiedes in sich vertilgt [Self-consciousness experiences what absolute freedom is. In itself it is simply this abstract self-consciousness, which obliterates all difference and all continuance of difference in itself] (437).

39. Žižek, *Tarrying with the Negative*, 24–26.

40. *Phänomenologie*, 435–36. See also Jean Hyppolite, *Genesis and Structure of Hegel's Phenomenology of Spirit*, trans. Samuel Cherniak and John Heckman (Evanston: Northwestern University Press, 1974), 459.

41. Žižek sees in this interiorized negative a prefiguration of the Freudian super-ego's sadistic force and the subject's failure to meet its impossible demands (*Tarrying with the Negative*, 25).

42. Ronald Paulson, "Gothic Fiction and the French Revolution," *ELH* 48 (1981): 532–54.

43. The absolute freedom to remember differently may feel far more traumatic than liberating. The French Revolution is also the Terror. Dialectically, as simple negation, absolute freedom has the devastating force of a compulsion, the not-I of the "foreign force" that acts upon the subject. To be free to remember things differently and to do so is disturbing, uncanny, and alienating, because revolutionary remembering is also to be absolutely forgotten, i.e., is subjective death. It is far more comfortable to be "forget-full," as it were, than memory-less. Negating the negation, we arrive at the following: the subject recognizes himself as this "not-I." He is constituted as the one who knows that freedom feels like compulsion because of his terror of being "free from" himself, the terror of what it would be like to forget absolutely (to be absolutely forgotten). In Hegel, one is liberated to forget. Finally, absolute freedom and absolute knowing as impulses of *Erinnerung* (memory) are experienced as uncanny: absolute freedom, be-cause it feels more like compulsion, and absolute knowing, because it feels more like forgetting. As an ironic Hegel shows again and again, however, just as one is not com-pelled to remember, one is never free to forget, absolutely.

44. Napoleon's troops were marching into Jena after the Prussian defeat, as Hegel penned the conclusion of the *Phenomenology*. Hegel did not support Prussia and wel-comed Napoleon's arrival. It could be argued that the unacknowledged "other" of the subject of Absolute Knowing is Napoleon (Absolute Knowing as a "French" Revolu-tion), and that the unrecognizable present is a result of the political upheaval taking place. In the complex negation of the concluding scene, Napoleon, the intruding foreign force, figures as the negative moment. He dispossesses our subject of a German national identity (as defined by Prussia), reinvesting him with a European one that he has yet to legitimate as his own (hence, the submersion in the night of self-consciousness). The conclusion would dramatize Hegel's negation of Prussia's absolutist claims to legitimate what would count as a German identity.

45. Narrative continuity equals subjective discontinuity.

46. The best treatment of gothic disinheritance is April Alliston's chapter on Sophia Lee's *The Recess*, in *Virtue's Faults* (Stanford: Stanford University Press, 1996). Alliston

relates gender to genre as she connects the narrative blockage of the gothic genre with the heroine's inability to possess a legitimizing inheritance.

47. In this context, Hegel is pointing to the fact that mind, as a universal, has predicates, in other words, is a substantial universal, but that it lacks self-reflexivity. As property, it does not yet pertain to any particular subject. In Hegel, property is communal before it is private; private property is as labor-intensive and inconclusive an achievement as self-consciousness.

48. I refer to the concluding section, where Hegel mentions twice in the same sentence that these spirits move slowly because they are weighted down (attired) with the entire wealth of Mind as the entire wealth of his substance.

49. *Phänomenologie*, 317–18.

50. "Das Sein . . . ist absolut vermittelt;—es ist substantieller Inhalt, der ebenso unmittelbar Eigentum des Ichs . . . ist" [Being is absolutely mediated; it has a substantial content that is also the immediate property of the I] (39).

51. "Schon ein Gedachtes, ist der Inhalt *Eigentum* der Substanz . . . die Gestaltung [ist] bereits auf ihre Abbreviatur, auf die einfache Gedankenbestimmung, herabgebracht" [What is already thought is, concerning its content, the property of (the subject as) substance . . . the form is already reduced to its abbreviation, to its simple determination by thought] (34).

52. Clark Butler points this out in his commentary in *Hegel: The Letters*, trans. Clark Butler and Christiane Seiler (Bloomington: Indiana University Press, 1984), 97. Since I am interested in calling attention to the relevance of Savigny's work for Hegel's conception of legal possession in *The Phenomenology*, I do not go into the substantial differences between Hegel's and Savigny's later understandings and positions on law. These differences became a full-fledged dispute and aligned Hegel with Thibaut as a "progressive" proponent for a universal civil code much like Napoleon's, against Savigny's historical conservatism (see Butler, *Hegel*, 504–5 and Jacques D'Hondt, *Hegel in his Time* 76). For the discussion here, see Savigny, *Das Recht des Besitzes. Eine civilistische Abhandlung* (Vienna: Carl Gerold, 1865). The English edition I cite from is *Von Savigny's Treatise on Possession; or the Jus Possessionis of the Civil Law*, trans. Sir Erskine Perry (London: Sweet, 1848). Karl Rosenkranz, one of Hegel's first biographers, indicates that in the 1790s Hegel read a great deal of English writings on acquisition and possession, and considered the state and its laws (after Locke) as the embodiment of the principle of property; *Georg Wilhelm Friedrich Hegel's Leben* (Berlin: Dunker und Humblot, 1844), 85, 87. In light of this, the simultaneity of the defeat of the German state by Napoleon with the stage of Absolute Knowing in the *Phenomenology* encourages the reader to see Absolute Knowing as a quasi-absolute divestment of national identity.

53. "Western inheritance law . . . illustrates a more individualistic, voluntaristic spirit. . . . Greek law anticipates that of Rome by allowing for inheritance based on nonnatural volition in the form of adoption. But Rome—which practiced disinheritance as well as adoption—fully displays the self-seeking private person uprooted from tradition and nature" (commentary by Clark Butler in *Hegel: The Letters*, 505).

54. In Perry's translation, see especially 170–71 and 177. For Savigny's treatment of the loss of the will to possess as a contrary mental act, see 266–67; for categories of those unfit to possess (children, the insane, slaves), see 85–87 and 180–81. For the possession of incorporeal things such as rights, see 131–34.

55. When Hegel speaks of specific determinations as immanent, he recognizes them as having "einheimische und eigentümliche Selbsterzeugung und Darstellung" [a native

and unique way of producing and presenting themselves] (52). He again links the native (*einheimische*) with property (what is proper to or the property of something, *eigentümliche*). Unsurprisingly perhaps, given the conjunction of opposites in the uncanny, in this moment of appropriation and familiarization, the negative still slips in: what is *eigentümlich* is also strange, queer, odd, not recognizable.

56. Theodor Adorno suggests an alignment of *Museum* with *Mausoleum* in his essay "Valery-Proust Museum," in *Prisms*, trans. Samuel and Shierry Weber (Cambridge: MIT Press, 1981), 175. Condemning the safety enjoyed by the museum visitor, Adorno offers an implicit critique of Hegel's voyeuristic subject of absolute knowing: "It is only when the distance necessary for enjoyment to be possible is established between an observer and works of art that the question of their continuing validity can arise. It would probably never occur to anyone . . . who was not a mere visitor," 179. In the gallery of ancestral portraits, Hegel imagines his protagonist as a museum and as its visitor. He enjoys his contents (their substantial wealth), having the leisure to ponder their continuing validity. Whether they possess a vital relationship to him is precisely the question Hegel raises.

57. Herbert Marcuse, "A Note on Dialectic," *The Essential Frankfurt School Reader*, ed. Andrew Arato and Eike Gebhardt (New York: Continuum, 1988), 451.

58. "Der vollkommene Nihilist—das Auge des Nihilisten . . . das Untreue übt gegen seine Erinnerungen—es läßt die fallen, sich entblättern; es schützt sie nicht gegen leichenblasse Verfärbungen, wie sie die Schwäche über Fernes und Vergangenes gießt; und was er gegen sich nicht übt, das übt er auch gegen die ganze Vergangenheit des Menschen nicht,—er läßt sie fallen," in Friedrich Nietzsche, *Werke* (*Nachgelassene Fragmente*), ed. Giorgio Colli and Mazzino Montinari, vol. 8, part 2 (Berlin: Walter de Gruyter, 1970), 142.

59. "Das besondere Individuum ist der unvollständige Geist, eine konkrete Gestalt, in deren ganzem Dasein *eine* Bestimmtheit herrschend ist und worin die anderen nur in verwischten Zügen vorhanden sind" (The particular individual is incomplete mind, a concrete shape, in whose entire existence *one* determination predominates and wherein the others are present only as blurred features, 32).

60. This puts the protagonist amidst those who, in Savigny's treatise, are unable to possess: slaves, the insane, sons still subject to paternal control, and, most obviously, if only because they do not need to be named, women.

61. *Typography: Mimesis, Philosophy, Politics*, ed. Christopher Fynsk (Cambridge: Harvard University Press, 1989), 129. Philippe Lacoue-Labarthe's discussion here concerns the unsettling of the notion of an originary masculine subject through mimesis; it is possible to read the phenomenological subject's dialectical passage through history as an example of mimesis par excellence.

62. Žižek also calls the Hegelian subject hysterical: "the dialectic . . . follows the matrix of hystericization: the subject escapes into activity . . . from the void of absolute self-contradiction" (*Tarrying with the Negative*, 34–35).

63. Peter Brooks, *Reading for the Plot* (New York: Knopf, 1984). For an excellent comparative analysis of the narrative mode of the gothic and the "male plot of ambition," see April Alliston, *Virtue's Faults*, chapter 5.

Chapter 2. The Male Romantic Poet as Gothic Subject

1. Quotations from John Keats's *Hyperion* and *The Fall of Hyperion: A Dream* refer to *Complete Poems*, ed. Jack Stillinger (Cambridge: Harvard University Press, 1982).

2. For an analysis of the social and socializing intersection of language, power, and politics, see Pierre Bourdieu, *Language and Symbolic Power*, ed. John Thompson, trans. Gino Raymond and Matthew Adamson (Cambridge: Harvard University Press, 1991).

3. Marlon Ross, "Beyond the Fragmented Word: Keats at the Limits of Patrilineal Language," *Out of Bounds: Male Writers and Gender[ed] Criticism*, ed. Laura Claridge and Elizabeth Langland (Amherst: University of Massachusetts Press, 1990), 110–11. Both Marjorie Levinson and Ross note in their essays that this notion of poetic maturation is figuratively aligned with physical maturation; when Keats becomes a poet, he will have become a man; see *The Romantic Fragment Poem: A Critique of Form* (Chapel Hill: University of North Carolina Press, 1986).

4. Critics, from Walter Jackson Bate to Harold Bloom to Karen Swann, question Keats's response to inclusion within a community of male poets. What he seems to disclose above all is uncertainty, as he fluctuates between unadulterated enthusiasm and desire, uncanny dissociation, or refusal, as he ambivalently faces the risks and rewards of homosocial belonging: how to reconcile singularity or separateness with incorporation and sameness. See Walter Jackson Bate, *The Burden of the Past and the English Poet* (New York: Norton, 1972). Harold Bloom discusses Keats's questioning of Milton and Wordsworth (and thereby himself) in *The Anxiety of Influence* (New York: Oxford University Press, 1973), 126–28; Carl Plasa argues that Keats's relation to Milton in *Hyperion*, Books One and Two, amounts to a repossession or revision of the tradition (Keats fills Miltonic language with himself as Satan does the serpent). In Book Three, Keats evades or represses the Miltonic influence, and his failed quest for an autonomous subjectivity is charted as the movement from a dialogue with Milton to a radical discontinuity. See "Revision and Repression in Keats's *Hyperion*: 'Pure Creations of the Poet's Brain,'" *Keats-Shelley Journal* 44 (1995): 117–46. Karen Swann's essay, "Harassing the Muse," reads *La Belle Dame sans merci* as an allegory for Keats's ambivalent initiation into a community of male poets; *Romanticism and Feminism*, ed. Anne K. Mellor (Bloomington: Indiana University Press, 1988): 81–92.

5. Marjorie Levinson, *The Romantic Fragment Poem*; John Whale, "Sacred Objects and the Sublime Ruins of Art," *Beyond Romanticism*, ed. S. Copley and J. Whale (London: Routledge, 1982), 236; and Marlon B. Ross situates Keats's fragmented discourse within larger issues of cultural politics (the capacity to perform "the discursive rituals of his culture") and the individual's power over his own discourse ("Beyond the Fragmented Word: Keats at the Limits of Patrilineal Language," 110–31). In a more dialectical reading, Adrienne Donald contends that, within Romanticism, the surest sign of cultural centrality is to be situated on the margins; in "Coming Out of the Canon: Sadomasochism, Male Homoeroticism, Romanticism," *Yale Journal of Criticism* (1991): 239–52. Thomas McFarland also sees the fragment as a form intentionally chosen, but one which transcends "forms of fragmentation," i.e., the consciousness of fragmentation and the poetic expression of that consciousness; *Romanticism and the Forms of Ruin: Wordsworth, Coleridge, and Modalities of Fragmentation* (Princeton: Princeton University Press, 1981. Edward Bostetter, rejecting the notion of Keats's fragments as either intentional or as mastery, sees them as the recognition of his inability to control a poetry that suggests wholeness; *The Romantic Ventriloquists* (Seattle: University of Washington Press, 1975.

Within Romanticism, critical work on poetic election began with Walter Jackson Bate's biography *John Keats* (Cambridge: Harvard University Press, 1963) and *The Bur-*

den of the Past and the English Poet. Jackson Bate presents an image of Keats attempting to negotiate the inherited literary tradition and his place in it in the *Hyperion* fragments, which Harold Bloom's Oedipal model of literary history further elaborates as Keats's difficulty with writing epic after Milton in *The Anxiety of Influence*. The question of Keats's ability or failure (deliberate or not) to master the epic form—specifically in the *Hyperion* fragments—becomes the vexed question of his status as a poet.

6. The "first" English Gothic novel, Horace Walpole's *The Castle of Otranto*, also features a gigantic, if campy, intrusion of the epic past—the enormous helmet of the paternal ancestor—into the diminished space of the present.

7. Robert Gittings notes Keats's references to the landscapes of Radcliffe and William Beckford's gothic-oriental novel *Vathek* as they influence the settings of the *Hyperion* fragments; *John Keats* (London: Heinemann, 1968), 255–56.

8. Michelle Massé's *In the Name of Love: Women, Masochism and the Gothic* (Ithaca: Cornell University Press, 1992) studies the centrality of sadomasochism to gothic novels and the alignment of its positions with cultural and fictional expectations about heterosexual gender roles for women. According to Massé, the gothic sets up a fantasy of paternal omnipotence to which the "normal" woman responds passively, disavowing her desires in response to his.

9. Three of the best-known examples occur in Ann Radcliffe's *The Italian*, Matthew Lewis's *The Monk*, and Charles Maturin's *Melmoth the Wanderer*.

10. Chloe Chard, in her introduction to Ann Radcliffe, *The Romance of the Forest* (Oxford: Oxford University Press, 1986), xvii. Steven Bruhm argues that gothic representations of torture allowed the British reading public the fantasy of an impermeable English body; *Gothic Bodies: The Politics of Pain in Romantic Fiction* (Philadelphia: University of Pennsylvania Press, 1994).

11. Bruhm points to something similar when he argues that Romanticism foregrounds this contradictory relation in its recurring representations of being both within and outside the pained object and thereby processes the gothic violence it represents by adopting the transcendent consciousness of the spectator (*Gothic Bodies*, xvi, xx).

12. Geoffrey Hartman, *The Fate of Reading and Other Essays* (Chicago: University of Chicago Press, 1975).

13. Lee Edelman, *Homographesis: Essays in Gay Literary and Cultural Theory* (New York: Routledge, 1994), 99.

14. When Keats represents the hierarchical relations between men that govern poetic election in the *Hyperions*, he does not maintain a hard and fast demarcation between the homosocial and the homoerotic. This is not simply because male passivity is sometimes eroticized, but, more broadly, because of the gothic subtext Keats incorporates into the epic narrative, through which gender and sexual transgression, by men, exist as a norm rather than as an exception (see the Introduction). See also Susan Wolfson's fine essay in which she examines the extent to which Keats's effeminacy became a way for male and female writers and readers to define changing norms of masculinity and a masculine style over the course of the last two centuries; "Feminizing Keats," in *Critical Essays on John Keats*, ed. Hermione de Almeida (Boston: G. K. Hall and Co., 1990), 317–56 and "Keats and the Manhood of the Poet," *ERR* 6.1 (1995), 1–37.

I use the term effeminacy here in Keats to signal: 1) an indulgence of sensation, concern for elegance and refinement, and a desire to live a "luxurious, endless dream" as William Hazlitt defines it in "On Effeminacy of Character," in *Table-Talk* (London: Oxford University Press, 1901), 333; 2) the absence of an autonomous and agential self in men, as discussed by Anne K. Mellor in *Romanticism and Gender* (New York: Routledge, 1993); and 3) as the adoption of a passive sexual role, since "active and passive sexual roles are equated in the eighteenth century with masculine and feminine roles"; Theo van der Meer, "Sodomy and the Pursuit of a Third Sex in the Early Modern Period," *Third Sex Third Gender: Beyond Sexual Dimorphism in Culture and History*, ed. Gilbert Herdt (New York: Zone Books, 1994), 162.

15. Keats's sources for Hesiod's epic, according to Robert Gittings, are the accounts in Lemprière's *Dictionary* and Tooke's *Pantheon*.

16. Oceanus's historicized rationalization and Clymene's aestheticization of power is not necessarily identical to Keats's perspective; what they respond to and find compelling, as Keats does, I would argue, is power in its sublimated, symbolic guises.

17. In relation to the *Hyperion* fragments, Hazlitt's essay on Shakespeare's *Coriolanus* and his comments on the Elgin Marbles are telling. Writing on *Coriolanus*, Hazlitt draws an analogy between the rhetoric of power and the rhetoric of poetry; *Miscellaneous Works of William Hazlitt*, vol. 3 (New York: Derby and Jackson, 1859), 48–49:

> The insolence of power is stronger than the plea of necessity. The tame submission to usurped authority, or even the natural resistance to it, has nothing to excite or flatter the imagination; it is the assumption of a right to insult or oppress others, that carries an imposing air of superiority with it. We had rather be the oppressor than the oppressed. . . . The language of poetry naturally falls in with the language of power. . . . The principle of poetry is a very anti-levelling principle. It aims at effect, it exists by contrast. . . . It is everything by excess. . . . It puts might before right.

If Keats is in agreement with Hazlitt, as his quoting of Hazlitt's defense of this essay in the letter to his brother George of 13 March 1819 suggests, then it provides additional support for reading *Hyperion* anti-sympathetically (i.e., Keats is not siding with the Titans's "tamed submission" but is fascinated with the Olympians' "imposing air of superiority"). On the Elgin Marbles, Hazlitt says "they have no sympathy with us," to which Davud Bromwich, writing of Hazlitt's influence on Keats, adds that they are "instances of power rather than sympathy . . . a kind of Coriolanus among art objects" (Bromwich, "'Keats," *Critical Essays on John Keats*, 248–49).

18. Eve K. Sedgwick writes: "Of all the Gothic conventions dealing with the sudden, mysterious, seemingly arbitrary, but massive inaccessibility of those things that should normally be most accessible, the difficulty the story has in getting itself told is of the most obvious structural significance. This difficulty occurs at every level of the novels"; *The Coherence of Gothic Conventions*, second revised edition (New York: Methuen, 1986), 13–14.

19. I want to thank Claudia Brodsky Lacour for calling my attention to the idea of gratuitous language in *Hyperion*, as well as to its presence in the opening of Keats's *Ode To Psyche* when Keats implores the goddess Psyche to "pardon that thy secrets should be sung / Even into thine own soft-conched ear" (3–4). Like Thea to Saturn, Keats puts himself into the role of the apologetic speaker whose violation is the telling to his listener, Psyche, what she already knows. Like the *Hyperion*s, too, this speech of self-effacement or inaction in *Psyche* is set within a larger context of the questioning of authorial agency.

20. In her reading of the gothic, April Alliston discusses the protagonist's crisis as the dilemma of how to alter inherited familial history; introduction, *Virtue's Faults* (Stanford: Stanford University Press, 1996).

21. This expression comes from Elaine Scarry, *The Body in Pain: The Making and Unmaking of the World* (New York: Oxford University Press, 1985).

22. David Hume in his *Treatise of Human Nature* calls attention to the revulsion occasioned by seeing great distress, specifically mentioning the torture of the rack; because it destroys sympathy in the one afflicted and in the onlooker, the sight of excessive pain is an anti-socializing experience, he concludes; David Hume, Treatise of *Human Nature*, ed. L. A. Selby-Bigge (Oxford: Clarendon Press, 1973), 388. Page duBois in *Torture and Truth* asserts that lyricizing the tortured body is an act of dispossession since it then inevitably becomes the inscribed body of the master (New York: Routledge, 1991), 141. See also Scarry, 53.

23. Edward Peters, *Torture* (Oxford: Oxford University Press, 1985), 164.

24. Theo van der Meer points out that active and passive sexual roles are equated in the eighteenth century with masculine and feminine roles. Both the so-called sodomites and prosecutors of sodomy referred to the assumption of a passive sexual role as "being used as a woman." Van der Meer points out that since effeminacy became the hallmark or sign of the sodomite, men became increasingly concerned to avoid effeminacy for fear of being suspected of engaging in "unnatural acts" (*Third Sex Third Gender: Beyond Sexual Dimorphism in Culture and History*, 162 and 149).

25. Keats's aesthetic handling of this moment may well reflect increasing pressures to render invisible the attributes of the third gender, or sodomite. The historian Randolph Trumbach points out that, during this time, men are negatively defined as masculine, i.e., by their avoidance of sex with other men. See Randolph Trumbach, "London's Sapphists: From Three Sexes to Four Genders in the Making of Modern Culture," *Body Guards: The Cultural Politics of Gender Ambiguity* (New York: Routledge, 1991), 112–41 and "The Birth of the Queen: Sodomy and the Emergence of Gender Equality in Modern Culture, 1660–1750," *Hidden from History: Reclaiming the Gay and Lesbian Past*, ed. Martin Duberman, Martha Vicinus and George Chauncey, Jr. (New York: New American Library, 1989), 129–40.

26. Jeff Nunokawa's essay "Homosexual Desire and the Effacement of the Self in *The Picture of Dorian Gray*" calls attention to a similar sublimating strategy in Wilde's representation of homoerotic desire. In *American Imago* 49.3 (1992): 33–34.

27. Even Keats's friend Leigh Hunt, who stood accused of lacking a proper virility (both by nasty reviewers and by Byron), condemned the deification scene: according to Hunt, there is "something too effeminate and human in the way Apollo receives the exaltation which his wisdom is giving him. He weeps and wonders somewhat too fondly"; in the *Indicator* 2 (9 August 1820), 352.

28. Gittings indicates Keats's familiarity with Tooke (see note 21). See also Andrew Tooke's *The Pantheon* for Apollo's androgynous appearance and the accounts of his erotic affairs with the young men Hyacinth and Cypress (London: Bathurst, 1784), 29–33).

29. Edelman, *Homographesis*, 128. Although Edelman doesn't draw the connection between gothic dispossession and sodomy, he interestingly describes the terrors of sodomy through a gothic metaphor, namely, as the fear of speaking with a foreign tongue (127). Limiting her focus to Keats's gender transgression without calling attention to its impact on the representation of erotic desire, Anne K. Mellor notes that "in the medical discourse of the Romantic era . . . the absence of an autonomous or agential self in men became a symptom of gender-crossing and of disease" (in *Romanticism and Gender*). Michele Cohen points to increasing cultural anxieties during the eighteenth century

centering around British men speaking in a foreign tongue; *Fashioning Masculinity* (New York: Routledge, 1996), 98–110.

30. Hazlitt's critique of Keats addresses his poetic shortcomings as the shortcomings of an effeminate character. He contrasts Keats's representations of the avoidance of pain in favor of an indulgence in pleasure: "instead of voluntarily embracing pain, or labour, or danger, or death, every sensation must be would up to the highest pitch of voluptuous refinement, every motion must be grace and elegance; they live in a luxurious, endless dream" ("On Effeminacy of Character," 333). In the *Hyperion*s, interestingly, Keats outdoes Hazlitt by imbuing pain, labour, danger, and even death with "voluptuous" pleasure.

31. Gittings outlines in detail Keats's debt to William Beckford's gothic-oriental tale *Vathek* for the dwelling of Hyperion, the temple in *The Fall of Hyperion*, and the link between the Titans's subterranean recesses and Beckford's halls of the underworld Eblis, where "preadamite" kings suffer eternal torments (*The Mask of Keats*, 101–4). Of greater significance are the thematic resemblances that Gittings does not mention. Common to both is the obsession with secret knowledge—Vathek's "insolent curiosity of penetrating the secrets of heaven" and the narrator of *The Fall of Hyperion* aching "to see what things the hollow brain behind enwombed." The ambition for forbidden knowledge is inseparable in Beckford's novel from sensuality and perverse pleasures, whose mutual fulfillments lead to punishment, a narrative trajectory Keats also traces as he moves from *Hyperion* to *The Fall of Hyperion*.

32. Homans discusses Keats's compensatory wish to assert his own masculine authority when he is faced with women's real and imagined power over him; in the context of this essay, this response seems to emerge, not in response to women, but to his own perceived effeminacy. John Lockhart's scathing review in *Blackwood's Magazine* ridicules Keats for his effeminate lisping; we might say that in *The Fall of Hyperion* Keats is chastising Apollo's tongue by getting rid of the bower scenario's "lisp." See Homans, 368. Both Susan Wolfson and Nicholas Roe direct attention to the ways that criticism of Keats's poetry during his lifetime frequently coupled the accusation of an effeminate style (his "lisping" poetry) with his "inferior" class, a double-pronged attack evident in the prosecutions of sodomy throughout the eighteenth and early nineteenth centuries as well. Wolfson, "Feminizing Keats," 320 and Nicholas Roe, "Keats's Lisping Sedition," *Essays in Criticism* 42, no. 1 (January 1992): 36–55 and also Mellor, "Ideological Cross-Dressing in Keats," 172.

33. Adrienne Donald defines Romanticism's notion of poetic vocation as the broader alignment of intellectual power and physical (homoeroticized) suffering in her essay, "Coming Out of the Canon," 245.

34. See Massé for the masochist's role in establishing the hierarchy of authority in the gothic, 43.

35. Pierre Bourdieu, *Language and Symbolic Power*, 123, my italics.

36. In the eighteenth century, Horace Walpole and William Beckford serve as examples where a reputed aristocratic homosexual identity is associated with the exaggerated impulse to collect art and antiquities. This also lies behind *Blackwood's* Z's implications of effeminacy in Hunt's "vulgar" form of this activity (thanks to Susan Wolfson for calling this to my attention). The proximity of the gothic impinges once again, not only because of Walpole's and Beckford's own novels, but because it is the genre most closely associated at that time with impediments to inheritance and the transmission of symbolic value.

37. This concept can be found in Karl Marx's *The German Ideology*, in *Literary Theory: An Anthology*, ed. Julie Rivkin and Michael Ryan (Malden, Mass.: Blackwell, 1998), 254.

38. Jonathan Dollimore writes about this constitutive paradox of male Eurowestern homosexual identity: regarded as asocial or antisocial—the "unsocialized libido at the expense of the social order"—and at the same time representative of the highest civility—as Freud observes, "practicing homosexuals may be especially civilized"; *Sexual Dissidence: Augustine to Wilde, Freud to Foucault* (Oxford: Clarendon Press, 1991), 172 and 193.

39. Bourdieu, *Language and Symbolic Power*, 217.

40. See Anne K. Mellor, "Ideological Cross-Dressing in Keats," 185; Marlon Ross, "Beyond the Fragmented Word," 128–30; and Barbara Shapiro, *The Romantic Mother: Narcissistic Patterns in Romantic Poetry* (Baltimore: Johns Hopkins University Press, 1983), esp. 55–60.

41. Such a positioning corresponds to masochism as theorized by Gilles Deleuze in *Masochism: An Interpretation of Coldness and Cruelty*, trans. Aude Willm (New York: Braziller, 1971). Anne K. Mellor argues that Keats rejects the "all-male" preserve of poetry by casting Moneta as a feminine/mother figure. Moneta, according to Mellor, represents female reproductive biology as sacred and prior to male poetic creation; she is also the figure who articulates the "cultural meaning [of the reproductive process], the meaning of life itself" ("Ideological Cross-Dressing," 185). What Mellor overlooks is that the site of Moneta's vaunted "reproductive" capacity is her brain, which contains the Olympian hegemony: she reproduces the dominance of the father's symbolic legacy.

42. Anne K. Mellor points to the identification of Mnemosyne with Minerva or Athena in eighteenth-century antiquarian history in "Keats's Face of Moneta: Source and Meaning," *Keats-Shelley Journal* 25 (1976): 66.

43. Revealing the intimate connection between pain and mastery as he mounts the stairs or bears the burden of Moneta's vision, the poet-narrator uncovers the "learned misrecognition of injury as nurture . . . toward a position of sadism and cultural 'authority'"; Eve K. Sedgwick, "A Poem is Being Written," *Representations* 17 (Winter 1987): 125.

44. Interpreting Freud's notion of the uncanny, Neil Hertz observes that whatever formally reminds us of this compulsion to repeat is perceived as uncanny; "Freud and the Sandman," *Textual Strategies*, ed. Josue Harari (Ithaca: Cornell University Press, 1979), 301.

CHAPTER 3. SHARING GOTHIC SECRETS

1. Andrew Elfenbein, "Stricken Deer: Secrecy, Homophobia, and the Rise of Suburban Man," *Genders* 27 (1998): paras. 27–28. Online at: <http://www.genders.org/g27_stdr.html>.

2. The role of the narrator is key in shifting the emphasis from the exploration of character to an exploration of point of view and is primarily accomplished through a rhetoric of insinuation. Jean Hall's essay "The Evolution of the Surface Self: Byron's Poetic Career," is an example of the criticism that focuses on Byron's constitution of an interior and an exterior self, one an "affair of depth . . . [and] of integrity," and the other, a "surface self," a mode of activity in the world, a fragmented self; *Keats-Shelley*

Journal 36 (1987): 134–57. See also Daniel Watkins's dialectical reading of a public/private dichotomy of self in *Social Relations in Byron's Eastern Tales* (Rutherford, N.J.: Fairleigh Dickinson University Press, 1987), and Peter L. Thorslev's tracing of the literary antecedents of the Byronic hero in *The Byronic Hero: Types and Prototypes* (Minneapolis: University of Minnesota Press, 1962).

3. David Seed, "'Disjointed Fragments': Concealment and Revelation in *The Giaour*," *The Byron Journal* 18 (1991): 14. Seed argues that Byron is exploring the productive possibilities of multiperspectivism. Peter Manning's essay "*Childe Harold* in the Marketplace," *MLQ* 52.2 (June 1991): 170–90, offers a fine discussion of this strategy in relation to the reviews of *Childe Harold* which noted Byron's illusion of confiding in his readers.

4. Seed, "Disjointed Fragments," 25.

5. Eve Kosofsky Sedgwick, *Epistemology of the Closet* (Berkeley: University of California Press, 1990), 73. Gender-crossing and sexually transgressive behavior are clearly not equivalent, although certain forms of gender-crossing and cross-dressing began to be suggestive of an emerging homosexuality in England during the eighteenth century (see Introduction). Cross-dressing as such did not constitute a crime, if expressed during sanctioned or ritualized occasions for such carnivalesque inversions. Further, male cross-dressing in Byron's time proved to be more threatening than female cross-dressing; in men, gender effeminacy was increasingly aligned with the sexually receptive position, e.g., with the so-called sodomite. See Vern Bullough and Bonnie Bullough, *Cross Dressing, Sex, and Gender* (Philadelphia: University of Pennsylvania Press, 1993).

6. Dyer looks at Byron's employment of the slang of boxing and thievery as a coded language for sodomy in "Thieves, Boxers, Sodomites, Poets: Being Flash to Byron's *Don Juan*," *PMLA* 116.3 (2001): 563.

7. Cheryl Giuliano emphasizes that Byron identifies with the page figures, but only as the expression of the difficult consequences with gender inversion, not with its possibilities. Although she alludes to the dynamic of inversion in relation to Byron's bisexuality, her focus on gender remains framed by a heterosexual presumption; "Gulnare/Kaled's 'Untold' Feminization of Byron's Oriental Tales," *SEL* 33 (1993): 785–807.

8. Jerome McGann, "Byron and 'the Truth in Masquerade,'" *Romantic Revisions*, ed. Robert Bunkley and Keith Hanley (Cambridge: Cambridge University Press, 1992), 207.

9. Christensen reads the cryptic rhetoric used in the letters as the production of a gay literary identity, not as a response to persecution; *Lord Byron's Strength: Romantic Writing and Commercial Society* (Baltimore: Johns Hopkins University Press, 1993), 60–61. Within the *Tales*, I would argue, this implicative mode is represented as a response to real, possible, or even imagined persecution or suffering. Dyer too notes that speaking in secrets is as often an emblem of constraint than the sign of liberation (563). Crompton discusses the use of a code as well in Byron's *Oriental Tales*; see *Byron and Greek Love: Homophobia in Nineteenth-Century England* (Berkeley: University of California Press, 1985), 127–29 and 160–63.

10. I am not disputing Byron's sexual attraction to men *and* women, his lived bisexuality; when I refer to his homoerotic desires, I am focusing on the then socially unacceptable "component" of that bisexuality.

11. For the stanza on Beckford, see *The Complete Poetical Works*, ed. McGann, vol. II, note to ll. 270–78. All citations of Byron's poetry refer to this edition; line numbers will be cited parenthetically within the text.

12. Letter to John Hanson, *Byron's Letters and Journals*, ed. Leslie A. Marchand (London: John Murray, 1973), 1:232; see also Marchand's note to 1:232 and Crompton, *Byron and Greek Love*, 124. For Byron's mention of the apostrophe of *The Cornelian*, see *BLJ* 1:110.

13. In Malcolm Elwin, *Lord Byron's Wife* (London: MacDonald, 1962), 231, 413. This mention of mysteries could also refer to his affair with Augusta.

14. Eve K. Sedgwick, "The Character in the Veil: Imagery of the Surface in the Gothic Novel," *PMLA* 96.2 (March 1981): 256, 260–91.

15. For the cultural obsession with seeing and writing the difference of the homosexual, see Lee Edelman's *Homographesis: Essays in Gay Literary and Cultural Theory* (New York: Routledge, 1994).

16. *Byron: The Critical Heritage*, ed. A. Rutherford (New York: Barnes & Noble, 1970), 66–67.

17. Sedgwick, "The Character in the Veil," 256, 260–61.

18. James Creech, *Closet Writing/Gay Reading: The Case of Melville's Pierre* (Chicago: University of Chicago Press, 1993), 59. Creech extends the question to how certain texts could have been "discovered" as gay by some, while remaining unacknowledged as such by scores of readers: "At a time when homophobia was as unquestioned a touchstone of American culture as virtually any other defining feature, it is a literary-historical problem of significant proportions to discern precisely how *Billy Budd* or *Moby Dick*, like *Leaves of Grass*, could ever have become staples of high school and college English courses. In a word, how could Melville's writings achieve their unquestioned status at the core of the American literary canon at all when they are marked by homoerotic content that was—at least to some—recognizable to the point of being distinctive?" (78–79).

19. Jerome McGann, "Byron, Mobility and the Poetics of Historical Ventriloquism," in *Romanticism, Past and Present* 9 (1985): 69.

20. The closet itself is as central a subject to the *Oriental Tales* as the expressions of same-sex desire and gender-crossing to which they allude.

21. Leslie Marchand, Jerome McGann, and Louis Crompton all emphasize that Byron began writing *The Giaour* primarily for personal reasons and was overwhelmed at the response the first tale elicited; see Marchand, *Byron: A Biography*, 3 vols. (New York: Knopf, 1957) 1:408–9; Jerome McGann, *Fiery Dust* (Chicago: University of Chicago Press, 1968), 148; Louis Crompton, *Byron and Greek Love*, 205–6. Publishing these tales (and *Childe Harold* before them), the literary marketplace served Byron well: his personal concerns turned an unexpected profit. Jerome Christensen explores how the literary market itself reflected Byron's "perversion" (as used in contemporary psychoanalytic discourse, to refer to the mobility of desire and to obsessive fixations) and made his identity into a commodity, against which Byron's attempts at oppositional writing failed (*Lord Byron's Strength*, chapter 3). Christensen stresses the inappropriateness of a vocabulary of authorial strength for what, in the *Oriental Tales*, he sees as the mechanical forces of literary production.

22. For a reading of *The Old Manor House* as a parody and critique of the gothic, see Joseph Bartolomeo, "The Subversion of Romance in *The Old Manor House*," *SEL* 33.3 (Summer 1993): 645–57.

23. Dorothy Langley Moore, *Lord Byron: Accounts Rendered* (New York: Harper, 1974), 444.

24. Byron's *Oriental Tales* represent sexual behaviors that are equally "deviant," or

anti-paternal (e.g., heterosexual incest in *The Bride of Abydos* and *Parisina*), but without a rhetorical emphasis on "the secret" or the socius's supernaturalization of that gendered and sexual transgression as one affiliated with male effeminacy or male homoeroticism. For that reason, I have not introduced them in the discussion here, although in the world of Byron's "secrets," incest certainly plays a significant role.

25. *Complete Poetical Works*, III, 52.

26. Jerome McGann points to a source for the *The Giaour* in Samuel Rogers's *Voyage of Columbus*, where a similarly fictive historical collection of fragments is intended, according to Rogers's own preface, to "[leave] much to be imagined by the reader." McGann also notes the simultaneity of the drama and the creation of the drama through the narrator's adoption of the voices of various persona (*Fiery Dust*, 143–47).

27. Watkins, *Social Relations*, 37–39. McGann, like Watkins, because he does not identify a social reality that would generate such obscurantist discourses, sees Byron, through the figure of the Giaour, naturalizing and mythologizing incompletion and unfulfillment as part of his subjective condition—and that of the sociopolitical world he inhabits (*Fiery Dust*, 161–64).

28. McGann convincingly presents this tale as one told by a single narrator (instead of multiple narrators), who adopts different voices, including the Turkish fisherman, the monk, and the Giaour (*Fiery Dust*, 143–47).

29. Eric Meyer reads *The Giaour* as a thinly veiled political allegory of Romantic Orientalism, wherein political and ideological issues defined as constituting the difference between East and West are figured through the struggles of the Giaour (the embodiment of the West) and Hassan (the Western fantasy of the Eastern despot) over Leila. While the Giaour may represent the impulses of western Europe to "liberate" the orient from patriarchal tyranny (a kind of Napoleon according to Meyer), I would argue that the Giaour is dominated as much as he dominates and ultimately assimilates Hassan's difference. Even within the limits of her role, Leila is not reducible to the Giaour's "conquest" nor is she simply a "passive" object or victim as both Meyer and Watkins argue; "'I Know Thee Not, I Loathe Thy Race': Romantic Orientalism in the Eye of the Other," *ELH* 58 (1991): 657–99. For other treatments of *The Giaour*'s orientalism, see Marilyn Butler's "The Orientalism of Byron's *The Giaour*," in *Byron and the Limits of Fiction*, ed. Beatty and Newey (Liverpool: Liverpool University Press, 1988), 78–96 and Caroline Franklin's *Byron's Heroines* (Oxford: Clarendon Press, 1992), 39–47. I agree with Caroline Franklin that Leila's sexual autonomy is an aspect of Byron's conception of a liberal subject, but that such autonomy is relegated to the briefest of interludes in his verse narratives (35).

30. By "wink," I refer to Creech's use of the term (*Closet Writing/Gay Reading*, 96). Crompton points to Beckford's use of the cross-dressed woman as a vehicle to represent homosexuality in his "Story of Prince Alesi" (*Byron and Greek Love*, 210).

31. As we shall see in *Lara*, Lara's identity is clearly mirrored in his page, Kaled. Christensen reads the Byronic hero's serial infidelity and narcissism as interiorized reflections of economic production. Narcissism and infidelity read very differently if a virulently homophobic society is the generative context in which these traits are said to characterize same-sex desire. While the shifting of objects of desire from one tale to the next may represent serial infidelity, a reflection of a narcissistic market economy, for example, it also reflects a society where the expression of same-sex desire was confined to the most sporadic of encounters. One could argue that it is the page figure in the *Oriental Tales* who expresses a longing for fidelity between men: a demand unthinkable

in Georgian England where expressions of same-sex desire were confined, as far as has been ascertained, to brief and limited encounters.

32. The term "equivocal being" as a signifier for male effeminacy comes from Mary Wollstonecraft's *Vindication of the Rights of Woman*. The opening setting of the tale, Greece, is often a symbolic displacement for an unnameable homoeroticism in Byron's works. Greece, where one could be a man and love another boy/man, cannot be narrated, having "no legend" or "theme" (143–44); like Leila, its existence is comparable to, if not worse than a slave's (150–51); like her, its beauty is phantasmagorical, "the loveliness in death / That parts not quite with parting breath" (94–95). Byron thus sets political oppression on the same continuum with sexual and gender oppression, as critics have noted (Christensen, Eric Meyer). For Byron, Greece functions analogously to the fleeting entrance of Leila cross-dressed: as the desire to maintain some liberating expression in an otherwise oppressive reality. Speaking of the confusion of political and sexual liberation in Byron's life, Christensen notes that political repression becomes the ground whereby Byron could imagine his own sexual liberation: the degraded masculinity of the effeminate boy, the consequence of political oppression, allows the lifting of Byron's sexual repression. Political oppression and sexual liberation are dialectically related; the self-loathing Byron privately expresses in relation to his boy lovers, however, is absent in his idealized representations of the page figures in the *Oriental Tales*.

33. In the newspapers, journals, and pamphlets of Byron's time, homosexual acts — not heterosexual infidelity — are alluded to as "nameless crimes" and as "unspeakable." See Crompton, *Byron and Greek Love*, chapter 1; Theo van der Meer, "Sodomy and the Pursuit of a Third Sex in the Early Modern Period," in *Third Sex/Third Gender*, ed. Gilbert Herdt (New York: Zone Books, 1994): 137–212; that Byron should have chosen a cross-dressed woman for an exploration of these issues can be attributed to the relative "safety" afforded by such a representation, since women cross-dressers were not subject to the same vilification and stigmatization as men.

34. Seed, "Disjointed Fragments," 19 (my italics).

35. As McGann writes: "The Giaour, who is the prime object of interest to all the people in the story, is dramatized largely through the responses he elicits from those who watch him . . . and realized in the emotional reactions which he provokes" (*Fiery Dust*, 150). The transference of the secret from Leila to the Giaour would make sense within a homoerotic relationship, in which both participants would be implicated.

36. Susan Wolfson explores how clear markers of differentiation between the masculine and feminine break down in *Don Juan* (in the harem, the humor is provoked by Juan's heterosexual prowess being greatest at the moment when he appears as a woman, i.e., as Juana). Wolfson calls attention to cross-dressing in the epic as Byron's strategy to make visible the cultural basis of normative masculine and feminine gender identities and the psychological constraints such categories impose; see " 'Their She Condition': Cross-Dressing and the Politics of Gender in *Don Juan*," *ELH* 54 (Fall 1987): 585–617. As Marchand outlines, during his travels Byron was repeatedly exposed to a culture where male effeminacy was accepted (*Byron*, I, chapters 7 and 8). Adam Potkay notes that "paradise contains beautiful boys in the Koran, and pederasty figures more generally in both the Islamic literature and the oriental tales available to Beckford and Byron"—and a British culture; see "Beckford's Heaven of Boys," *Raritan* 13.1 (Summer 1993): 77. In a deleted stanza to *Childe Harold*, II, Byron speaks of "boyish minions of unhallowed love," preferred above women, whose "forms for Nature's gentler errors fit / All frailties mote excuse save that which they commit" (quoted in

Crompton, *Byron and Greek Love*, 139). Note Byron's ambivalence, expressed as the attractive nature of the "gentler errors" of boyish effeminacy in contrast to the "unhallowed" act of sodomy.

37. Alan Richardson suggests that cross-dressing in *Don Juan* functions as a series of negations, the evasion of ordinary gender norms: "not simply a temporary exchange of sexual roles, but the vehicle of a more profound questioning of the grounds of sexual difference"; see "Escape from the Seraglio: Cultural Transvestism in *Don Juan*," in *Re-reading Byron*, ed. Alice Levine and Robert N. Keane (New York: Garland, 1993), 183 and 170. Christensen emphasizes that this holds a specifically aesthetic value in Byron. Speaking of Romantic scenes of fascination, he calls attention to the "more than" equivocal figures (in Byron, more than boy or woman) that ultimately point to the fascination with the mobile nature of signification (51).

38. "Lord Byron's Embarrassment: Poesy and the Feminine," *Bulletin of Research in the Humanities* 86.3 (1983–85): 281. Byron's own body was made over to a femininized one numerous times during his travels: see especially the visit to the Ali Pacha, the "strange Englishman," and the Ali Pacha's son, the Veli Pasha (Marchand, *Byron*, I, 208–11, 242, 248–49). Cecil Lang's essay assesses the crucial sexual and authorial significance of this episode by way of Byron's literary reformations of it during his lifetime: "Narcissus Jilted: Byron, *Don Juan*, and the Biographical Imperative," in *Historical Studies and Literary Criticism*, ed. Jerome McGann (Madison: University of Wisconsin Press, 1985), 143–79. For his experiences of seraglios of boys, see Marchand, *Byron*, I, 202, 206 and Lang.

39. See *BLJ*, 1:227–28. The "ambrosial curls hanging down his amiable back" are cited from Byron, *S-P*, I, 75–76). In a letter to Matthews, Byron writes that he is "surrounded by Hyacinths & other flowers most fragrant [na]ture, & I have some intention of culling a handsome Bouquet" (the homoerotic significance is discussed in Crompton, *Byron and Greek Love*, 127–29). Some forty-six years after the event, Hobhouse recalls the boys who served Byron and himself during their visit to the Pacha, having "their hair flowing half way down their backs"; see Lord Broughton [John Cam Hobhouse], *Travels in Albania and Other Provinces of Turkey in 1809 and 1810*, New Edition, 2 vols. (London: John Murray, 1855), 1:97. Leila's eyes' "dark charm" recall his statement about the young Mahmout Pacha's "large black eyes, which our ladies would purchase at any price" (*LJ*, 1:280). Jonathan Gross shows how in *Don Juan* double entendres or comic puns not only provide the poem with a homoerotic thematics but fashion a gay narrator; "'One Half What I Should Say': Byron's Gay Narrator in *Don Juan*," in *Mapping Male Sexuality: Nineteenth-Century England*, ed. Jay Losey and William D. Brewer (Madison, N.J.: Fairleigh Dickinson University Press, 2000), 91–122.

40. In the "Thyrza" lyrics, as Crompton points out, Byron cross-dresses a lyrical vocabulary, writing of Edleston's "form so soft, and charms so rare," as a "flower in ripen'd bloom unmatch'd" ("Stanzas," ll. 3 and 37, in *Complete Works*, vol. III).

41. Proust will do this in *A la recherche du temps perdu* where Albertine can be read as Albert; see Mark Guenette, "Le Loup et le narrateur: The Masking and Unmasking of Homosexuality in Proust's *A la recherche du temps perdu*," *Romantic Review* 80.2 (March 1989): 229–46. Guenette argues with considerable subtlety that Albertine is a displacement for Robert de Saint-Loup. This practice, where an author changes a character's gender to conceal homosexual sensibilities is commonly called "the Albertine strategy." Writing about Melville's *Pierre*, both John D. Seelye and James Creech show how Melville collapses the character of Isabel with the figure of Hawthorne; see Seelye, "'Un-

graspable Phantom': Reflections of Hawthorne in *Pierre* and *The Confidence-Man*," *Studies in the Novel* 1.4 (Winter 1969): 439 and Creech, 88.

42. The vampire undermines the nuclear family by killing off its members one by one. In the nineteenth and twentieth centuries, vampires become the abject creatures that society destroys in order to preserve the home and the institution of marriage with its transmission of patrilineal names and properties.

43. Similarly, when the monk later imagines that the Giaour is haunted by the ghostly severed hand of Hassan, it is a projection of the monk's fears rather than the Giaour's, since the Giaour does not share/see the delusion himself. Like the fantastic figure of the vampire in *The Giaour*, other genders in Georgian England occupied the social position of the "outsider inside" whose stigmatization was bound up with public fascination and revulsion; they frequently elected self-exile over the risk of a "social death" for their family and friends. Beckford, as well as other rumored homosexuals including Byron's friend Richard Heber and Thomas Beddoes, were either forced into exile or chose it as the only alternative. It is perhaps not surprising that, immediately preceding the lines in *The Giaour* on the unspeakable torment of vampirism, Eblis is mentioned, the Muslim underworld made famous in Beckford's *Vathek*: "But thou, false Infidel! shalt writhe / Beneath avenging Monkir's scythe; / And from its torment 'scape alone / To wander round lost Eblis' throne; / And fire unquench'd, unquenchable— / Around—within—thy heart shall dwell, / Nor ear can hear, nor tongue can tell / The tortures of that inward hell" (747–54). Byron lived the last eight years of his life in exile, due to numerous rumors, the most serious of which concerned his homosexuality. See Crompton, *Byron and Greek Love*, 37, 43, 45.

Sexual "deviance" and vampirism become aligned in the early nineteenth century in an association that has lasted up to the present. Byron may have been the first to link vampirism with the social marginalization/exile exercised upon homosexuals, a linkage explored in numerous works of the nineteenth century, including *Christabel*, *Carmilla*, and *Dracula*. For critical essays on this linkage, see Sue-Ellen Case, "Tracking the Vampire," *differences* 3.2 (1991): 1–20; Christopher Craft, "'Kiss me with those red lips': Gender and Inversion in Bram Stoker's *Dracula*," *Representations* 8 (1984): 107–33; Bram Dijkstra, *Idols of Perversity: Fantasies of Feminine Evil in Fin-de-siècle Culture* (Oxford: Oxford University Press, 1986); and Ellis Hanson, "Undead," in *inside/out*, ed. Diana Fuss (New York: Routledge, 1991), 324–40. In a work such as *Dracula*, the vampiric threat is exciting by virtue of its appearance inside Britain, as a libidinous force that drains its national-sexual-racial-imperial health. Marjorie Garber, though not the first, points out that J. W. Polidori, Byron's doctor, is accredited with the first vampire novel, *Vampyre*, with a protagonist supposedly based upon Byron; *Vice Versa* (New York: Simon and Schuster, 1995), 97–104. Byron anticipates Polidori by having the Giaour be represented within the tale as a quasi-vampiric figure.

44. *Complete Works*, III, 419, my italics.

45. While he does not mention Byron, Richard Dellamora's work on the Gorgon in Percy Bysshe Shelley, Dante Gabriel Rossetti, and particularly, in Walter Pater, emphasizes the Gorgon's positive transformative effect; in Pater, Dellamora argues, through its hermaphroditic (or "deviant") nature, the Gorgon initiates the (assumed male) viewer into a "liminal state that is both 'masculine' and 'feminine.'" See *Masculine Desire: The Sexual Politics of Victorian Aesthetics* (Chapel Hill: University of North Carolina Press, 1990), 136–39.

46. *The Monk* (Oxford: Oxford University Press, 1980), 433.

47. The bird charmed by a snake will reappear in one of Byron's last poems, "Last Words," as a figure for this lyric speaker's consuming desire for a young man: "I am the fool of passion—and a frown / Of thine to me is as an Adder's eye / To the poor bird whose pinion fluttering down / Waft unto death the breast it bore so high— / Such is the maddening fascination grown, / So strong thy Magic—or so weak am I" (5–10).

48. Otto Fenichal, "The Scoptophilic Instinct and Identification," in *Collected Papers*, vol. 1 (New York: Norton, 1953), 389–92.

49. In "Stanzas," Edleston's memory is what proves to be most real and most unreal: "The all of time that cannot die / Through dark and dread Eternity / Returns again to me, / And more thy buried love endears / Than aught, except its living years" (68–72). Without effacing the ambiguity with which Byron imbues this moment, the fate of the Giaour-Leila pair echoes that of the stigmatization of same-sex desire: a love simultaneously desired and criminalized, its invisibility the result of patriarchal, public vilification.

50. I wonder whether Leila, the Muslim orphan whom Juan adopts, is Byron's way of rewriting Leila's fate, so that Leila survives (as Gulnare in *The Corsair* and Kaled in *Lara* do). Relating Juan's love for Leila, the narrator takes up a suggestive tone: "Don Juan loved her, and she loved him, as / Nor brother, father, sister, daughter love. / I cannot tell exactly what it was" (10.53).

51. This echoes D. A. Miller's assertion that although secrets seemingly afford the subject a private or indeterminate space from the culture that otherwise determines him, these secrets usually prove to be no more than a cultural prescription or cliché; see "Secret Subjects, Open Secrets," *Dickens Studies Annual* 14 (New York: AMS Press): 19.

52. For critical essays that discuss *The Giaour*'s fragmentation as a productive experiment in multiple perspectivism instead of a failure, see McGann's *Fiery Dust*, Robert Gleckner's *Byron and the Ruins of Paradise* (Baltimore: Johns Hopkins University Press, 1967) and David Seed's "'Disjointed Fragments': Concealment and Revelation in *The Giaour*."

53. Meyer, "Romantic Orientalism in the Eye of the Other," 672.

54. Byron makes such an alignment in one of the "Thyrza" lyrics. The shattered cornelian heart Edleston had given him as a gift becomes a metaphor for the unrealized possibility of their love: "Yet precious seems each shatter'd part / And every fragment dearer grown / Since he who wears thee, feels thou art / A fitter emblem of his own"; "On a Cornelian Heart which was Broken" (ll. 5–8), *Collected Works*, vol. III.

55. Gleckner points to *Lara*'s affinity with *The Giaour*; he suggests it functions as a kind of sequel to *The Giaour* insofar as it adopts and mediates various points of view (*Byron and the Ruins of Paradise*, 155–58). I would argue that this similarity is extended to both *The Giaour* and *Lara* with their emphasis on the social nature of the protagonists' secrets. Crompton discusses the pederastic overtones of the tale in connection with Byron's life (*Byron and Greek Love*, 206–10).

56. About *Lara*, Christensen writes that it exhibits a "terminal exhaustion." As "the purest sequel," it becomes "an allegory of blame for having nothing to say and for having to say it again and again" (Christensen, *Lord Byron's Strength*, 125–26).

57. Edelman compares the common metaphor for the reading process, the opening of a box to discover a truth inside, to the reading of the gay body (*Homographesis*, 21).

58. Eric Daffron, "Disorienting the Self: The Figure of the White European Man in Byron's *Oriental Tales* and Travels," in *Mapping Male Sexuality*, 81.

59. Andrew Elfenbein, *Byron and the Victorians* (New York: Cambridge University Press, 1995), 207.

60. Sedgwick, *Between Men*, 83–96.

61. Gross, "'One Half What I Should Say,'" 114.

62. Christensen, *Lord Byron's Strength*, 136.

63. Gleckner, *Byron and the Ruins of Paradise*, 163–64. Robert Gleckner calls Kaled "Byron's most intensely rounded human," but he also reads Kaled as the externalization of Lara's own destroyed humanity.

64. The private language in *Lara* recalls Byron's and Matthews's coded language for homosexual desires and experiences in the so-called "Greek epistles," which served a need for self-protection *and* self-disclosure. The idea of a language incomprehensible to others and used as a code for the expression of homosexual desire functions as a discursive "gay underground" within the gay community—and for others outside the community who are "in the know." Judy Grahn's *Another Mother Tongue: Gay Words, Gay Worlds* (Boston: Beacon Press, 1984) writes a gay cultural history through the various encoded discourses used to describe gay or lesbian identity.

65. *The Monk*, 277, 432.

66. Byron's own identification with the feelings that such effeminate boy figures as Kaled express emerges in his aphoristic *Detached Thoughts*. In what are taken to be comments on Edleston, Byron's declaration of love in #72 sounds very much like Kaled's in *Lara*. In #74 and #76, he points to homoeroticism in a language resonant with the secret and its import, as in the *Tales*:

#72: "I could have left or lost the world with or for that which I loved."

#74: "I have written my memoirs—but omitted *all* the really *consequential and important* parts."

#76: "I must not go on with these reflections—or I shall be letting out some secret or other—to paralyze posterity" (quoted in Crompton, *Byron and Greek Love*, 247–48). This last resonates with the paralysis supposedly induced by the sight of the Giaour/Gorgon.

George Haggerty's work on the "man of feeling" emphasizes how the melancholia of one man mourning another was a way of culturally diffusing the threatening import of male-male love, since the desire is for something permanently lost or inaccessible (*Men in Love*, 173).

67. Christensen, *Lord Byron's Strength*, 127.

68. Watkins emphasizes the power of the narrator's rejection of accepted gender conventions, but then undermines the strength of that insight by concluding that Kaled's identity "is the only information *of substance* that is ever revealed" (*Social Relations*, 105–6, my emphasis). Thus, the sustained ambiguity, or distance from gender norms is reduced to a knowledge "without substance," as Watkins perversely engages in the same kind of social mystification he claims to deplore.

69. Claudia Johnson, *Equivocal Beings: Politics, Gender, and Sentimentality in the 1790s* (Chicago: University of Chicago Press, 1995), 53.

70. Haggerty, *Men in Love*, 20.

71. Crompton points to the aristocratically inflected, paternalistic component in Byron's sexual attractions to adolescent boys, both those in England (in *Childe Harold* the referent is Robert Rushton, "Robin") and those in the Mediterranean and the Levant (*Byron and Greek Love*, 130–31).

72. It goes without saying, or with what will always be "half" saying, that an eroticized desire for a male soul mate and companion could not be imagined, much less represented, unequivocally (if it could, it would implicitly attribute to Byron an acceptance of his own desire and its difficult consequences, the loss of both family and country).

73. The expression comes from Edelman, *Homographesis*, 7.

74. Wolfson, "'Their She Condition,'" 594.

75. This rhetorical strategy has been adopted by many gay and lesbian writers; portraying same-sex love, they dissolve the relationship tragically or otherwise. Depending on how you read it, this move either concedes or critiques a homophobic society, or both.

CHAPTER 4. "THIS DREAM IT WOULD NOT PASS AWAY"

1. *Collected Letters of Samuel Taylor Coleridge*, ed. Earl Leslie Griggs (Oxford: Clarendon Press, 1956–71), I: 378–79.

2. By way of contrast, Coleridge reviews the works of Ann Radcliffe more favorably, but trivializes them as "amusement." Coleridge writes of the schematic nature of the gothic romance, using Radcliffe as the model: "I amused myself, on reading a Romance in Mrs. Radcliffe's style, with marking out a scheme, which was to serve for all romances a-priori—only varying the proportions: a Baron or Baroness . . . Castle—on a Rock— . . . Deserted Rooms— . . . a Ghost, so believed—a written record—blood on it!—A wonderful cut throat, etc." (*Collected Letters*, III: 294–95). Michael Gamer points to Coleridge's review of Radcliffe's *Mysteries of Udolpho* and subsequent addendum as evidence of Coleridge's ambivalence about the gothic as a genre more concerned with pleasure than edification. According to Coleridge's review, *Udolpho* peaks the reader's curiosity to excess, without being able adequately to gratify that curiosity. Further, no lasting interest is generated; once the book is completed, the interest is gone as well. In response to overwhelming criticism by readers of the *Critical Review*, Coleridge balanced his criticism in an addendum by calling the novel "the most interesting novel in the English language." See 'The Most Interesting Novel in the English Language': An Unidentified Addendum to Coleridge's Review of *Udolpho*," *The Wordsworth Circle* 24.1 (Winter 1993): 53–54.

3. See Coleridge's review of *The Monk* in *A Wiltshire Parson and His Friends: The Correspondence of William Lisle Bowles, Together With Four Hitherto Unidentified Reviews by Coleridge*, ed. Garland Greever (London: Constable), 192–95.

4. *A Wiltshire Parson and His Friends*, 195 and 197.

5. Donald Tuttle points to the parallels between *Christabel* and another of Lewis's works, *The Monk*, in "*Christabel*'s Sources in Percy's *Reliques* and Gothic Romance," *PMLA* 53 (1938): 445, and Andrew Cooper mentions the gender confusion common to *The Monk* and *Christabel*, in *Doubt and Identity in Romantic Poetry* (New Haven: Yale University Press, 1988), 107–29.

6. In her excellent essay, "'Christabel': The Wandering Mother and the Enigma of Form," *Studies in Romanticism* 23 (Winter 1984): 533–53, Karen Swann argues that *Christabel* reveals how culture genders its formal questions. The subject's autonomy is played out as an opposition between "authentic, contained 'manly' speech and 'feminine' bodies—the utterly conventional yet licentiously imaginative female characters, readers, and genres of the circulating libraries." Coleridge then goes on to deconstruct this opposition and suggest that all subjects in discourse exhibit such uncontained, or hysterically feminine, responses.

7. Camille Paglia suggests a connection between the poem and Coleridge's homo-

eroticism in her essay in *Samuel Taylor Coleridge*, ed. Harold Bloom (New York: Chelsea House, 1986), 225–26.

8. Tillotama Rajan, "Coleridge, Wordsworth, and the Textual Abject," *The Wordsworth Circle* 24.2 (Spring 1993): 65.

9. Judith Butler, *Bodies That Matter: On the Discursive Limits of "Sex"* (New York: Routledge, 1993), 12.

10. Throughout this essay, and specified by the immediate context, I use identification in two senses: 1) as a perceived similarity and 2) as an absence of awareness of separation or difference.

11. Part One of *Christabel* was composed by Coleridge in 1797 and Part Two in 1800. The poem was never completed, but it circulated widely in manuscript form and spawned a number of imitations before its publication as a fragment in 1816. One of the critical issues about *Christabel* concerns whether Geraldine's rape is a fact or a performance. Reading this poem as "camp" obviates such hard and fast distinctions, since camp identifies with what it stages.

12. Samuel Taylor Coleridge, *Poems*, ed. John Beer (London: J. M. Dent and Sons, 1991). All citations of Coleridge's poetry refer to this edition. Line numbers will be indicated parenthetically within the text.

13. Michael Taussig traces the effects (the "history") of embodiment and sensuousness as hallmarks that characterize mimetic forms of otherness. See *Mimesis and Alterity: A Particular History of the Senses* (New York: Routledge, 1993), 176.

14. *The Notebooks of Samuel Taylor Coleridge*, ed. Kathleen Coburn, vol. 1, 1794–1804 (New York: Pantheon, 1957), entry 523. While such a depersonalizing experience occurs in *Christabel*, a will capable of restoring the self's "substantiality" is not imagined.

15. The glittering eyes in *Christabel*, recurring in a whole range of poems Coleridge was writing in the late 1790s, symbolize the imagination as 1) possession by another's vision and 2) the power to compel others to see as the artist does. Karen Swann points to Hazlitt's review of *Christabel* in which "the danger of this 'dim, obscure, and visionary' poem is that it threatens to hold the reader as if it were his *own* dream"; "Literary Gentlemen and Lovely Ladies: The Debate on the Character of *Christabel*," *ELH* 52 (Spring 1985): 406.

16. Charles J. Rzepka gives a Lacanian reading of *Christabel* and argues that Christabel is entrapped in the mirror stage, which prevents her from speaking herself; "*Christabel*'s 'Wandering Mother' and the Discourse of the Self: A Lacanian Reading of Repressed Narration," *Romanticism Past and Present* 10.1 (1986): 17–43.

17. For a compelling account of mimesis and subjectivity as the experience of "being other," see Mikkel Borch-Jacobsen's *The Emotional Tie* (Stanford: Stanford University Press, 1992), 101; see esp. 98–120.

18. *The Notebooks of Samuel Taylor Coleridge*, ed. Kathleen Coburn, vol. 1 (New York: Pantheon, 1957), entry 257.

19. "General Character of the Gothic Literature and Art," in *Coleridge's Miscellaneous Criticism*, ed. Thomas Middleton Raysor (Cambridge: Harvard University Press, 1936), 12.

20. Unlike *The Nightingale*, however, *Christabel* has a thoroughly gothicized landscape of spectral mothers, disturbing dreams, and the confusion of pleasure and fear.

21. *Notebooks* 1: entry 189.

22. Geraldine's expulsion from the society is signaled by the adjective "forlorn." Because of her rape, Geraldine is forlorn; Christabel will become forlorn when she is

alienated from language and when her father rejects her. Geraldine shares an affinity with Coleridge's "fallen" woman in his poem *The Outcast*: "the pale roamer through the night, [the] poor forlorn," who projects the same eerie or unreal quality that Geraldine does.

23. "True thoughts are those alone which do not understand themselves"; Theodor Adorno, *Minima Moralia* (London: Verso, 1978), 192. See also Taussig, *Mimesis and Alterity*, 46.

24. Two critical articles on *Christabel* interpret the relationship between Geraldine and Christabel as one between mother and child. In the poem's ambivalence about Geraldine's goodness or evil, Barbara Shapiro sees the child's intense desire and terror of fusion with the mother. "'Christabel': The Problem of Ambivalent Love," *Literature and Psychology* 30, nos. 3 and 4 (1980): 119–32. Margery Durham also focuses on Geraldine as mother-figure and Christabel as the embodiment of conflicting infantile impulses to identify and separate; she reads the powerful affective responses in the context of Coleridge's interest and ideas concerning the child's achievement of language and a sense of morality; "The Mother Tongue: *Christabel* and the Language of Love," *The (M)other Tongue: Essays in Feminist Psychoanalytic Interpretation*, ed. Shirley Nelson Garner, Claire Kahane, and Madelon Sprengnether (Ithaca: Cornell University Press, 1985): 169–93. While Geraldine adopts certain maternal features and Christabel certain infantile features, I do not believe the self-dissolving homoerotic experiences of *Christabel* need to be conceptualized only as regressive fantasies to a pre-oedipal phase. Coleridge also presents another mother in the poem, one who would prohibit or block such regression—the spectral mother who encourages her daughter to marry and recreate the family unit, or even the mother who dies in childbirth, the consequence of her (hetero)sexual initiation.

25. Coleridge excises the line that describes Geraldine's breasts as "lean and old and foul of hue," which would establish Spenser's Duessa as the antecedent for Geraldine. It would be difficult to imagine that these breasts of Duessa could be the same as Geraldine's "heaving breasts" on the morning after, which Christabel gazes upon with renewed desire and guilt.

26. Richard Dellamora speaks of the use of the dash in Gerard Manley Hopkins's writings on Walt Whitman as a substitution for the "proscribed terms of desire": " . . . the dash exemplifies the figure of aposiopesis and substitutes for the proscribed terms of desire. Aposiopesis, in Greek 'a becoming silent,' is 'a conscious anacoluthon, that is, a speaker's abrupt halt midway in a sentence, accountable to his being either too excited to give further articulation to his thought . . . or thinking to impress his addressee the more with this kind of vague hint of an idea too awesome to be put into words.' In writing that deals with illicit subjects, aposiopesis—even against a writer's intention—turns the ban on expression against itself in order to express what otherwise remains silenced"; *Masculine Desire: The Sexual Politics of Victorian Aestheticism* (Chapel Hill: University of North Carolina Press, 1990), 88. Andrew Elfenbein sees the blank as a figure for the sublime horror of lesbianism, an event which usurps the imagination, but one which Coleridge exploits to demonstrate his poetic originality; *Romantic Genius: The Prehistory of a Homosexual Role* (New York: Columbia University Press, 1999), 181.

27. James Creech writes of the importance of seeing such blanks as more than literariness: "politically and ideologically enforced blanks are not, in the first instance, a sign of literature. Rather, it is legitimate to see them as signs of repression" (*Closet Writing/Gay Reading*, 21).

28. In this light, it is interesting to consider Coleridge's fascination with outcast women who cannot speak for themselves in light of cultural discourses about homosexuality. In his work on cultural constructions of the "effeminate male," Randolph Trumbach points out that they shared the status of outcast women of the lowest standing and viewed themselves as a species of outcast women. Randolph Trumbach, "Gender and the Homosexual Role in Modern Western Culture: The Eighteenth and Nineteenth Centuries Compared," in *Homosexuality, Which Homosexuality* (London: GMP, 1989), 157 and "The Birth of the Queen: Sodomy and the Emergence of Gender Equality in Modern Culture, 1660–1750," in *Hidden From History: Reclaiming the Gay and Lesbian Past,* ed. Martin Duberman, Martha Vicinus and George Chauncey, Jr. (New York: Modern American Library, 1989), 137.

29. Susan Eilenberg speaks of the narrator being held in thrall or victim to the kind of speech threat that Geraldine imposes upon Christabel; "'Michael,' 'Christabel,' and the Poetry of Possession," *Criticism* 30.2 (Spring 1988): 214. Charles Rzepka observes that what the narrator can or cannot tell is a reflection of what Christabel herself can or cannot ("*Christabel*'s 'Wandering Mother'," 21–23). Richard Harter Fogle writes that the poetry performs "a kind of hypnotism," whereby reader and narrator alike are entranced; *The Idea of Coleridge's Criticism* (Berkeley: University of California Press, 1962), 138.

30. Karen Swann, "'Christabel': The Wandering Mother and the Enigma of Form," 541.

31. Michael Warner's essay, "Homo-narcissism; or, Heterosexuality" criticizes the view that assumes the distinction of self and Other is founded on gender difference. Warner challenges the position (epoused by many, including Freud and Lacan), that homosexuality is ultimately narcissism, a desire to see oneself in the guise of another, and deconstructs this with Freud's work on the ego-ideal, where the projection of one's ego ideals onto a love object characterizes all erotic relationships. What lies behind this will to see homosexuality as a collapse into sameness is a cultural system in which heterosexual identity, despite its own narcissism, assumes the difference between self and other is founded on the difference between genders. In *Engendering Men: The Question of Male Feminist Criticism,* ed. Joseph A. Boone and Michael Cadden (New York: Routledge, 1991).

32. The further development of this idea in the course of the nineteenth-century Britain and into the twentieth makes same-sex desire overtly vampiristic, as has been suggested in the chapter on Byron's *Oriental Tales,* especially *The Giaour,* and can be seen further in Sheridan LeFanu's *Carmilla,* Bram Stoker's *Dracula,* and Anne Rice's *The Vampire Chronicles.*

33. "On the Mimetic Faculty," in *Reflections,* ed. Peter Demetz, trans. E. Jephcott (New York: Harcourt Brace Jovanovich, 1979), 333.

34. The formulation is Taussig's, *Mimesis and Alterity,* 86.

35. If everyone is impelled by mimesis, then everyone or no one would be forlorn.

36. In the context of Leoline's failed attempts to be consoled for this first loss, it is interesting to consider Judith Butler's work on the impossibility of mourning the loss of primary homosexual love objects: see *Gender Trouble* (New York: Routledge, 1990), 57–72 and "Melancholy Gender/Refused Identifications," *Psychoanalytic Dialogues* 5.2 (1995): 165–80.

37. Anne Williams notes the opposition of the symbolizable and non-symbolizable inherent in the meanings of the word "spell"; on the one hand, "to spell" pertains to the

ordering and meaning of discourse: to make clear (spell out); to write the letters of a word; to comprehend by study; to puzzle out. The word comes from the Middle English meaning "discourse," and its old English root signified "story" or "fable." In its contrary senses, a spell is incantational or formulaic, indicative of a trance state, or that which fascinates and attracts without being nameable (*Art of Darkness*, 179–80).

38. Coleridge, *Biographia Literaria*, vol. 7, no. 2 in *The Collected Works of Samuel Taylor Coleridge* (Princeton: Princeton University Press, 1983), 6–7.

39. William Wordsworth, *The Letters of William and Dorothy Wordsworth: The Early Years, 1787–1805*, ed. Ernest de Selincourt, 2nd edition, rev. Chester L. Shaver (Oxford: Clarendon Press, 1967), 1:309.

40. Alison Hickey is the latest in a substantial critical tradition that examines the nervousness Coleridge's collaborative projects unleashed for him, his co-authors, and his critics, specifically his collaboration with Southey, because of its challenge to the singular nature of writerly authority. "'Coleridge, Southey and Co.': Collaboration and Authority," *Studies in Romanticism* 37.3 (Fall 1998): 305–39. In his chapter on Wordsworth's and Coleridge's collaboration on the 1798 volume of the *Lyrical Ballads*, Koestenbaum mentions Coleridge's recurring desire to "mingle identities with other men." In the context of a homoerotics of literary collaboration between Wordsworth and Coleridge, he focuses primarily on Wordsworth's echoing of Coleridge's *Rime of the Ancient Mariner*. *Double Talk: The Erotics of Male Literary Collaboration* (London: Routledge, 1989), 71. Richard Matlak connects Coleridge's propensity for psychological imitation in his friendships with men to his imitative "compositional strategies," which peak in his plagiarisms, in *"Licentia Biographica*: or, Biographical Sketches of Coleridge's Literary Life and Plagiarisms," *European Romantic Review* 4.1 (Summer 1993): 57–70. Susan Eilenberg notes the mystery surrounding the circumstances that led to *Christabel*'s suppression in the second volume of the *Lyrical Ballads* and argues that, with Wordsworth's insertion of "Michael" in its place, Wordsworth uncannily imitates what he wanted to replace. Not only does Wordsworth incorporate images and details from Coleridge's poem, but like *Christabel*, *Michael* "contends with the earlier poem's failure of voice. The fragmentary state of 'Christabel,' its mistrust of representation, and its fear of the foreign become problems for Wordsworth's poem" ("The Poetry of Possession," 213). Karen Swann's "Literary Gentlemen and Lovely Ladies: The Debate on the Character of *Christabel*" discusses the effect of *Christabel* on Wordsworth's and Coleridge's *Lyrical Ballads* and suggests it can be seen as a hysterical symptom—just one example of the disruptive (read: feminizing) effect that the poem exerted on writers, readers, and critics alike (399–403). For the motif of ventriloquism in Wordsworth and its function in relation to Coleridge's assessment of the figure of the poet, see Reeve Parker, "'O Could You Hear His Voice!': Wordsworth, Coleridge, and Ventriloquism," in *Romanticism and Language*, ed. Arden Reed (Ithaca: Cornell University Press, 1984), 125–43.

41. From *The Pretty Gentleman: or, Softness of Manners Vindicated from the false Ridicule exhibited under the Character of William Fribble, Esq.* (1747), reprinted in *Secret Sexualities: A Sourcebook of 17th- and 18th-Century Writing*, ed. Ian McCormick (New York: Routledge, 1997), 154.

42. Ibid., 155.

43. Ibid., 118.

44. Lee Edelman, *Homographesis*, 121–28.

45. Randolph Trumbach, "London's Sapphists: From Three Sexes to Four Genders in the Making of Modern Culture," in *BodyGuards: The Cultural Politics of Gender Ambigu-

ity (New York: Routledge, 1991), 135. On the subject of Coleridge and plagiarism as theft, as a compositional strategy, as a psychological need, as marginal exegesis, and as the fulfillment of an ego-ideal, respectively, see: Norman Fruman, *Coleridge, The Damaged Archangel* (New York: Braziller, 1971); James Engell, "Introduction," *CBL* 2: cxiv–cxxxii; Thomas McFarland, *Romanticism and the Forms of Ruin* (Princeton: Princeton University Press, 1981), 127; Jerome Christensen, *Coleridge's Blessed Machine of Language* (Ithaca: Cornell University Press, 1981), 105; and Matlak, "Licentia Biographica," 59.

Thomas De Quincey's treatment of Coleridge's literary thieving is interesting in this regard. De Quincey avoids any insinuation of Coleridge's plagiarism as a form of unmanliness in two ways: he casts Coleridge's intellect as so capacious and masterful that it already contains the capacities, if not the thoughts, of all other men, so that his theft is not based on need or insufficiency; and, he avoids "criminalizing" the behavior by infantilizing him: as the child who pickpockets from others, Coleridge is playing an innocent game. In fact, Coleridge becomes the one violated or abused as De Quincey, or anyone else, (posing as a prying, obtuse, quasi-pederastic, and "deviant" rationality) rifles through his pockets as he naps, in order to find out what he has taken:

> Had Coleridge any need to borrow from Shelling [*sic*]? Did he borrow *in forma pauperis*? Not at all:—there lay the wonder. He spun daily and at all hours, for mere amusement of his own activities, and from the loom of his own magical brain, theories more gorgeous by far, and supported by a pomp and luxury of images, such as Shelling [*sic*]—no, nor any German that ever breathed, not John Paul—could have emulated in his dreams. With the riches of El Dorado lying about him, he would condescend to filch a handful of gold from any man whose purse he fancied; and in fact reproduced in a new form, applying itself to intellectual wealth, that maniacal propensity which is sometimes well known to attack enormous proprietors and *millionaires* for acts of petty larceny . . . . did the reader . . . ever amuse himself by searching the pockets of a child—three years old, suppose, when buried in slumber after a long summer's day of out-a-door's activity? I have done this; . . . Philosophy is puzzled, conjecture and hypothesis are confounded, in the attempt to explain the law of selection which *can* have presided in the child's labours: stones remarkable only for weight, old rusty hinges, nails, crooked skewers, . . . rags, broken glass, tea-cups having the bottom knocked out, and loads of similar jewels . . . Such in value were the robberies of Coleridge; such their usefulness to himself or anyone else . . . . (*Recollections of the Lakes and the Lake Poets*, ed. David Wright [New York: Penguin, 1970, 40–41]).

46. Herman Melville expressed a wish for an authorship that was both unowned and unowning; the transgressive idea of a text that belongs to no one and everyone is aligned with an alternative masculine interpersonal (eroticized) economy, as the following review of Hawthorne's *Mosses from an Old Manse* suggests:

> To what infinite height of loving wonder and admiration may I yet be borne, when by repeatedly banquetting on these Mosses [Hawthorne's "Mosses from an Old Manse"], I shall have thoroughly incorporated their whole stuff into my being,—that, I can not tell. But already I feel that this Hawthorne has dropped germinous seeds into my soul. He expands and deepens down, the more I contemplate him; and further, and further, shoots his strong New-England roots into the hot soil of my Southern soul.

Ellen Weinauer's essay investigates Melville's negotiations of competing views of authorship, one of nonproprietary affiliation that erases notions of ownership and one that emphasizes the Lockean notions of authorial property and origin. "Plagiarism and the

Proprietary Self: Policing the Boundaries of Authorship in Herman Melville's 'Hawthorne and His Mosses,'" *American Literature* 69.4 (December 1997): 697–717.

47. Coleridge anticipates poststructural thinking on textuality that emphasizes the lack of clear boundaries between texts as well as Northrop Frye's assertion of the conventionality of literature which copyright law and theory disguises; see Mark Rose, *Authors and Owners: The Invention of Copyright* (Cambridge: Harvard University Press, 1993), 2–3.

48. Karen Swann, "Literary Gentlemen and Lovely Ladies," 404, and Susan Sontag, "Notes on Camp," *Against Interpretation* (New York: Dell, 1969).

49. Swann, "Literary Gentlemen and Lovely Ladies," 404.

50. Michael Gamer, *Romanticism and the Gothic* (New York: Cambridge University Press, 2000), 71.

51. Butler, *Gender Trouble*, 142–49.

52. Sontag, "Notes on Camp," 293.

53. While the typical heroine of the gothic is innocent, curious, and guided by providence, Christabel's attempts at piety and innocence are presented as derivative or merely feigned. If she constantly "prays," the narrator mocks her, as Dramin notes, with his deliberate pun on "prey": Christabel lures Geraldine in as her prey and then gives herself up to Geraldine's seductive powers in a deliberate pursuit of her own sexual desires. See Edward Dramin, "'Amid the Jagged Shadows': *Christabel* and the Gothic Tradition," *The Wordsworth Circle* 13.4 (Autumn 1982): 221–28.

54. Alison Hickey writes of parody as a double-voiced mode, both "beside" and "against" its original in "'Coleridge, Southey, and Co.,'" 309. Zora Neale Hurston's comments on race and mimicry articulate the subject's control over, not the subjection to, the impulse that characterizes mimesis: "The Negro, the world over, is famous as a mimic. But this in no way damages his standing as an original. Mimicry is an art in itself [and] he does it as the mocking-bird does it, for the love of it, and not because he wishes to be like the one imitated"; *The Sanctified Church*, (Berkeley: Turtle Island, 1983). Coleridge too has it both ways, reflecting the ambivalence of camp's critics when they try to resolve whether camp is ultimately serious or ridiculous, high or low, elite or popular, conservative or liberatory. Andrew Cooper's chapter on *Christabel* is alert to the parodic bent of the text which he links to Coleridge's moral mission: to raise his reader's consciousness about Christabel's (and the genre's) passive attitude toward sin. What I find missing in Cooper's account of *Christabel* is an attentiveness to Coleridge's own psychological and formal proclivity for unconscious imitation and states of suspended identity.

55. Taussig, *Mimesis and Alterity*, 151.

56. In a letter to Coleridge, Byron writes that "[the details of the poem] took a hold on my imagination which I never shall wish to shake off," quoted in *Collected Letters of Samuel Taylor Coleridge*, IV:601.

57. Swann notes the alarm concerning gender that this kind of "feminized" pleasure—feminized because it was associated with the predominantly female-authored literature of the lending libraries and a popular female reading audience—might provoke in "a man of culture": "In moments of imaginative generosity, of voluntary relinquishment of self to fictions, writers and readers flirt with the possibility of going too far, . . . of acceding to 'holds' they might 'never wish to shake off'. . . . [Coleridge] casts the pleasure one takes in certain kinds of books as a feminine pleasure: the implicit message is that to read is to behave like a woman, an axiom that the man of culture might find

both alarming and alluring to contemplate" ("Literary Gentlemen and Lovely Ladies," 416).

58. Quoted in Gamer, "'The Most Interesting Novel in the English Language,'" 53.

CHAPTER 5. THE GOTHIC ROMANCE OF SIGMUND FREUD AND WILHELM FLIESS

1. Sigmund Freud, "The Psychotherapy of Hysteria," in *Standard Edition of the Complete Psychological Works of Sigmund Freud*, ed. and trans. by James Strachey, 24 vols. (London: Hogarth Press, 1953–1958), II:283. All subsequent citations from the Standard Edition will refer to this edition and will be abbreviated as *SE*. "Der Fall ist etwa mit dem Aufschließen einer versperrten Türe zu vergleichen," *Studien über Hysterie* (Frankfurt: Fischer, 1991), 300; citations from the German *Studies on Hysteria* refer to this edition. All other German citations are drawn from the *Studienausgabe*, 11 vols. (Frankfurt: Fischer, 1969–75).

2. Ibid., *SE* II:281 ("So bald er dies vollzogen hat, schwindet das Bild, wie ein erlößter Geist zur Ruhe eingeht").

3. Freud to Stefan Zweig, 2 June 1932, *Letters of Sigmund Freud*, ed. Ernst L. Freud, trans. Tania and James Stern (New York: Basic Books, 1960), 413.

4. Ernest Jones, *The Life and Work of Sigmund Freud*, 3 vols., *The Formative Years and the Great Discoveries 1856–1900* (New York: Basic Books, 1953–57), I: 224–25.

5. "Studies on Hysteria," *SE* II:134.

6. The phrase "erotic, self-surrendering dimension" is John Toews's; "Fashioning the Self in the Story of the 'Other': The Transformation of Freud's Masculine Identity between 'Studies on Hysteria' and 'Dora,'" in *Proof and Persuasion*, ed. Marchand and Lunbeck (Turnhout, Belgium: Brepols, 1997), 196–218. Toews's essay is an overview of the culturally determined limitations and biases in Freud's early representations of masculinity. It draws on work done by both feminists and scholars interested in Freud's Jewish identity. Shirley Nelson Garner calls the Freud-Fliess correspondence "love letters" ("Freud and Fliess: Homophobia and Seduction," in *Seduction and Theory: Readings of Gender, Representation, and Rhetoric*, ed. Dianne Hunter (Urbana: University of Illinois Press, 1989), 86. In the introduction to the letters, Jeffrey Moussaiff Masson notes that Freud rarely mentions Fliess except in a few letters, until late in his life; *The Complete Letters of Sigmund Freud to Wilhelm Fliess, 1887–1904*, ed. and trans. by Jeffrey Moussaiff Masson (Cambridge: Harvard University Press, 1985), 4. Mention of Fliess is rare in Freud's own accounts of the history of psychoanalysis, and the reference is not by name, but as "a colleague"; see *Origin and Development of Psychoanalysis* (Chicago: Gateway Editions, 1955) and "An Autobiographical Study," *SE* XX.

7. All English citations from the letters of Freud to Fliess refer to *The Complete Letters of Sigmund Freud to Wilhelm Fliess, 1887–1904*, while all German citations refer to the following edition: *Briefe an Wilhelm Fliess 1887–1904* (Frankfurt am Main: Fischer, 1986). The period of conflict in the Freud-Fliess friendship, the late 1890s, overlaps with Freud's development of the Oedipal story and the developmental model of human sexuality (Toews).

8. The unraveling of the friendship occurred over a period of years, beginning as

early as 1896. For the paranoid plot attributed by Freud to Breuer and Ida, see the letters of 5.30.1896, 8.12.1896, 3.11.1900, and especially 8.7.1901.

9. Fliess kept Freud's letters to him, and when he [Fliess] died, Ida Fliess sold them to Marie Bonaparte. Freud admitted to Marie Bonaparte that he was extremely nervous about the incriminating material he remembered in them, should they come under public scrutiny. He was anxious that she should purchase them whatever the cost. One of the most glaring, unresolved secrets of this history is what Freud did with Fliess's letters. He claims to have forgotten whether he burned them or not—a hardly innocent amnesia. For the story of the letters from their writing to eventual publication, see Masson's introduction to the correspondence, 4–13.

10. Two essays specifically relate the homoerotics of the Freud-Fliess relationship to the hysterical case studies of the 1890s: Wayne Koestenbaum, "Privileging the Anus: Anna O. and the Collaborative Origin of Psychoanalysis," *Genders* 3 (Fall 1988): 57–81 and Madelon Sprengnether, "Freud, Fliess, and Emma Eckstein," in *The Spectral Mother* (Ithaca: Cornell University Press, 1990), 22–38. Koestenbaum argues that Freud's collaboration with Breuer, and then with Fliess, fuse male bonding with an appropriation of the power of female reproduction; it is particularly Anna O. who is the object of exchange between men. Koestenbaum argues that Freud uses the language of the woman's body to describe his intellectual and emotional affairs with men and makes the anus the primary originary site of creativity, not the uterus. Madelon Sprengnether uses the Emma Eckstein episode and the figure of Emma Eckstein to illuminate the ambivalent consequences for Freud's masculine identity that his identification with Eckstein precipitates.

11. Bersani, "Is the Rectum a Grave?" (especially 215–22), and Edelman, *Homographesis*, 99.

12. As a result of his work with Charcot, Freud was from early on a firm adherent of the idea that hysteria was not just a woman's disease, but one that men suffered from as well. In the letters he refers to a number of hysterical male patients. Freud also gave a talk on male hysteria in 1886 to the Vienna Medical Society. For a compilation of the minutes of that meeting, see "Quellentexte," *Luzifer-Amor* 1.1 (1988): 156–75 and Henri Ellenberger's critical assessment of the meeting (which includes Freud's response to it): "La conference de Freud sur l'hysterie masculine (15 octobre 1886): Étude critique," *L'information psychiatrique* 44. 10 (1968): 921–34. There is a great deal of recent critical work on male hysteria: see especially Jan Goldstein, "The Uses of Male Hysteria: Medical and Literary Discourse in Nineteenth-Century France," *Representations* 34 (Spring 1991): 134–65; *The Hysterical Male: New Feminist Theory*, ed. Arthur and Marielouise Kroker (New York: St. Martin's Press, 1991); Mark Micale's "Hysteria Male/Hysteria Female: Reflections on Comparative Gender Construction in Nineteenth-Century France and Britain," in *Science and Sensibility: Gender and Scientific Enquiry, 1780–1945* (Cambridge, Mass.: Blackwell, 1991), 200–239 and his *Approaching Hysteria: Disease and Its Interpretations* (Princeton: Princeton University Press, 1995); Janet Oppenheim's fifth chapter on "Manly Nerves" in *Shattered Nerves: Doctors, Patients, and Depression in Victorian England* (New York: Oxford University Press, 1991) and Elaine Showalter's *Sexual Anarchy: Gender and Culture at the Fin-de-siècle* (New York: Viking, 1990).

13. All of these theories find an enactment in Freud's epistolary representation of his relationship with Fliess. Among the critics who focus on the influence of Fliess on Freud's theorizing on bisexuality, Patrick Mahoney throws his net wider than the others and claims that "through and in spite of him [Fliess], Freud learned the theory of paranoia," "Friendship and Its Discontents," *Contemporary Psychoanalysis* 15 (1979): 64.

14. This last encounter in 1906 concerned a publicly waged plagiarism dispute which is treated later in this chapter.

15. For example, in the 1905 edition of Freud's *Three Essays on Sexuality*, Fliess is mentioned as the originator of the idea of an inherent bisexuality; by the next edition in 1915, Fliess's name is dropped (*SE* VII:220, Fn. 1).

16. In order, the quotes are from the following letters: 5.28.88, 10.7.93, 7.24.95, 4.26.95, 10.7.93, and 6.22.94 ("denn die Gewalt über die Geister, die Ihnen gebührt, läßt sich nicht übertragen"; "drittens hoffe ich noch auf Dich als auf den Messias"; "Daimonie!"; "Lieber Zauberer"; "Mit der Anfrage, wann und wo heuer, bist Du mir nur um wenige Tage zuvorgekommen"; "ich glaube nämlich im geheimen, daß Du sehr genau weißt, was es ist").

17. As we shall see, after his "abandonment" of hypnosis in favor of free association, such occult appellations record Freud's ambivalence, evidencing his affection for Fliess and his dismissal of him as a serious scientist: when he calls Fliess a "seer" and "honorary astrologer" or claims to want to indulge in some "new magic" with him, these compliments also convey a veiled insult, much as Fliess's imputation that Freud's scientific technique is based on thought-reading, i.e., the doctor reading his thoughts into his patients. Letters of 5.4.96, 10.9.96, 7.15.96, and 9.19.1901 ("Seher"; "Ehrenastrolog"; "den neuen Zauber von Dir hören").

18. In spite of this rejection, the impulses underlying suggestion continue to have a long afterlife in his writings on the transference relationship in analysis. Freud states in his Clark Lectures: "the study of transfer can also give you *the key* to the understanding of hypnotic suggestion . . . You must not think that the phenomenon of transfer . . . is created by the *influence* of psychoanalytic treatment. The transfer arises spontaneously in all human relations and in the relations of the patient to the physician; it is everywhere the especial bearer of therapeutic influences, and it works the stronger the less one knows of its presence. Accordingly, psychoanalysis does not create it, it merely discloses it to consciousness" (*Origin and Development of Psychoanalysis*, 63–64). When Freud writes that "I have had good reason for asserting that everyone possesses in his own unconscious an instrument with which he can interpret the utterances of the unconscious in other people," he is obviating the need for a conscious consent to, or creation of, a hypnotic/suggestive state, since the unconscious means for tapping into it are already there and active ("The Disposition to Obsessional Neurosis," *SE* XII:320; "Aber ich habe nicht ohne gute Gründe behauptet, daß jeder Mensch in seinem eigenen Unbewußten eine Instrument besitzt, mit dem er die Äußerungen des Unbewußten beim anderen zu deuten vermag").

19. "Psychical (or Mental) Treatment," *SE* VII:283, 292; "Ein solches Mittel ist vor allem das Wort, und Worte sind auch das wesentliche Handwerkszeug der Seelenbehandlung. Der Laie wird es wohl schwer begreiflich finden, daß krankhafte Störungen des Leibes und der Seele durch 'bloße' Worte des Arztes beseitigt werden sollen. Er wird meinen, man mute ihm zu, an Zauberei zu glauben. Er hat damit nicht so unrecht; die Worte unserer täglichen Reden sind nichts anderes als abgeblaßter Zauber. Es wird aber notwendig sein, einen weiteren Umweg einzuschlagen, um verständlich zu machen wie die Wissenschaft es anstellt, dem Worte wenigstens einen Teil seiner früheren Zauberkraft wiederzugeben. . . . Wir beginnen nun auch den 'Zauber' des Wortes zu verstehen. Worte sind ja die wichtigsten Vermittler für den Einfluß, den ein Mensch auf den anderen ausüben will; Worte sind gute Mittel, um seelische Veränderungen bei dem hervorzurufen, an den sie gerichtet werden, und darum klingt es nicht länger

rätselhaft, wenn behauptet wird, daß der Zauber des Wortes Krankheitserscheinungen beseitigen kann, zumal solche, die selbst in seelischen Zuständen begründet sind").

20. "Psychical Treatment," *SE* VII:298, 291–92 ("Wundermann"; "Zauberformeln, die Reinigungsbäder, die Hervorlockung von Orakelträumen"). Interestingly, Freud refers to suggestion as historically the oldest form of medicine; in a (soon to be characteristic) move where antiquity confers authority, here an unestablished young doctor with disputed techniques goes back in time to establish the priority of his practices over contemporary medical ones that summarily dismiss hypnosis.

21. "Review of August Forel's *Hypnotism*," *SE* I:99. Freud at times advertises hypnosis as much for the authoritative image it confers upon the doctor as for the alleviation of symptoms: "But in order to gauge the practical importance of the new discoveries we must put a physician in place of the hypnotist and a patient in place of the hypnotic subject. Hypnosis would then seem pre-ordained *to fulfil all the physician's requirements*, in so far as he seeks to act towards the patient as a 'mind-doctor.' Hypnosis endows the physician with an authority such as was never possessed by the priest or the miracle man, since it concentrates the subject's whole interest upon the figure of the physician"; "Psychical (or Mental) Treatment," *SE* VII:297–98 ("Um nun aber die praktische Bedeutung der neuen Erkenntnisse zu würdigen, wolle man an Stelle des Hypnotiseurs den Arzt, an Stelle des Hypnotisierten den Kranken setzen. Scheint da die Hypnose nicht berufen, alle Bedürfnisse des Arztes, insoferne er als 'Seelenarzt' gegen den Kranken auftreten will, zu befriedigen? Die Hypnose schenkt dem Arzt eine Autorität, wie sie wahrscheinlich niemals ein Priester oder Wundermann besessen hat, indem sie alles seelische Interesse des Hypnotisierten auf die Person des Arztes vereinigt"). With his characteristic wit, Sandor Ferenczi comments on the hypnotist's smug enjoyment of his patriarchal power: "the suggester wishes to impress the patient. He adopts the self-satisfied expression of scientific and moral authority, of altruistic benevolence, and looks upon his patients in this way, giving them tranquillizing explanations or issuing commands to them. He even wishes to impress them with his outward appearance, with the size of his beard and with his ceremonial garb"; in *Further Contributions to the Theory and Technique of Psychoanalysis*, ed. John Rickman, trans. Jane Suttie and others (New York: Basic Books, 1952), 63.

22. Freud, "An Autobiographical Study," *SE* XX:17.

23. Letters of 6.12.95 and 8.29.88 ("Nun überraschest Du mich mit einer ernstgemeinten Diskussion jener Phantasien"; "die stärksten Eindrücke von der Möglichkeit mächtiger seelischer Vorgänge, die doch dem Bewußtsein des Menschen verborgen bleiben").

24. In what appears to be a one-way exchange of treatment, Fliess acts as Freud's consulting physician for a variety of ailments over the years, including his addiction to cigars and cocaine, his heart ailment, impotence, depression, and migraine. Fliess performs nasal surgery on Freud at least once. I can find no indication that Freud served in the capacity of doctor to Fliess. In the letter of 8.29.94, he admits: "I wish I were a 'doctor' . . . and would not have to leave you in strange hands. . . . I must rely on you in this as in everything else" [Ich wollt', ich wäre ein "Doktor," . . . und Dich in solchen Lagen keiner fremden Hand überlassen zu müssen. . . . Ich muß mich auf Dich verlassen, hierin wie in allem übrigen"]. For a summary of the various critical readings on the nature of the transference underlying the Freud-Fliess relationship, see Mahoney, "Friendship and Its Discontents," 68–73.

25. "Review of August Forel," *SE* I:94. Here I am describing identification in hyp-

nosis as a one-way phenomenon, as the transfer of the doctor's conscious and unconcious impulses into the patient. In doing so I am simplifying the matter for the moment. Freud's understanding of suggestibility, and its after-life in transference phenomenon, indicates that, in fact, it goes both ways, as transitivity implies. If we can speak of the patient's transference onto the doctor, we can also speak of the doctor's receptivity and countertransference. This has a profound effect on the subject (both doctor and patient) as constituted through the transference in the psychoanalytic situation. By far the best work on this is Francois Roustang's chapter "Suggestion Over the Long Term," in his book *Psychoanalysis never lets go* (Baltimore: Johns Hopkins University Press, 1983), 43–65. Also excellent is the work of Mikkel Borch-Jacobsen which treats the political and psychosocial implications of Freud's views on suggestion: see *The Freudian Subject*, trans. Catherine Porter (Stanford: Stanford University Press, 1988) and *The Emotional Tie: Psychoanalysis, Mimesis, and Affect* (Stanford: Stanford University Press, 1993), esp. 39–122. Ruth Leys has a fascinating essay on the use of hypnosis in psychoanalysis's constitution of a gendered subject. She looks at a case of multiple personality disorder in "The Real Miss Beauchamp: Gender and the Subject of Imitation," in *Feminists Theorize the Political*, ed. Judith Butler and Joan Scott (New York: Routledge, 1992), 167–214. Drawing on extensive clinical experience, the psychoanalytic work on pre-oedipal relations should also be mentioned here, since it looks at the affective disturbances in the preverbal infant environment that lead to an inability to distinguish self from other (a disturbance that surfaces in hysteria and hypnoid states as Freud describes them). See especially the work of D. H. Winnicott, Michael Balint, Sandor Ferenczi, and Christopher Bollas.

26. *Group Psychology and the Analysis of the Ego, SE* XVIII:127 ("passiv-masochistisch [einstellt]").

27. Freud, "Psychical (or Mental) Treatment," *SE* VII:295 ("in fast schrankenloser Weise").

28. Sandor Ferenczi, a pupil of Freud, writes on the dangers of hypnotism years later, criticizing its powerful eroticism in contrast to what he deems the relative safety of free association and the transference. Ferenczi interprets the expression of the wish to be under hypnosis as a mask for the patient's unconscious desire, namely, the sexual fantasy of being overpowered in sleep by the doctor. For his complicitous part, the hypnotist "zealously cherishes" the patient's "pathological love," (*Further Contributions to the Theory and Technique of Psychoanalysis*, pp. 250, 65). Since it suppresses scepticism and autonomy, for Ferenczi, the sexual element hypnosis unleashes undermines its validity as an analytic (and thus as a therapeutic) tool.

Freud himself attempts to address the general public's and his colleagues' misperceptions about its unsavory reputation. Freud begins his entry on hypnosis for Bum's medical encyclopedia by emphasizing the difficulty of the technique of hypnosis and claims it can provide not merely a useful, but a necessary service in healing. He concludes by simply dismissing any inherent dangers: "Everything that has been said and written about the great *dangers* of hypnotism belongs in the realm of fable," "Hypnosis," *SE* I:113; "Alles, was über die grossen *Gefahren* der H. gesagt und geschrieben wurde, gehört in's Reich der Fabel," "Hypnose," in Sigmund Freud, *Ausgewählte Texte*, ed. Ingrid Kästner and Christina Schröder (Berlin: Uberreuter, 1990), 166.

For Freud's bitter public dispute over the use of hypnosis with the eminent physician Theodor Meynert, see Stephanie Kiceluk, "The Disenchantment of Freud: Erasure and the Problem of Narrative Construction in the Case of Emmy von N.," in *Proof and*

Persuasion, 173–95. See also Peter Gay, *Freud: A Life for Our Time* (New York: Doubleday, 1989).

29. "Psychical (or Mental) Treatment," *SE* VII:296; "Nebenbei bemerkt, eine solche Gläubigkeit, wie sie der Hypnotisierte für seinen Hypnotiseur bereit hat, findet sich außer der Hypnose im wirklichen Leben nur *beim Kinde gegen die geliebten Eltern*, und eine derartige Einstellung des eigenen Seelenlebens auf das einer anderen Person mit ähnlicher Unterwerfung hat ein einziges, aber darin vollwertiges Gegenstück in manchen *Liebesverhältnissen* mit voller Hingebung. Das Zusammentreffen von Alleinschätzung und gläubigem Gehorsam gehört überhaupt zur Kennzeichnung des Liebens."

30. Letter of 5.21.94 ("Du [bist] der einzige Andere, der alter"). Freud calls Fliess his "other" in the letters of 5.18.98 and 9.21.99 as well.

31. Letter of 8.1.90 ("ich [kann] Sie nicht in Berlin sehen. . . . da ich die Reise im Sinne eines großen Vergnügens sehe, das ich mir bereite, bin ich veranlaßt worden, auf dieses Vergnügen zu verzichten. . . . ich hatte mir von dem Verkehr mit Ihnen sehr viel erwartet. . . . Wenn ich mit Ihnen sprach und merkte, daß Sie so von mir denken, pflegte ich sogar selbst was von mir zu halten, und das Bild der überzeugungsvollen Energie, das Sie boten, war nicht ohne Eindruck auf mich").

32. In anticipation of a meeting, Freud, referring to Fliess, mentions the ontological stakes of their rapport: "I have done too long without *ens* [being]" (7.25.94; "Ich habe das Ens zu lange entbehrt").

33. Letters of 3.10.98 and 11.6.98 ("Deine Schläfrigkeit erklärt mir jetzt mein gleichzeitiges Befinden. Unser Protoplasma hat sich durch den gleichen Zeitknoten durchgearbeitet. Wie schön wäre es, wenn diese verwandtschaftliche Übereinstimmung eine durchgehende wäre"; "Infolge der geheimen biologischen Sympathie, von der Du oft gesprochen hast, haben wir um ähnliche Zeit das Messer des Chirugen in unseren Leibern verspürt und an genau den nämlichen Tagen gestöhnt oder gewimmert vor Schmerzen").

34. Letters of 6.30.96 and 7.15.96 ("Ich . . . kann nur sagen, ich freue mich auf den Kongreß wie auf die Befriedigung von Hunger und Durst. Ich bring nichts als zwei offene Ohren und einen zur Aufnahme geschmierten Schläfenlappen"; "dieser Furcht opfere ich das brennende Bedürfnis, wieder einmal ganz zu leben mit dem Kopf und dem Herzen zugleich, *zoon politikon* zu sein und zu alledem noch—Dich zu sehen").

35. In order, see Draft C (postmarked 5.30.93) and the letters of 1.1.96, 5.21.94, 6.22.94, and 6.22.95 ("unsere ätiologische Formel"; "Es ist der erfreulichste Gedanke, den ich derzeit fassen kann, daß uns beide die gleiche Arbeit beschäftigt"; "Gedankenaustausche"; "das Echo meines eigenen"; "Deine Entdeckung dann in Ehren, Du wärst der stärkste Mann, hieltest die Zügel der Sexualität in der Hand, welche die Menschen regiert, könntest alles machen und alles verhüten"). That holding the "reins of sexuality which governs all mankind" is his own fantasy is apparent in an earlier letter of 5.21.94. Freud had written of his work on the neuroses: "I have the distinct feeling I have touched upon one of the great secrets of nature" ("ich habe die deutliche Empfindung, an eines der großen Geheimnisse der Natur gerührt zu haben"). In numerous letters, Freud claims himself to have found "the key" or "the secret" that will unlock and reveal everything.

36. Letter of 12.17.96 ("Als mir dann die Sache einfiel, hatte ich einen glücklichen Tag, ohne recht zu wissen, warum, einen Art seligen Nachgeschmacks wie nach einem schönen Traum").

37. Letter of 12.17.96 ("Hoffentlich kommt es soweit, daß wir auf ihm gemeinsam

Endgiltiges aufführen und dabei unsere Beiträge bis zur Eigentumsverkennung vereinigen").

38. The phrase "group of two" (eine Masse zu zweit) appears in *Group Psychology and the Analysis of the Ego*, *SE* XVIII:127; "Psychical (or Mental) Treatment," *SE* VII:295 ("Während der Hypnotisierte sich gegen die Außenwelt sonst verhält wie ein Schlafender, also sich mit all seinen Sinnen von ihr abgewendet hat, ist er *wach* für die Person, die ihn in Hypnose versetzt hat, hört und sieht nur diese, versteht sie und gibt ihr Antwort. Diese Erscheinung, die man den *Rapport* in der Hypnose heißt, findet ein Gegenstück in der Art, wie manche Menschen, z.B. die Mutter, die ihr Kind nährt, schlafen. Sie ist so auffällig, daß die uns das Verständnis des Verhältnisses zwischen Hypnotisiertem und Hypnotiseur vermitteln sollte").

39. As Borch-Jacobsen writes: "the other, in hypnosis, does not appear *as other*, and if the subject does recognize himself in the other, it is rather by totally *identifying* with him. . . . It would be totally false to claim that an *I* is submitting or responding to another here. In reality, 'I' am *spoken by* the other, I come into the place of the other— who, by the same token, is no longer an *other* but rather 'myself' in my undecidable identity," *The Emotional Tie*, 49–50.

40. Twenty years later, Freud will write in a footnote to the Dora case: "I have already indicated that the majority of hysterical symptoms, when they have attained their full pitch of development, represent an imagined situation of sexual life—such as a scene of sexual intercourse, pregnancy, childbirth, confinement, etc." "Fragment of an Analysis of a Case of Hysteria," *SE* VII:103; "Ich habe schon angedeutet, daß die meisten hysterischen Symptome, wenn sie ihre volle Ausbildung erlangt haben, eine phantasierte Situation des Sexuallebens darstellen, also eine Szene des sexuellen Verkehrs, eine Schwangerschaft, Entbindung, Wochenbett, u. dgl."

41. Letters of 5.25.95, 4.27.95, 6.12.95, 7.13.95, and 3.7.96 ("das Konzeptionsproblem"; "[ein] sechsmonatig[er] Foetus"; "aufnahmsgierig nach allen Deinen Novis, selbst mit Rudimenten und Embryonalkeimen beladen"; "Nachweis einer 23tägigen Periode für sexuelle Vorgänge . . . Nachweis der Notwendigkeit einer nicht über dreimonatlichen Periode für Freundschaftsangelegenheiten").

42. As Toews writes of Freud's position on an organic bisexuality, "the 'predisposition toward bisexuality' is described in 'Dora' as one of the 'organic bases' of unconscious psychic relations, i.e., it seems to constitute the necessary condition for the fluidity of aims and objects of desire and of models of identification in the psychic unconscious." I would argue that in hypnosis this gender fluidity and identificatory indeterminacy was already in place. See also the following articles on gender fluidity as that which undermines or opposes oedipal tendencies: Parveen Adams, "Per Os(cillation)," *Camera Obscura* 17 (1988): 7–29; Neil Hertz, "Dora's Secrets, Freud's Techniques," *Diacritics* 13.1 (Spring 1983): 65–76; and Madelon Sprengnether, "Enforcing Oedipus: Freud and Dora," in *In Dora's Case*, ed. Bernheimer and Kahane (New York: Columbia University Press, 1985), 254–75.

43. See Fliess's "Die nasale Reflexneurose," in *Verhandlungen des Kongresses für innere Medizin* (Wiesbaden: J. F. Bergmann, 1893), 384–94, as well as *Die Beziehungen zwischen Nase und weiblichen Geschlechtsorganen* (Leipzig and Vienna: Franz Deuticke, 1897). In footnotes two and three to the letter of 3.1.96, Masson cites Fliess's statement on male menopause. For a summary of Fliess's theories and their reception, see Frank J. Sulloway, *Freud: Biologist of the Mind: Beyond the Psychoanalytic Legend* (New York: Basic Books, 1983), 135–70.

44. Madelon Sprengnether, "Freud, Fliess, and Emma Eckstein," 26.

45. For Charcot's work on male hysteria and its influence on Freud, see Micale, *Approaching Hysteria*, 164–66. In his "Hysteria Male/Hysteria Female," Micale argues that instead of effeminizing the male body in a misogynistic or homophobic way, Charcot's transposition of the symptomatology onto the male body contributed to a gender relativization that sought to bring the male and female body into closer similarity; Micale suggests that this similarity enabled Freud to react more comfortably to Fliess's idea of an innate bisexuality (213–14).

46. 10.8.95 ("Ich bin allein mit einem Kopf, in dem so vieles keimt und vorläufig sich durcheinander wirrt"). In 1895, the time of the greatest intensification of these metaphors, both Ida Fliess and Martha Freud were pregnant. Freud wanted to name the child Wilhelm, if it was a boy, after Fliess (it was Anna Freud who was born). Freud's attraction to these tropes indicates a rivalry with Ida, who could give Fliess a child.

47. Letter of 2.8.93 ("Vor Deiner jungen Frau wirst Du das Manuskript ja doch verwahren").

48. Letter of 8.20.93 ("Anfangs [starrte ich sie] wie eine Erscheinung an").

49. In Masson's division of the letters into sections, he calls one "The Emma Eckstein Episode." For other extensive analyses of this event, see especially: Max Schur's "Some Additional 'Day Residues' of 'The Specimen Dream of Psychoanalysis,'" *Psychoanalysis—A General Psychology: Essays in Honor of Heinz Hartmann*, ed. Rudolph M. Loewenstein et al. (New York: 1966), 45–85; Peter Gay's *Freud: A Life for Our Time* (New York: Doubleday, 1989) chapter 2; and Mahoney, "Friendship and Its Discontents," 55–109.

50. "Since Freud himself was suffering from discharges and bleeding from the nose due to his own operation under Fliess, the identification between doctor and patient is often striking in the letters, as Freud shifts back and forth between describing his own and Eckstein's symptoms and his own anxieties and his anxieties about her" (Toews). See also Madelon Sprengnether, "Freud, Fliess, and Emma Eckstein," where she explores the relationship between Freud and Eckstein in order to interrogate Freud's changing relationship to the mother, from one of identification with the suffering female body, to the fear of castration, and thereby paving the way for his attraction to the Oedipus myth.

51. For the cultural attitudes on male homosexuality, historians distinguish between protestant Wilhelmine Germany and fin-de-siècle Vienna (Fliess lived in Berlin, Freud in Vienna). For the German context, the most thorough work is John Fout's "Sexual Politics in Wilhelmine Germany: The Male Gender Crisis, Moral Purity, and Homophobia," *Journal of the History of Sexuality* 2.3 (January 1992): 388–421. Fout compares the opposition between an emerging gay activism (centered around Magnus Hirschfeld) and the Protestant moral purity organizations. He argues that the virulent homophobia expressed a general concern about eroding gender boundaries, due to the strength of the women's movement; the image of the male homosexual as passive and emotionally and physically weak was constructed out of fear of any concomitant change in male gender roles. For the Viennese context, see Jacques Le Rider, *Modernité viennoise et crises de l'identité* (Paris, 1990). Sander Gilman's work highlights the convergence of discourses on femininity and on judaism (constructing the Jew as "other") in the representation of masculine identity: see "Freud, Race and Gender," *American Imago* 49 (Summer 1992): 155–83, as well as his four books, *The Jew's Body* (New York:

Routledge, 1991); *The Case of Sigmund Freud: Medicine and Identity at the Fin-de-siècle* (Baltimore: Johns Hopkins University Press, 1993); *Freud, Race and Gender* (Princeton: Princeton University Press, 1993); and *Jewish Self-Hatred: Anti-Semitism and the Hidden Language of the Jews* (Baltimore: Johns Hopkins University Press, 1986).

52. Letter of 3.8.95 ("Ich . . . bat also Rosanes, mit mir zusammenzutreffen. Das war mittags. Es blutete mäßig fort aus Nase und Mund, der Foetor war sehr arg. Rosanes reinigte sich die Umgebung der Öffnung, zog Blutgerinnsel heraus, die anhafteten, und plötzlich zog er an etwas wie einem Faden, zog weiter an; ehe einer von uns Zeit zum Überlegen gehabt hatte, war ein gut 1/2 Meter langes Stück Gaze aus der Höhle herausbefördert. Im nächsten Moment folgte ein Blutstrom, die Kranke wurde weiß, mit hervorquellenden Augen und pulslos. Allerdings im nächsten wieder hatte er frische Jodoformgaze hineingestopft, und die Blutung stand. . . . Dazwischen, d.h. darnach eigentlich, geschah noch etwas. In dem Moment, da der Fremdkörper herauskam und mir alles klar wurde und ich gleich darnach den Anblick der Kranken hatte, wurde mir übel; nachdem sie ausgestopft war, flüchtete ich ins Nebenzimmer, trank eine Flasche Wasser aus und kam mir kläglich vor. Die tapfere Doktorin brachte mir dann ein Gläschen Kognak, und ich wurde wieder ich. . . . Sie ist seither außer Gefahr, natürlich sehr bleich und elend mit frischen Schmerzen und Schwellung. Sie hatte während der Verblutungsszene ihre Besinnung nicht verloren; als ich etwas wankend ins Zimmer kam, empfing sie mich mit der überlegenen Bemerkung: Das ist das starke Geschlecht. . . . Ich glaube nicht, daß mich das Blut überwältigt hat; es drängten sich damals bei mir die Affekte. Wir hatten ihr also unrecht getan; sie war gar nicht abnorm gewesen, sondern ein Stück Jodoformgaze war Dir beim Herausziehen abgerissen, 14 Tage lang liegen geblieben und hatte die Heilung verhindert, zum Schluß losgerissen die Blutung provoziert. Daß dieses Malheur Dir geschehen konnte, wie Du darauf reagieren wirst, es zu hören, was die anderen daraus machen können, wie ungerecht ich gehabt, Dich zu einer Operation in der Fremde zu drängen, wo Du nicht nachbehandeln kannst, wie meine Absicht, dem armen Mädchen das Beste anzutun, tückisch vereitelt worden und sich Lebensgefahr für sie daran geknüpft, dies alles kam zusammen über mich. . . . Ich war nicht klar genug, um auch gleich damals einen Vorwurf für Rosanes zu konzipieren. Das fiel mir erst zehn Minuten später ein, daß er sofort hätte denken sollen: Da ist etwas darin ich zieh es nicht heraus, sonst kommt eine Blutung. . . . Jetzt, nachdem ich es verarbeitet, bleibt davon nichts übrig als herzliches Mitleid mit meinem Schmerzenskind. Ich hätte Dich freilich hier nicht quälen sollen, allein ich durfte Dir dergleichen und mehr zutrauen. Du hast es so gut gemacht, als man kann. Das Abreißen der Jodoformgaze bleibt unter den Zufällen, die dem glücklichsten und umsichtigsten Chirugen passieren. . . . Es macht Dir natürlich niemand einen Vorwurf, ich wüßte auch nicht, woher").

53. Freud later arrives at the conclusion that the addictions to alcohol, tobacco, masturbation, etc., are hysterical substitutions (letter of 12.22.97).

54. Sprengnether argues that Freud's identification with Emma Eckstein horrified him because of the gender confusion—his own—that a violation of the nose implies, since it could be either vagina/anus ("Freud, Fliess, and Emma Eckstein," footnotes pp. 29 and 31). She focuses on Freud's distress at finding himself "a woman." I read Freud's distress as localized around the thought of being a man penetrated by another man, which puts him in a feminine position, but is not equivalent to finding himself a woman.

55. Freud's own reproach and guilt toward Fliess has a precedent in Emma's treat-

ment of Freud: as the letter of 1.24.95 makes clear, Emma reproaches herself instead of the doctor (in Freud's draft H included with this letter, the self-reproach of hysteria will be contrasted with paranoia—paranoia is disavowed self-reproach through projection onto external agents). The price of this self-reproach is hysteria, the incompatible idea—a doctor who can't be idealized—"retained in a segregated compartment," as draft H suggests. Freud's repression of the episode is eminently clear in the letters that follow-up this episode over the course of the next year. The reproach of Fliess and of himself disappears ("For me you remain the physician, the type of man into whose hands one confidently puts one's life and that of one's family," one for whom "a reproach is in clear contradiction to [his] feelings," 4.20.95; "Für mich bleibst Du der Arzt, der Typus des Mannes, dem man vertrauensvoll sein Leben und das den Seinigen in die Hände legt;" "Dir etwas vorwerfen . . . wäre dumm, unberechtigt und im hellen Widerspruch mit all meinem Gefühl") and Emma is demonized (she is, according to Freud, "my tormenter and yours," letter of 4.26.95; "mein und Dein Quälgeist"). See also the letters of 4.26.96 and 5.4.96 where the hemorrhaging is considered a symptom of Emma Eckstein's hysteria, a bleeding "out of longing" for the doctor's attention and not the sign of any medical malpractice. Emma, according to Freud, produces her bleeding herself. Freud's intense attachment to Fliess as his physician may well be the source of this projection and provides another identificatory link between Emma Eckstein and Freud: for his helplessness and need to have Fliess by his bedside, see the letters of 8.7.94, 8.29.94, and 4.20.95. Garner argues that Freud's health problems were psychosomatic; she further notes that his fears of death became occasions for his greatest attestations of love for Fliess, especially visible in the letters of 4.25.94 and 8.7.94 ("Homophobia and Seduction," 101 and 98).

56. Freud, *The Interpretation of Dreams*, SE IV:107; "Eine große Halle—viele Gäste, die wir empfangen.—Unter ihnen Irma, die ich sofort beiseite nehme, um gleichsam ihren Brief zu beantworten, ihr Vorwürfe zu machen, daß die die 'Lösung' noch nicht akzeptiert. Ich sage ihr: Wenn du noch Schmerzen hast, so ist es wirklich nur deine Schuld.—Sie antwortet: Wenn du wüßtest, was ich für Schmerzen jetzt habe im Hals, Magen und Leib, es schnürt mich zusammen.—Ich erschrecke und sehe sie an. Sie sieht bleich und gedunsen aus; ich denke, am Ende übersehe ich da doch etwas Organisches. Ich nehme sie zum Fenster und schaue ihr in den Hals. Dabei zeigt sie etwas Sträuben wie die Frauen, die ein künstliches Gebiß tragen. Ich denke mir, sie hat es doch nicht nötig.—Der Mund geht dann auch gut auf, und ich finde rechts einen großen weißen Fleck, und anderwärts sehe ich an merkwürdigen krausen Gebilden, die offenbar den Nasenmuscheln nachgebildet sind, ausgedehnte weißgraue Schorfe.—Ich rufe schnell Dr. M . hinzu, der die Untersuchung wiederholt und bestätigt . . . Dr. M. sieht ganz anders aus als sonst; er ist sehr bleich, hinkt, ist am Kinn bartlos . . . Mein Freund Otto steht jetzt auch neben ihr, und Freund Leopold perkutiert sie über dem Leibchen und sagt: Sie hat eine Dämpfung links unten, weist auch auf eine infiltrierte Hautpartie an der linken Schulter hin (was ich trotz des Kleides wie er spüre) . . . M. sagt: Kein Zweifel, es ist eine Infektion, aber es macht nichts; es wird noch Dysenterie hinzukommen und das Gift sich ausscheiden . . . Wir wissen auch unmittelbar, woher die Infektion rührt. Freund Otto hat ihr unlängst, als sie sich unwohl fühlte, eine Injektion gegeben mit einem Propylpräparat, Propylen . . . Propionsäure . . . Trimethylmin (dessen Formel ich fettgedruckt vor mir sehe) . . . Man macht solche Injektionen nicht so leichtfertig . . . Wahrscheinlich war auch die Spritze nicht rein").

57. Ibid, *SE* IV:115–17; "Am selben Abend, nach welchem ich an der Krankenge-

schichte geschrieben und darauf geträumt hatte, öffnete meine Frau eine Flasche Likör, auf welcher 'Ananas' zu lesen stand und die ein Geschenk unseres Freundes Otto war. . . . Diesem Likör entströmte ein solcher Fuselgeruch, daß ich mich weigerte, davon zu kosten . . . [mich zu] vergiften. . . . Der Fuselgeruch (Amyl . . .) hat nun offenbar bei mir die Erinnerung an . . . Propyl, Methyl usw. geweckt. . . . Ich habe dabei allerdings eine Substitution vorgenommen, Propyl geträumt, nachdem ich Amyl gerochen. . . . Worauf führt mich nun Trimethylamin, auf das ich in solcher Weise aufmerksam gemacht werde? Auf ein Gespräch mit einem anderen Freunde, der seit Jahren um all meine keimenden Arbeiten weiß, wie ich um die seinigen. Er hatte mir damals gewisse Ideen zu einer Sexualchemie mitgeteilt und unter anderem erwähnt, eines der Produkte des Sexualstoffwechsels glaube er im Trimethylamin zu erkennen . . . Trimethylamin ist nicht nur eine Anspielung auf das übermächtige Moment der Sexualität, sondern auf eine Person, an deren Zustimmung ich mich mit Befriedigung erinnere").

58. Freud remembers thinking that "injections of that sort ought not to be made so thoughtlessly [leichtfertig]. . . . how easily [leicht] his thoughts are introduced! How thoughtlessly [leicht] he jumps to conclusions!," connecting injections with the ease of introjected thoughts (*SE* IV:117; "Man macht solche Injektionen nicht so leichtfertig. . . . Wie leicht er sich beeinflüssen läßt; wie leicht er mit seinem Urteil fertig wird").

59. Given the context, it is hard to resist reading into the word, "Ananas," for the stinking liqueur, a pun on anality.

60. *Studies on Hysteria*, *SE* II:48–105.

61. Borrowed from Goethe's *Faust*, the epigraph to Freud's 1901 *The Psychopathology of Everyday Life* also hints at such a ghostly reflection: "Nun ist die Luft von solchem Spuk so voll, / Daß niemand weiß, wie er ihn meiden soll" [Now fills the air so many a haunting shape, That no one knows how best he may escape] (trans. Bayard Taylor, *SE* VI:vii).

62. *SE* II:160 ("es berührt mich selbst noch eigentümlich, daß die Krankengeschichte, die ich schreibe, wie Novellen zu lesen sind"). Dorrit Cohn's essay, "Freud's Case Histories and the Question of Fictionality," in *Telling Facts: History and Narrative in Psychoanalysis* (Baltimore: Johns Hopkins University Press, 1992), 21–47, takes on numerous critics who read Freud's case studies as fiction. She proposes the following position: Freud's case studies are narratives (in the sense of theoretical constructs that feature a kind of emplotment), but they are not fictions. Acknowledging their fiction-likeness, she argues persuasively for their claims to referentiality (their heuristic and theoretical functionality), emphasizes passages where Freud distinguishes his work from creative writers, and positions Freud as narrator in the role of "witness biographer," a biographer who knows the subject but doesn't have the creative writer's direct access to his or her inner life.

63. *SE* II:49. ("Um so befremdender ist es, daß sie alle paar Minuten plötzlich abbricht, das Gesicht zum Ausdrucke des Grausens und Ekels verzieht, die Hand mit gespreizten und gekrümmten Fingern gegen mich ausstreckt und dabei mit veränderten, angsterfüllter Stimme die Worte ruft: 'Seien Sie still—reden Sie nichts—rühren Sie mich nicht an!' Sie steht wahrscheinlich unter dem Eindrucke einer wiederkehrenden grauenvollen Halluzination und wehrt die Einmengung des Fremden mit dieser Formel ab.")

64. Freud, *The Origin and Development of Psychoanalysis*, 15, my italics.

65. The essay where Freud discusses the notion of the counterwill at length is "A Case of Successful Treatment by Hypnotism, with some Remarks on the Origin of Hys-

terical Symptoms through 'Counterwill,'" *SE* I:117–28. The hysteric's dilemma is occasioned by her perception that she is committing a crime against the socius. The crime can take two forms, the first being occasioned by the split between an individual's particular desire and the societal prohibition of that desire (and the illness, by keeping something separate from it). Unable to rid herself of that desire, the hysteric makes herself "sick of" society, as it were. Here is the core of Freud's later contention that culture exacts an enormous price by making us ill. The pressure of consciously resisting or attempting to disavow one's desires in accordance with the norms of society is what causes the illness: i.e., the oppositional desires themselves are not pathological. Hence, Freud at times can construe that hysterics suffer, not from their "demonic" desires, but rather from the devilish torments of social conscience embodied in their own "excess of conscience." Second, in order not to reduce all hysteria to repressed desires and in doing so, negate the reality of the traumas suffered by some patients, hysteria, as an illness, is more than the expression of socially prohibited desires. The other conflict which precipitates hysteria is the pathological inability of society to incorporate the traumatic knowledge that its members suffer or experience into its public consciousness or memory. The split consciousness of the hysteric makes visible the traumatic split in the social psyche between the reality of its members' experiences and society's unwillingness to hear them—and take responsibility for its own contribution to the illness (the hysteric's need to be heard). If we look at the studies on hysteria, virtually all the examples point to an etiology provoked by an incident where something that constitutes private desire/knowledge becomes traumatic by being exhibited as public knowledge/property, without being able to be symbolized as such.

66. Ibid., *SE* I:127. ("Die Frage: Was wird aus den gehemmten Vorsätzen [des Gegenwillens]? scheint für das normale Vorstellungsleben sinnlos zu sein. Man möchte darauf antworten, sie kommen eben nicht zu Stande. Das Studium der Hysterie zeigt, dass sie dennoch zu Stande kommen, d.h. dass die ihnen entsprechenden materielle Veränderung erhalten bleibt, und dass sie aufbewahrt werden, in einem Art von Schattenreich eine ungeahnte Existenz fristen, bis sie als Spuk hervortreten und sich des Körpers bemächtigen, der sonst dem herrschenden Ichbewusstsein gedient hat").

67. Freud's case study of Emmy von N., where he outlines her many resistances to hypnosis (see esp. pp. 77–82), differs considerably from his summary of her case in the essay "Psychotherapy of Hysteria," in which he claims Emmy von N. exhibited no resistance (*SE* II:284).

68. Kiceluk writes: "Freud set forth his new idea of 'defense' hysteria, in which he postulated that the ego inadvertently splits off part of itself in attempting to defend itself. Confronted with an idea so distressing that it must be disowned, the ego tries to get rid of it by pushing it away and 'forgetting' about it. The ego, in short, sets itself the impossible task of treating 'the incompatible idea as *non arrivée*,' a foreign body. Remarkably, we see Freud himself enacting this very process in the case of Emmy von N. His technique of 'wiping out,' of not ascribing reality to the continuing existence of the distressing idea, in effect, replicated the very mechanism of repression that gave rise to Emmy's symptoms in the first place. In hypnosis, the pathological processes of getting rid of and of splitting were reproduced by precisely those 'therapeutic' measures that were meant to undo the original repression. In both cases—in hypnosis and in hysteria—the intolerable idea was treated essentially as *'non arrivée,'*" "The Disenchantment of Freud," 192–93.

69. "Preface to the Translation of Bernheim's *Suggestion*," *SE* I:82 ("die Suggestion

kennzeichnet sich vor anderen Arten der psychischen Beeinflussung, dem Befehl, der Mittheilung oder Belehrung und Anderem dadurch, dass bei ihr in einem zweiten Gehirn eine Vorstellung erweckt wird, welche nicht auf ihre Herkunft geprüft, sondern so angenommen wird, als ob sie in diesem Gehirne spontan entstanden wäre").

70. Christopher Bollas uses this term to describe the unconscious and partially conscious transference relationships between analyst and analysand in *The Shadow of the Object* (New York: Columbia University Press, 1987).

71. For the similarity between the state of consciousness in a hysterical acting out and in hypnoid states, see "The Neuro-Psychoses of Defence," *SE* III:50.

72. The conflict between female patient and male doctor as a conflict over sex and gender roles has been treated extensively in the feminist critical literature on Freud. See especially: Jan Goldstein, *Console and Classify: The French Psychiatric Profession in the Nineteenth Century in France* (Cambridge: Cambridge University Press, 1987); Dianne Hunter, "Hysteria, Psychoanalysis and Feminism: The Case of Anna O," *Feminist Studies* 9 (1983): 465–88; Elizabeth Lunbeck, *The Psychiatric Persuasion: Knowledge, Gender, and Power in Modern America* (Princeton: Princeton University Press, 1994); Elaine Showalter, *The Female Malady: Women, Madness, and English Culture, 1830–1980* (New York: Pantheon, 1985); and Carroll Smith-Rosenberg, "The Hysterical Woman: Sex Roles and Role Conflict in Nineteenth-Century America," in Smith-Rosenberg, *Disorderly Conduct: Visions of Gender in Victorian America* (New York: Knopf, 1985).

73. *SE* II:99 and 82 ("weil *Sie* es verlangen" and "nur weil Sie es sagen").

74. *SE* II:66 ("Sie nimmt diese Lehre nicht viel besser auf als irgendein asketischer Mönch des Mittelalters, der den Finger Gottes und die Versuchung des Teufels in jedem kleinsten Erlebnisse sieht").

75. *SE* II:81 ("sie [sei] in voller Auflehnung begriffen").

76. *SE* II:97. Kiceluk recounts a similar experience outside the therapy proper: "Freud stopped at Emmy's estate in Zurich, and we have some interesting information about this visit. As Ellenberger discovered, Emmy asked all her guests to sign an album; when she had a falling out with one of her visitors, she would paste a little piece of paper over his name. There, on 18 July 1889, is Freud's signature relegated to this ignominious fate. Apparently, Emmy had her own way of wiping out disagreeable things" ("The Disenchantment of Freud," 185). In "Psychical (or Mental) Treatment," one can sense Emmy's presence when Freud applies the adjective "widerspenstig" (the English "recalcitrant" misses the German sense of "actions of a contrary spirit"), to characterize the resistance to hypnosis (*SE* VII:301). Freud aligns this recalcitrance with the patient's neurotic desire to remain sick.

77. Letter of 1.17.97 (my italics); "Was sagst Du übrigens zu der Bemerkung, daß meine ganze neue Hysterie-Urgeschichte bereits bekannt und hundertfach publiziert ist, allerdings vor mehreren Jahrhunderten? Erinnerst Du Dich, daß ich immer gesagt, die Theorie des Mittelalters und der geistlichen Gerichte von der Besessenheit sei identisch mit unserer Fremdkörpertheorie und Spaltung des Bewußtseins? Warum aber hat der Teufel, der die Armen in Besitz genommen, regelmäßig Unzucht mit ihnen getrieben und auf ekelhafte Weise? Warum sind die Geständnisse auf der Folter so ähnlich den Mitteilungen meiner Patienten in der psychischen Behandlung?" For Freud's further development of the pre-history of hysteria, see David Thurn, "Fideikommißbibliothek: Freud's 'Demonological Neurosis,'" *MLN* 108 (1993): 849–74.

78. "Die Eckstein hat eine Szene, wo ihr der Diabolus Nadeln in die Finger sticht. . . . Nun stechen die Inquisitoren wieder mit Nadeln, um die Stigmata Diaboli zu fin-

den. . . . So erinnerten sich dabei nicht nur die Opfer, sondern auch die Henker an ihre erste Jugend." Freud may be remembering Emmy von N.'s protest against him, when she reveals her vivid antipathy to doctors with needles: "I won't be given any antipyrine injections; I would rather have my pains!" she objects (*SE* II:78; "Ich will keine Antipyrininjektion, ich will lieber meine Schmerzen haben").

79. All of this will be addressed much later, with a different vocabulary, in Freud's writings on negative transference.

80. Anna O's hysterical childbirth can be read similarly, after Breuer's discontinuation of therapy, as an act of expulsion or rejection: not the sign of love, but its refusal.

81. "Studies on Hysteria," *SE* II:98.

82. Freud differentiates between secrets and foreign bodies in the "Studies," making clear that the basis of their difference is that foreign bodies are unconsciously held and preserved from public knowledge or view while secrets are consciously withheld. As he says, "From the beginning it seemed to me probable that Fräulein Elisabeth was conscious of the basis of her illness, that what she had in her consciousness was only a secret and not a foreign body," *SE* II:138–39. ("Bei Fräulein Elisabeth war mir von Anfang an wahrscheinlich, daß sie also nur ein Geheimnis, keinen Fremdkörper im Bewußtsein habe").

83. The idea of the "talking cure" is Anna O.'s: see "Studies on Hysteria," *SE* II: 40 and 43; Anna O.'s case study is not considered here because she was Breuer's patient; however, her use of language as a medium and strategy for cooperation and resistance exceeds Emmy von N.'s.

84. *SE* II:63 and 62 ("Nun sagte sie recht mürrisch, ich solle nicht immer fragen, woher das und jenes komme, sondern sie erzählen lassen, was sie mir zu sagen habe. . . . ich [nahm] ihre Erzählung für vollendet und [unterbrach] sie durch meine abschließende Suggestion. . . . Wahrscheinlich wollte sie mir den Vorwurf machen, daß ich sie heute in der Erzählung störe").

85. For the production of false connections, see *SE* II:67–70 (footnote one).

86. "Psychotherapy of Hysteria," *SE* II:287 ("das pathogene psychische Material erscheint als *das Eigentum* einer Intelligenz, die der des normalen Ich nicht notwendig nachsteht. Der Schein einer zweiten Persönlichkeit wird oft auf das täuschendste hergestellt"). Freud shows sympathy for Emmy's resistance (perhaps because when he writes the essay, he is increasingly disenchanted with hypnosis). In "Studies," he criticizes the patient who evinces no resistance to hypnosis and correspondingly suggests a lack of integrity and seriousness on the part of the doctor who tries to cure with what amounts to a sleight of hand: "It would have to be a truly pathological brain from which it was possible to blow away by mere suggestion such well-founded products of intense psychical events" ("Studies," *SE* II:100). ("Es wäre nur ein wahrhaft pathologisches Gehirn, in dem es möglich war, so berechtigte Ergebnisse intensiver psychischer Vorgänge durch die Suggestion wegzublasen").

87. If he avoids the implicit, originary scenario with his symbiotic maternal-infant metaphor, Freud elsewhere concedes that the doctor using hypnosis needs to alleviate the patient's "fear and the embarrassing sensation of being overwhelmed [überwältigt]" ("Hypnosis," *SE* I:105; "[die] Angst des Kranken und [die] ihm peinlichen Empfindung, überwältigt zu werden"). Ferenczi goes so far to compare his actions to a mental rape by the father, metaphorically adding incestuous abuse to the imagination of hypnosis's psychological terrors: "Suggestion reduces people precisely to the level of a helpless child incapable of contradicting or of independent thought, whereby the suggestor

forces himself upon the medium's will with paternal authority" (*Further Contributions*, 56). The outcome of the encounter is not the beloved child who justifies and epitomizes mutual desires, but a forced incorporation of the father-doctor into the child-patient as a foreign presence or body, an unwanted pregnancy. Suggestion is

> the deliberate smuggling of sensations, feelings, thoughts, and decisions of the will into another person's psychic world, and this in such a way that the person influenced cannot of himself modify or correct the suggested thoughts, feelings, and impulses. Put briefly, suggestion is the *forcing* upon, or the unquestioning acceptance of, a *foreign psychic influence*. ("Suggestion and Psychoanalysis," 55)

Like a smuggler crossing into territory that does not belong to him, the doctor plants himself within the patient. The violation is not simply that the doctor's insinuation into the patient's mind is a forcing upon him or her under the misappropriated guise of healing. More disturbingly, as the paradoxical equivalence of "forcing upon" as the "unquestioning acceptance of" suggests, is that the patient, with the doctor's encouragement, agrees to put herself in a state where the act of consent to the trespass is bypassed, as well as any modifications or corrections of the introduced thoughts and impulses.

Ferenczi's early perspectives on the dangers of hypnosis should be contrasted with his subsequent, substantial work with regressed patients; there he seems to foster and encourage precisely the kind of dependence and overwhelming of subject-object boundaries that he rejected with hypnosis. See Michael Balint, *The Basic Fault* (Evanston: Northwestern University Press, 1992), 149–58.

88. The "sexual shock" reference occurs in the letter of 11.2.95; the explanation of "fright hysteria" occurs in Draft K (*The Neuroses of Defense*) that accompanies the letter of 1.1.96. In the letter of 2.8.97, Freud concludes that his father has abused him; in the letter of 9.21.97, Freud abandons the seduction theory. The widespread occurrence of hysteria would be evidence of an equally widespread perversion against children; something Freud decides is impossible. Instead, he construes the traumatic moment as a fantasy construction imposed by the patient upon the past, a fantasy allows for the gratification of repressed desires (Freud's way to have Fliess is to make him into an abusive father, i.e. the punishment goes along with maintaining the source of the gratification). For an in-depth reading of the significance of the seduction theory and its abandonment, see Jeffrey Moussaiff Masson, *The Assault on Truth: Freud's Suppression of the Seduction Theory* (New York: Farrar, Straus, and Giroux, 1984).

89. I am condensing a great deal of theoretical terrain here that Freud covers in the letters from the end of May 1897 to the end of September 1897: see esp. Draft M (*The Architecture of Hysteria* enclosed with letter of 5.25.97) and the letter of 5.31.97 for fantasies and repression as protective structures; for the abandonment of the seduction theory, see the letter of 9.21.97; for the pederastic element, see Draft M.

90. Letter of 1.1.96 (the italics are my addition); "Deine Briefe, so der letzte wieder, enthalten eine Fülle von wissenschaftlichen Einsichten und Ahnungen, zu denen ich leider nichts sagen kann, als daß sie mich packen und überwältigen. Es ist der erfreulichste Gedanke, den ich derzeit fassen kann, daß uns beide die gleiche Arbeit beschäftigt." Cf. with the letter of six months earlier (5.25.95), where Freud uses the word "gap" not so much to signify absence, but as the testimony of Fliess's great hold over his emotions: "Your letter gave me much pleasure and caused me to regret anew what I feel is the great gap in my life—that I cannot reach you in any other way" ("Dein

Brief hat mich herzlich gefreut und mich neuerdings bedauern gemacht, was ich als die große Lücke in meinem Leben empfinde, daß Du für mich nicht anders erreichbar bist").

91. Letter of 7.7.97 (". . . irgend etwas aus den tiefsten Tiefen meiner eigenen Neurose hat sich einem Fortschritt im Verständnis der Neurosen entgegengestellt, und Du warst irgendwie mit hineingezogen. Denn die Schrieblähmung scheint mir bestellt, um unseren Verkehr zu hemmen," my italics).

92. In the letter of 1.11.97, Freud calls such "amentia" or "confusional psychosis" (his twilight states) a "psychosis of being overwhelmed," which he will attribute first to abuse by his father, then to a nurse. Freud makes further references to his hysteria in the letters of 8.31.98 and 12.21.99.

93. Letter of 1.24.97 ("Letzterer knüpft an die charakteristische Unbestimmtheit betreffs der Übeltäter an, die ja durch die Abwehr verhüllt werden"). Freud is talking about paranoics, who defend themselves against self-reproaches by projecting both the aggression and the punishing agent into the external world — hence the characteristic vagueness of the persecuting object, which is really their own conscience. Freud's confusional psychosis cloaks Fliess with such vagueness, identifying him and effacing him at the same time.

94. I would argue that for Freud, the paternal etiology that underlies the seduction theory and the Oedipal theory grows at least in part out of Freud's emerging awareness of his own homoerotic inclinations for Fliess. The "father" increases in importance in response to his growing suppression of those inclinations, which Freud at first casts as those between brothers and friends. Just as the father (sociocultural norms) steps in to punish the son for his desires, Freud the scientist brings on the father to punish the erotic pleasures of identification between brothers/men and then to relegate anal sexuality to a early phase. As the letters to Fliess make clear, it is much easier for Freud to remember or fantasize abuse by the father than to admit to homoerotic feelings between peers (pederasty is not subject to the intense degree of repression that same-generational, same-sex desire is).

95. Letter of 1.11.97.

96. Letter of 1.24.97 ("das Geld, was der Teufel seinen Opfern gibt, [verwandelt] sich regelmäßig in Kot"). Years later, in his essay on anal eroticism, Freud argues that baby, penis, gift, money and feces are "ill-distinguished from one another," and "easily interchangeable": "Faeces, penis, and baby are all three solid bodies; they all three, by *forcible entry or expulsion*, stimulate a membraneous passage, i.e., the rectum and the vagina"; "On Transformation of Instinct as Exemplified in Anal Eroticism," *SE* XVII:128 and 133; "Die Begriffe *Kot* (Geld, Geschenk), *Kind* und *Penis* [werden] schlecht auseinandergehalten und leicht miteinander vertauscht"; "Alle drei, Kotsäule, Penis und Kind, sind feste Körper, welche ein Schleimhautrohr [den Enddarm und die . . . Vagina] . . . bei ihrem Eindringen oder Herausdringen erregen." In the "Non-vixit" dream, Freud establishes the transitive immediacy of his (anal) connection to Fliess through an allusion to the following verse by Heine: "Selten habt ihr mich *verstanden*, / Selten auch verstand ich Euch, / Nur wenn wir im *Kot* uns fanden, / So verstanden wir uns gleich" (Rarely have you *understood* me, / and rarely too have I understood you. / Not until we both found ourselves in the mud [also dung, excrement]/ did we promptly understand each other), *The Interpretation of Dreams, SE* V:513.

97. Letter of 11.14.97; "nach der greulichen Wehen der letzten Wochen [wurde mir] ein neues Stück Erkenntnis geboren"; "Grob gesagt, die Erinnerung stinkt aktuell,

wie in der Gegenwart das Objekt stinkt. . . . [die normale Verdrängung liefert] die Affektgrundlage für eine Menge von intellektuellen Vorgängen der Entwicklung."

98. Letter of 12.22.97; "Ich kann Dir kaum ausführen, was sich mir alles (ein neuer Midas!) in—Dreck auflöst. Es stimmt ganz zur Lehre vom innerlichen Stinken. Vor allem das Geld selbst. Ich glaube, dies geht über das Wort 'schmutzig' für 'geizig.' Ebenso gehen alle Geburtsgeschichten, Fehlgeburt, Periode über das Wort 'Abort' (Abortus) auf den Lokus zurück. Es ist ganz toll. . . ."

99. Freud refers to his *Dreckology* reports in the letters of 12.29.97, 1.4.98, 2.23.98, and for the last time in 3.5.98. He actually uses the Greek, which, as Mahoney points out, Freud frequently does when he is making references to anality/homoeroticism: "There seems to be in general some overdetermination in Freud's recourse to Greek letters. He used them in private correspondence to designate anality" ("Friendship and its Discontents," 63, fn. 34).

100. "Fragment of an Analysis of a Case of Hysteria," *SE* VII:50; ("Wir dürfen doch nicht vergessen, daß uns widrigste dieser Perversionen, die sinnliche Liebe des Mannes für den Mann, bei einem uns so sehr kulturüberlegenen Volke wie den Griechen nicht nur geduldet, sondern selbst mit wichtigen sozialen Funktionen betraut war"). According to Freud, homosexuality was acceptable to the Greeks insofar as it also fulfilled important social functions. It is a perversion today because it represents only the inhibition of development, not any sublimation into "important social functions." According to Fout, homosexual activists in Germany used the cultural superiority of the Greeks to argue that many of culture's most gifted citizens were homosexuals ("Sexual Politics," 396).

101. Letter of 8.7.1901; "Ich teile aber Deine Verachtung der Männerfreundschaft nicht, wahrscheinlich weil ich in hohem Grade Partei bin. Mir hat, wie Du ja weißt, nie das Weib im Leben den Kamaraden, den Freund ersetzt. Wäre Breuers männliche Neigung nicht so verschroben, so zaghaft, so widerspruchsvoll, wie alles Seelische an ihm, es gäbe ein schönes Beispiel, zu welchen Leistungen sich die androphile Strömung beim Manne sublimieren läßt."

102. See Marjorie Garber, *Vice Versa*, 286–87.

103. Letter of 10.3.97; "Dieser Neffe und dieser jüngere Bruder bestimmen nun das Neurotische, aber auch das Intensive an allen meinen Freundschaften."

104. If he is hysterical about left-handedness, it is because the test will reveal "that [he has] been up to something that one can only do with the left hand," i.e., masturbate. Mahoney speculates on another interesting possibility: "In Greek, the name of Oedipus' father, Laius (laios) means *left*, and diverse Greek texts attribute to Laius the introduction of pederasty into Greece; being ascribed left-handedness, Laius was homosexual and effeminate" ("Friendship and Its Discontents," 81, footnote 102).

105. Letters of 12.29.97, 1.4.98, and 12.29.97; "[sein] Femininum"; "Mir kommt vor, ich sträube mich nur gegen die Durchdringung von Bisexualität und Bilateralität, die Du forderst"; "Übrigens ist die daran anschließende Frage die erste seit langer Zeit, in welcher unser beider Ahnungen und Neigungen nicht den gleichen Weg gehen." For Freud's conviction that Fliess is correct, see the letter of 1.22.98. It is unclear to me how to assess Freud's anxieties about bisexuality versus homosexuality. Is it the fluidity of gender and sexuality in bisexuality that is disturbing, or the effeminacy culturally associated with male same-sex desire? To complicate matters, the "between-ness" or destabilization of identity characteristic of hypnotic influence or "permeation" semantically dovetails with words used to designate bisexuality *and* homosexuality. For exam-

ple, Magnus Hirschfeld, drawing on existing studies, refers to homosexuality as "sexualle Zwischenstufen," sexually intermediate types (Fout, "Sexual Politics," 399). Bisexuality (Doppelgeschlechtigkeit) is called in the Freud-Fliess correspondence a "Zwischenreich," (an inbetween realm), a term Freud also used to designate the unconscious (Mahoney, "Friendship and its Discontents," 79). In the letter of 4.16.96, he refers to the realm of sexuality per se as the "inbetween realm."

106. See *The Interpretation of Dreams, SE* V:421.

107. Letter of 10.17.99; "Was meinst Du, wenn sich die Onanie auf Homosexualität reduzieren würde, diese, die Homosexualität, und zwar die männliche (bei beiden Geschlechtern), die primitive Art der Geschlechtssehnsucht wäre? (Das erste Sexualziel, analog dem infantilen, nicht über die Innenwelt hinausgehenden Wunsch)."

108. "Hysteria is alloerotic, since its main path is identification with the loved one [hence bisexuality underlies hysteria because each person can identify with persons of both genders]. Paranoia again dissolves the identification, and dissolves the ego itself into extraneous persons. So I have come to regard paranoia as a forward surge of the autoerotic current" (letter of 12.9.99; "Die Hysterie (und ihre Abart, die Zwangsneurose) ist alloerotisch, ihr Hauptweg ist ja die Identifizierung mit der geliebten Person. Die Paranoia löst die Identifizierung wieder auf . . . und löst das Ich selbst in fremde Personen auf. So bin ich darauf gekommen, die Paranoia als einen Vorstoß der autoerotischen Strömung zu betrachten"). Freud homophobically concludes that the homosexual can only love autoerotically; in loving other men, he really only loves himself.

109. There are a number of examples where an alienation from the "blissful dream" of imagined homoeroticized union gives way to the attempt to establish clear boundaries: "we parcel things out . . . you, the biological; I, the psychological" (6.22.97; "Wir teilen uns . . . Du das Biologische, ich das Psychische"); "your work is strange to me" and "I barely participate in your work and progress" (10.3.97 and 10.15.97; "meine eigene Fremdheit und Urteilsschwäche in Deinen Dingen nicht außer Rechnung lassen"; "An Deinen Arbeiten und Fortschritten habe ich leider so geringen Anteil"). Complaining of a long silence, Freud remarks, "It is my lot to wait, and in resignation I have given up my habit of complaining about the unbridgeable distance" (6.27.99; "Ich bescheide mich zu warten, die sonstige Klage über die unaufhebbare Entfernung habe ich mir resigniert abgewöhnt"). Of his proposal of a congress when that was no longer likely due to the strain in their friendship, Freud writes: "I knew very well that such a reminder was quite out of place at the moment. I was only escaping from the present into the most beautiful of my former fantasies, and I myself noticed which one it was. Meanwhile the congresses themselves have become relics of the past; I myself am doing nothing new and, as you write, have become totally estranged from what you are doing" (2.15.1901; "Ich wußte sehr wohl, daß diese Mahnung gerade jetzt übel angebracht ist. Ich flüchtete mich nur vor der Gegenwart in die schönste der damaligen Phantasien und merkte es selbst, in welche. Unterdes sind die Kongresse selbst Überlebsel geworden; ich mach selbst nichts Neues und bin, wie Du schreibst, dem völlig entfremdet, was Du machst").

110. Letters of 10.23.1900, 3.23.1900, and 5.28.99; "[das] Erstling des Traumbuches"; "das Traumkind"; "so autochthon war noch keine meiner Arbeiten").

111. Letter of 10.4.99; "Ich mußte es noch peinlicher verspüren, da es nicht Gedanken-, sondern Gefühlseigentum war, was sich loslöste."

112. Letters of 3.1.1900, 6.18.1900, and 11.21.1900.

113. See letters of 8.7.1901 and 9.19.1901.

114. Letter of 8.7.1901; "Nun die Hauptsache! Soviel ich erkenne, wird meine näch-ste Arbeit lauten 'Die menschliche Bisexualität,' wird das Problem an den Wurzel fas-sen und das letzte Wort sagen, das mir zu sagen vergönnt sein dürfte. Das letzte und tiefste. . . . ich [muß] eine lange ernsthafte Unterhaltung mit Dir haben. Die Idee selbst ist Deine. . . . Vielleicht muß ich also noch mehr von Dir entlehnen, vielleicht nötigt mich mein Ehrlichkeitsgefühl, Dich zu bitten, die Arbeit mit mir zu zeichnen. . . . Das ist also das nächste Zukunftsprojekt, das uns hoffentlich wieder recht ordentlich auch in wissenschaftlichen Dingen einigen wird."

115. Letter of 4.27.1904. Freud's proud claim to being the originator and teacher of Swoboda occurs in his letter of 4.26.1904.

116. Letter of 7.20.1904; "ein Mißbrauch mit fremdem Gut getrieben wurde." Ma-honey directs attention as well to Fliess's "paranoiac disposition and massive negation," citing his refusal, as late as 1904, to acknowledge that notion of permanent bisexuality was already part of psychoanalytical treatment and the scientific writings of the time ("Friendship and Its Discontents," 86).

117. Freud's letters to Fliess of 7.23.1904 and 7.27.1904 ("ein Einbrecher . . . mit einem gefundenen Schlüssel. . . . der [hat] sich angeblich den Tod aus Furcht vor seiner Verbrechernatur gegeben"; "Im Zusammenwirken mit meinem eigenen Versuch, Dir diese Originalität zu entwenden, verstehe ich dann mein Benehmen gegen Weininger"; "daß ich vergessen [habe] . . . daß ich durch Swoboda . . . Deine Idee ihm ausgeliefert hatte"; "Daß meine Freigebigkeit oder Unvorsichtigkeit mit Deinem Eigentum geschal-tet hat, habe ich mir offenbar damals dunkel zum Vorwurf gemacht wie heute in voller Klarheit"; "ein kleinlicher Anlaß"; "wenn man auf seine Priorität Wert legt"). For the public turn the dispute took in 1906, after the end of the correspondence, see Peter Gay's summary, 155–56.

118. Letter of 7.27.1904; "All mein Lebtag habe ich Anregungen ausgestreut, ohne zu fragen, was aus ihnen wird."

119. My disagreement with the overall thrust of Toews's essay lies with his assertion that Freud somehow masters or successfully overcomes his hysterical-homoerotic at-tachment to Fliess. I will argue that Freud never cured himself; in fact, as he said so often about his own patients, he does not want to be cured.

120. Letters of 11.19.99 and 7.4.1901; "Ein ungeborenes Stück hängt noch an dem bereitsgeborenen"; "wahrscheinlich erst halb geboren."

121. Freud speaks of primal fantasies being deeply buried in the letter of 12.21.99. I am reversing the temporal order: the primacy and depth of burial is a function of the repression they are subjected to in the present: the past is constructed out of the needs/ wishes of the present. Whatever is most unacceptable is projected farthest back, as the most primitive, infantile, the material most inaccessible—and unacceptable—to the ego.

122. "Analysis Terminable and Interminable," SE XXIII:250 and 252 ("ein Stück jenes großen Rätsels der Geschlechtlichkeit").

123. "Beyond the Pleasure Principle," SE XVIII:57 ("Sie leitet nämlich einen Trieb ab von dem Bedürfnis nach Wiederherstellung einer früheren Zustandes"). This phrase is taken in the context of Freud's reference to the myth of bisexuality recounted in Plato's Symposium.

124. Letter of 5.7.1900; "Aber den Verkehr mit dem Freund, den eine besondere— etwa feminine—Seite fordert, ersetzt mir niemand." In 1910, Fliess reappears as a "rev-enant" with Freud's work on Leonardo da Vinci as a homosexual (Jones, Life and Work of Sigmund Freud, 2:73). After a fainting episode in 1912 in a Munich hotel where he had

once visited Fliess, Freud explains to Jones that "some piece of unruly homosexual feeling" is the cause (Jones, 1:317). In two letters to Ferenczi, Freud states clearly— hoping to banish it—that his secret (and the secret that psychoanalysis does not resolve, its "child of sorrow") is homosexuality: "You probably imagine that I have secrets quite other than those I have reserved for myself, or you believe that my secrets are con- nected with a special sorrow, whereas I feel capable of handling everything and am pleased with the greater independence that results from having overcome my homosex- uality"; "That you surmised I had great secrets, and were very curious about them, was plain to see and also easy to recognize as infantile. Just as I told you *everything* on scien- tific matters I concealed very little of a personal nature . . . My dreams at that time were concerned, as I hinted to you, entirely with the Fliess affair" (Jones, *Life and Work*, 2:83–84). That the secret is associated with homosexual "trauma," surfaces in another letter: "You not only noticed, but also understood, that I *no longer* have any need to uncover my personality completely, and you correctly traced this back to the traumatic reason for it. Since Fliess's case, with the overcoming of which you recently saw me occupied, that need has been extinguished. A part of homosexual cathexis has been withdrawn and made use of to enlarge my own ego. I have succeeded where the para- noic fails" (Jones, 2:83–84). Significantly, it is only "a part of homosexual cathexis" that has been withdrawn. Given the notion of "incurability" in "Analysis Terminable and Interminable," it is clear that Freud does not in fact overestimate his mastery.

125. Letter of 7.10.1900; "im dunkelsten Kern die Umrisse von Luzifer-Amor sicht- bar."

Selected Bibliography

Abelove, Henry. "Some Speculations on the History of 'Sexual Intercourse' During the 'Long Eighteenth Century' in England." In *Nationalisms and Sexualities*. Ed. Andrew Parker, 335–42. New York: Routledge, 1992.

Abraham, Nicholas, and Maria Torok. "Introjection-Incorporation: Mourning or Melancholia." In *Psychoanalysis in France*. Ed. Serge Lebovici and Daniel Widlocher, 3–16. New York: International Universities Press, 1980.

— — —. "Notes on the Phantom: A Complement to Freud's Metapsychology." Trans. Nicolas Rand. *Critical Inquiry* 13 (Winter 1987): 287–92.

Abrams, M. H. *The Mirror and the Lamp*. New York: Norton, 1955.

— — —. *Natural Supernaturalism: Tradition and Revolution in Romantic Literature*. New York: Norton, 1971.

Adams, Parveen. "Per Os(cillation)." *Camera Obscura* 17 (1988): 7–29.

Adelman, Howard. "Facing the Preface." *Idealistic Studies* 14 (May 1984): 159–70.

Adorno, Theodor. *Hegel: Three Studies*. Trans. Shierry Weber Nicholsen. Cambridge: MIT Press, 1993.

— — —. *Minima Moralia*. Trans. E. F. N. Jephcott. London: Verso, 1978.

— — —. "Valéry-Proust Museum." *Prisms*. Trans. Samuel and Shierry Weber, 175–85. Cambridge: MIT Press, 1981.

Alliston, April. *Virtue's Faults: Correspondences in Eighteenth-Century British and French Women's Fiction*. Stanford: Stanford University Press, 1996.

Ashton, Rosemary. *The German Idea*. Cambridge: Cambridge University Press, 1980.

Bate, Walter Jackson. *The Burden of the Past and the English Poet*. New York: Norton, 1972.

Benjamin, Walter. *Reflections*. Ed. Peter Demetz. Trans. E. Jephcott. New York: Harcourt Brace Jovanovich, 1979.

Bersani, Leo. *Baudelaire and Freud*. Berkeley: University of California Press, 1977.

— — —. "Is the Rectum a Grave?" In *AIDS: Cultural Analysis/Cultural Activism*. Ed. Douglas Crimp, 197–222. Cambridge: MIT Press, 1988.

Berthold-Bond, Daniel. "Evolution and Nostalgia in Hegel's Theory of Desire." *Clio* 19.4 (1990): 367–88.

Bloom, Harold. *The Anxiety of Influence*. New York: Oxford University Press, 1973.

Bollas, Christopher. *The Shadow of the Object*. New York: Columbia University Press, 1987.

Bourdieu, Pierre. *Language and Symbolic Power*. Ed. John B. Thompson. Trans. Gino Raymond and Matthew Adamson. Cambridge: Harvard University Press, 1991.

Borch-Jacobsen, Mikkel. *The Emotional Tie.* Trans. Douglas Brick and others. Stanford: Stanford University Press, 1992.

———. *The Freudian Subject.* Trans. Catherine Porter. Stanford: Stanford University Press, 1988.

———. *Lacan: The Absolute Master.* Trans. Douglas Brick. Stanford: Stanford University Press, 1991.

Borges, Jorgé Luis, with Margarita Guerrero. *The Book of Imaginary Beings.* Trans. Norman Thomas di Giovanni. New York: Dutton, 1969.

Bostetter, Edward. *The Romantic Ventriloquists.* Seattle: University of Washington Press, 1975.

Botting, Fred. *Gothic.* New York: Routledge, 1996.

Brantley, Richard. *Coordinates of Anglo-American Romanticism.* Gainesville: University of Florida Press, 1993.

Bray, Alan. *Homosexuality in Renaissance England.* London: Gay Men's Press, 1982.

Brisman, Leslie. *Romantic Origins.* Ithaca: Cornell University Press, 1978.

Bromwich, David. "'Keats.'" *Critical Essays on John Keats.* Ed. Hermione de Almeida. Boston: G. K. Hall, 1990. 222–60.

Brooks, Peter. *Reading for the Plot.* New York: Knopf, 1984.

Brown, Marshall. "A Philosophical View of the Gothic Novel." *Studies in Romanticism* 26 (Summer 1987): 275–301.

———. *The Shape of German Romanticism.* Ithaca: Cornell University Press, 1979.

Bruhm, Steven. *Gothic Bodies: The Politics of Pain in Romantic Fiction.* Philadelphia: University of Pennsylvania Press, 1994.

Bullough, Vern, and Bonnie Bullough. *Cross Dressing, Sex, and Gender.* Philadelphia: University of Pennsylvania Press, 1993.

Butler, Judith. *Bodies That Matter: On the Discursive Limits of "Sex."* New York: Routledge, 1993.

———. *Gender Trouble: Feminism and the Subversion of Identity.* New York: Routledge, 1990.

———. "Melancholy Gender/Refused Identifications." *Psychoanalytic Dialogues* 5.1 (1995): 165–80.

———. *Subjects of Desire: Hegelian Reflections in Twentieth-Century France.* New York: Columbia University Press, 1987.

Butler, Marilyn. "The Orientalism of Byron's *The Giaour.*" In *Byron and the Limits of Fiction.* Ed. Bernard Beatty and Vincent Newey, 78–96. Liverpool: Liverpool University Press, 1988.

Byron, George Gordon. *The Complete Poetical Works.* Ed. Jerome McGann. Oxford: Oxford University Press, 1980– .

———. *Byron's Letters and Journals.* Ed. Leslie A. Marchand. London: John Murray, 1973.

Castle, Terry. *The Female Thermometer: Eighteenth-Century Culture and the Invention of the Uncanny.* New York: Oxford University Press, 1995.

———. "Phantasmagoria: Spectral Technology and the Metaphorics of Modern Reverie." *Critical Inquiry* 15.1 (1988): 26–61.

— — —. "The Spectralization of the Other in *The Mysteries of Udolpho.*" In *The New Eighteenth Century*. Ed. Felicity Nussbaum and Laura Brown, 231–53. New York: Methuen, 1987.

Chard, Chloe. Introduction. In *The Romance of the Forest*. By Ann Radcliffe. vii–xxiv. Oxford: Oxford University Press, 1986.

Charles, Robert Alan. "French Mediation and Intermediaries, 1750–1815." In *Anglo-German and American German Crosscurrents*. Ed. Philip Shelley, 1–38. Chapel Hill: University of North Carolina Press, 1957.

Christensen, Jerome. *Coleridge's Blessed Machine of Language*. Ithaca: Cornell University Press, 1981.

— — —. *Lord Byron's Strength: Romantic Writing and Commercial Society*. Baltimore: Johns Hopkins University Press, 1993.

Cohn, Dorrit. *Telling Facts: History and Narrative in Psychoanalysis*. Baltimore: Johns Hopkins University Press, 1992.

Coleridge, Samuel Taylor. *Collected Letters of Samuel Taylor Coleridge*. Ed. Earl Leslie Griggs. Oxford: Clarendon Press, 1956–71.

— — —. *The Collected Works of Samuel Taylor Coleridge*. Princeton: Princeton University Press, 1969– .

— — —. *The Notebooks of Samuel Taylor Coleridge*. Ed. Kathleen Coburn. New York: Pantheon, 1957.

— — —. *Poems*. Ed. John Beer. London: J. M. Dent and Sons, 1991.

Coleridge's Miscellaneous Criticism. Ed. Thomas Middleton Raysor. Cambridge: Harvard University Press, 1936.

Conger, Syndy. *Matthew Lewis, Charles Robert Maturin and the Germans. An Interpretive Study of the Influence of German Literature on Two Gothic Novels*. Salzburg: University of Salzburg, 1977.

Cooper, Andrew. *Doubt and Identity in Romantic Poetry*. New Haven: Yale University Press, 1988.

Craft, Christopher. "'Kiss Me with Those Red Lips': Gender and Inversion in Bram Stoker's *Dracula*." *Representations* 8 (1984): 107–33.

Creech, James. *Closet Writing/Gay Reading: The Case of Melville's* Pierre. Chicago: University of Chicago Press, 1993.

Crompton, Louis. *Byron and Greek Love: Homophobia in Nineteenth-Century England*. Berkeley: University of California Press, 1985.

Crosby, Christina. "Charlotte Brontë's Haunted Text." *Studies in English Literature* 24 (1984): 701–15.

Dean, Carolyn. "Law and Sacrifice: Bataille, Lacan, and the Critique of the Subject." *Representations* 13 (Winter 1986): 42–62.

Dellamora, Richard. *Masculine Desire: The Sexual Politics of Victorian Aesthetics*. Chapel Hill: University of North Carolina Press, 1990.

DeLamotte, Eugenia. *Perils of the Night: A Feminist Study of Nineteenth-Century Gothic*. New York: Oxford University Press, 1990.

De Quincey, Thomas. *Recollections of the Lakes and the Lake Poets*. Ed. David Wright. New York: Penguin, 1970.

Derrida, Jacques. "The Pit and the Pyramid." In *Margins of Philosophy*. Trans. Alan Bass, 69–108. Chicago: University of Chicago Press, 1982.

D'Hondt, Jacques. *Hegel in His Time*. Trans. John Burbidge. Peterborough, Ontario: broadview press, 1988.

Dolar, Mladen. "'I shall be with you on your wedding night': Lacan and the Uncanny." *October* 58 (1991): 5–23.

Dollimore, Jonathan. *Sexual Dissidence: Augustine to Wilde, Freud to Foucault*. Oxford: Clarendon Press, 1991.

Donald, Adrienne. "Coming Out of the Canon: Sadomasochism, Male Homoeroticism, Romanticism." *Yale Journal of Criticism* (1991): 239–52.

Dramin, Edward. "'Amid the Jagged Shadows': *Christabel* and the Gothic Tradition." *The Wordsworth Circle* 13.4 (Autumn 1982): 221–28.

duBois, Page. *Torture and Truth*. New York: Routledge, 1991.

Duncan, Ian. *Modern Romance and the Transformations of the Novel: The Gothic, Scott, Dickens*. New York: Cambridge University Press, 1992.

Durham, Margery. "The Mother Tongue: *Christabel* and the Language of Love." In *The (M)other Tongue: Essays in Feminist Psychoanalytic Interpretation*. Ed. Shirley Nelson Garner, Claire Kahane, and Madelon Sprengnether, 169–93. Ithaca: Cornell University Press, 1985.

Dyer, Gary. "Thieves, Boxers, Sodomites, Poets: Being Flash to Byron's *Don Juan*." *PMLA* 116.3 (2001): 562–78.

Edelman, Lee. *Homographesis: Essays in Gay Literary and Cultural Theory*. New York: Routledge, 1994.

Eilenberg, Susan. "'Michael,' 'Christabel,' and the Poetry of Possession." *Criticism* 30.2 (Spring 1988): 205–24.

Eimer, Manfred. "Einflüsse deutschen Räuber- und Schauerromantik auf Shelley, Byron." *Englische Studien* 48 (1915): 231–45.

Elfenbein, Andrew. *Byron and the Victorians*. New York: Cambridge University Press, 1995.

– – –. *Romantic Genius: The Prehistory of a Homosexual Role*. New York: Columbia University Press, 1999.

Ellenberger, Henri. "La conference de Freud sur l'hysterie masculine (15 octobre 1886): Étude critique." In *L'information psychiatrique* 44.10 (1968): 921–34.

Ellis, Kate. *The Contested Castle: Gothic Novels and the Subversion of Domestic Ideology*. Urbana: University of Illinois Press, 1989.

Engell, James. *The Creative Imagination*. Cambridge: Harvard University Press, 1981.

– – –. Introduction. *Biographia Literaria. The Collected Works of Samuel Taylor Coleridge*. Vol. 7, no. 1. Princeton: Princeton University Press, 1983.

Engendering Men: the Question of Male Feminist Criticism. Ed. Joseph A. Boone and Michael Cadden. New York: Routledge, 1991.

Ferenczi, Sandor. *Further Contributions to the Theory and Technique of Psychoanalysis*. Ed. John Rickman. Trans. Jane Suttie and others. New York: Basic Books, 1952.

Fletcher, Anthony. *Gender, Sex, and Subordination in England, 1500–1800*. New Haven: Yale University Press, 1995.

Fliess, Wilhelm. *Die Beziehungen zwischen Nase und weiblichen Geschlechtsorganen.* Leipzig and Vienna: Franz Deuticke, 1897.

———. "Die nasale Reflexneurose." In *Verhandlungen des Kongresses für innere Medizin,* 384–94. Wiesbaden: J. F. Bergmann, 1893.

Fogle, Richard Harter. *The Idea of Coleridge's Criticism.* Berkeley: University of California Press, 1962.

Fout, John. "Sexual Politics in Wilhelmine Germany: The Male Gender Crisis, Moral Purity, and Homophobia." *Journal of the History of Sexuality* 2.3 (January 1992): 388–421.

Franklin, Carolyn. *Byron's Heroines.* Oxford: Clarendon Press, 1992.

Freud, Sigmund. "Analysis Terminable and Interminable." *The Standard Edition of the Complete Psychological Works of Sigmund Freud.* Ed. and trans. by James Strachey, 216–53. Vol. XXIII. London: Hogarth Press, 1953–66.

———. "An Autobiographical Study." *SE* XX:7–74.

———. *Beyond the Pleasure Principle. SE* XVIII:7–64.

———. "A Case of Successful Treatment by Hypnotism, with some Remarks on the Origin of Hysterical Symptoms through 'Counterwill'." *SE* I:117–28.

———. " 'A Child is Being Beaten': A Contribution to the Study of the Origin of Sexual Perversions." *SE* XVII:179–204.

———. *Complete Letters of Sigmund Freud to Wilhelm Fliess, 1887–1904.* Ed. and trans. Jeffrey Moussaieff Masson. Cambridge: Harvard University Press, 1985.

———. "The Disposition to Obsessional Neurosis." *SE* XII:317–26.

———. "Fragment of an Analysis of a Case of Hysteria." *SE* VII:7–122.

———. *Group Psychology and the Ego. SE* XVIII:69–143.

———. "Hypnose." *Ausgewählte Texte.* Ed. Ingrid Kästner and Christina Schröder, 159–67. Berlin: Uberreuter, 1990.

———. "Hypnosis." *SE* I:105–14.

———. *The Interpretation of Dreams. SE* IV:1–338 and *SE* V:339–627.

———. *Letters of Sigmund Freud.* Ed. Ernst L. Freud. Trans. Tania and James Stern. New York: Basic Books, 1960.

———. "Negation." *SE* XIX:235–39.

———. "The Neuropsychoses of Defense." *SE* III:45–61.

———. "On Transformation of Instinct as Exemplified in Anal Eroticism." *SE* XVII:127–33.

———. *Origin and Development of Psychoanalysis.* Chicago: Gateway Editions, 1955.

———. "Preface to the Translation of Bernheim's *Suggestion*." *SE* I:75–87.

———. "Psychical (or Mental) Treatment." *SE* VII:283–302.

———. *The Psychopathology of Everyday Life. SE* VI:1–279.

———. "The Psychotherapy of Hysteria." *SE* II:253–305.

———. "Review of August Forel's *Hypnotism*." *SE* I:91–102.

———. *Studienausgabe.* 11 vols. Frankfurt: Fischer, 1969–75.

———. *Studies on Hysteria. SE* II:1–305.

———. *Three Essays on Sexuality. SE* VII:130–243.

———. "The Uncanny." *SE* XVII:219–52.

Fruman, Norman. *Coleridge, the Damaged Archangel*. New York: Braziller, 1971.

Fürst, Lilian. *The Contours of European Romanticism*. Lincoln: University of Nebraska Press, 1979.

———. "Mme de Staël's *De L'Allemagne*: A Misleading Intermediary." *Orbis Litterarum* 31 (1976): 43–58.

Gamer, Michael. "'The Most Interesting Language in the English Language': An Unidentified Addendum to Coleridge's Review of *Udolpho*." *The Wordsworth Circle* 24.1 (Winter 1993): 53–54.

———. *Romanticism and the Gothic: Genre, Reception, and Canon Formation*. New York: Cambridge University Press, 2000.

Garber, Marjorie. *Vice Versa: Bisexuality and the Eroticism of Everyday Life*. New York: Simon & Schuster, 1995.

Garner, Shirley Nelson. "Freud and Fliess: Homophobia and Seduction." In *Seduction and Theory: Readings of Gender, Representation, and Rhetoric*. Ed. Dianne Hunter, 86–109. Urbana: University of Illinois Press, 1989.

Gay, Peter. *Freud: A Life for Our Time*. New York: Doubleday, 1989.

German Literature in British Magazines, 1750–1860. Madison: University of Wisconsin Press, 1949.

Gilbert, Sandra, and Susan Gubar. *The Madwoman in the Attic: The Woman Writer and the Nineteenth-Century Imagination*. New Haven: Yale University Press, 1979.

Gilman, Sander. *The Case of Sigmund Freud: Medicine and Identity at the Fin-de-siècle*. Baltimore: Johns Hopkins University Press, 1993.

———. *Freud, Race and Gender*. Princeton: Princeton University Press, 1993.

———. *Jewish Self-Hatred: Anti-Semitism and the Hidden Language of Jews*. Baltimore: Johns Hopkins University Press, 1986.

———. *The Jew's Body*. New York: Routledge, 1991.

Gittings, Robert. *John Keats*. London: Heinemann, 1968.

———. *The Mask of Keats*. London: Heinemann, 1956.

Giuliano, Cheryl. "Gulnare's/Kaled's 'Untold' Feminization of Byron's Oriental Tales." *SEL* 33 (1993): 785–807.

Gleckner, Robert. *Byron and the Ruins of Paradise*. Baltimore: Johns Hopkins University Press, 1967.

Goldstein, Jan. *Console and Classify: The French Psychiatric Profession in the Nineteenth Century in France*. Cambridge: Cambridge University Press, 1987.

———. "The Uses of Male Hysteria: Medical and Literary Discourse in Nineteenth-Century France." *Representations* 34 (Spring 1991): 134–65.

Guthke, Karl. *Englische Vorromantik und deutscher Sturm und Drang: M. G. Lewis' Stellung in der Geschichte der deutsch-englischen Literaturbeziehungen*. Göttingen: Vandenhoeck & Ruprecht, 1958.

Hadley, Michael. *The Undiscovered Genre: A Search for the German Gothic Novel*. Bern, Switzerland: Peter Lang, 1978.

Haggerty, George. "Literature and Homosexuality in the Late Eighteenth Century:

Walpole, Beckford, Lewis." In *Homosexual Themes in Literary Studies*. Ed. Wayne Dynes and Stephen Donaldson, 167–79. New York: Garland Press, 1992.

— — —. *Men in Love. Masculinity and Sexuality in the Eighteenth Century*. New York: Columbia University Press, 1999.

Hall, Jean. "The Evolution of the Surface Self: Byron's Poetic Career." *Keats-Shelley Journal* 36 (1987): 134–57.

Harrold, C. F. *Carlyle and German Thought*. New Haven: Yale University Press, 1934.

Hartman, Geoffrey. *The Fate of Reading and Other Essays*. Chicago: University of Chicago Press, 1975.

Hazlitt, William. *Miscellaneous Works of William Hazlitt*. New York: Derby and Jackson, 1859.

— — —. "On Effeminacy of Character." *Table-Talk*, 332–41. London: Oxford University Press, 1901.

Hegel, Georg Wilhelm Friedrich. *The Letters*. Trans. Clark Butler and Christiane Seiler. Bloomington: Indiana University Press, 1984.

— — —. *Phänomenologie des Geistes*. Frankfurt am Main: Suhrkamp, 1970.

Hendershot, Cyndy. *The Animal Within: Masculinity and the Gothic*. Ann Arbor: University of Michigan Press, 1998.

Hertz, Neil. "Dora's Secrets, Freud's Techniques." *Diacritics* 13.1 (Spring 1983): 65–76.

— — —. "Freud and the Sandman." In *Textual Strategies*. Ed. Josue Harari, 296–321. Ithaca: Cornell University Press, 1979.

Hesiod. *Theogony*. Trans. Richard S. Caldwell. Newburyport: Focus Classical Library, 1987.

Hickey, Allison. " 'Coleridge, Southey, and Co.': Collaboration and Authority." *Studies in Romanticism* 37.3 (Fall 1998): 305–39.

Hilliard, David. "Unenglish and Unmanly: Anglo-Catholicism and Homosexuality." *Victorian Studies* 25.2 (Winter 1982): 181–210.

Hippolyte, Jean. *Genesis and Structure of Hegel's* Phenomenology of Spirit. Trans. Samuel Cherniak and John Heckman. Evanston: Northwestern University Press, 1974.

Hitchcock, Tim, and Michele Cohen. "Introduction." In *English Masculinities, 1660–1800*. Ed. Tim Hitchcock and Michele Cohen, 1–22. New York: Longman, 1999.

Hobhouse, John Cam. *Travels in Albania and Other Provinces of Turkey in 1809 and 1810*. 2 vols. London: John Murray, 1855.

Hoeveler, Diane Long. *Romantic Androgyny: The Woman Within*. University Park: Pennsylvania State University Press, 1990.

Hogle, Jerrold. "The Ghost of the Counterfeit in the Genesis of the Gothic." In *Gothick Origins and Innovations*. Ed. Allan Lloyd Smith and Victor Sage, Amsterdam: Rodolpi, 1994.

— — —. "Introduction: Gothic Studies Past, Present, and Future." *Gothic Studies* 1.1 (August 1999): 1–9.

Homans, Margaret. "Keats Reading Women, Women Reading Keats." *Studies in Romanticism* 29 (Fall 1990): 341–70.

Howells, Coral Ann. *Love, Mystery, and Misery: Feeling in Gothic Fiction*. London: University of London, Athlone Press, 1978.

Hull, Gloria T. "The Byronic Heroine and Byron's *The Corsair*." *Ariel* 9 (1978): 71–83.

Hume, David. *Treatise of Human Nature*. Ed. L. A. Selby-Bigge. Oxford: Clarendon Press, 1973.

Hunter, Dianne. "Hysteria, Psychoanalysis and Feminism: The Case of Anna O." *Feminist Studies* 9 (1983): 465–88.

The Hysterical Male: New Feminist Theory. Ed. Arthur and Marielouise Kroker. New York: St. Martin's Press, 1991.

Jaeck, Emma. *Madame de Staël and the Spread of German Literature*. London: Oxford University Press, 1915.

Jameson, Frederic. "The Imaginary and the Symbolic." *Yale French Studies* 55/56 (1977): 338–95.

Jones, Ernest. *The Life and Work of Sigmund Freud*. 3 vols. New York: Basic Books, 1953–57.

Kahane, Claire. "The Gothic Mirror." In *The (M)other Tongue*. Ed. Shirley Nelson Garner, Claire Kahane, and Madelon Sprengnether, 334–51. Ithaca: Cornell University Press, 1985.

Kant, Immanuel. *Träume eines Geistersehers, Erläutert durch Träume der Metaphysik*. In *Vorkritische Schriften bis 1768*, 923–93. Darmstadt: Wissenschaftliche Buchgesellschaft, 1983.

Keats, John. *Complete Poems*. Ed. Jack Stillinger. Cambridge: Harvard University Press, 1982.

———. *The Letters of John Keats*. Ed. Hyder Edward Rollins. Cambridge: Harvard University Press, 1958.

Kernberger, Katherine. "Power and Sex: The Implication of Role Reversal in Catherine's Russia." *Byron Journal* 8 (1980): 42–49.

Kiceluk, Stephanie. "The Disenchantment of Freud: Erasure and the Problem of Narrative Construction in the Case of Emmy von N." In *Proof and Persuasion*. Ed. Suzanne Marchand and Elizabeth Lunbeck, 173–95. Turnhout, Belgium: Brepols, 1997.

Kilgour, Maggie. *The Rise of the Gothic Novel*. New York: Routledge, 1995.

Klapper, Roxana. *German Literary Influence on Byron*. Salzburg: University of Salzburg, 1974.

Koch, John. "Sir Walter Scotts Beziehungen zu Deutschland." *Germanisch-romanische Monatsschrift* 15 (1927): 36–46.

Koestenbaum, Wayne. *Double Talk: The Erotics of Male Literary Collaboration*. London: Routledge, 1989.

———. "Privileging the Anus: Anna O. and the Collaborative Origin of Psychoanalysis." *Genders* 3 (Fall 1988): 57–81.

Kojève, Alexandre. "In Place of an Introduction." *Introduction to the Reading of Hegel*. Ed. Allan Bloom. Trans. James Nichols, Jr. New York: Basic Books, 1969.

Kristeva, Julia. *The Powers of Horror*. Ed. Leon Roudiez. New York: Columbia University Press, 1982.

Lacoue-Labarthe, Philippe. *L'Absolu littéraire: Théorie de la littérature du romantisme allemand*. Paris: Seuil, 1978.

———. *Typography: Mimesis, Philosophy, Politics*. Ed. Christopher Fynsk. Cambridge: Harvard University Press, 1989.

Lang, Cecil. "Narcissus Jilted: Byron, *Don Juan*, and the Biographical Imperative." In *Historical Studies and Literary Criticism*. Ed. Jerome McGann, 143–79. Madison: University of Wisconsin Press, 1985.

Laqueur, Thomas. "Orgasm, Generation, and the Politics of Reproductive Biology." In *The Making of the Modern Body*. Ed. Catherine Gallagher and Thomas Laqueur, 1–41. Berkeley: University of California Press, 1987.

Leary, David. "German Idealism and the Development of Psychology in the Nineteenth Century." *Journal of the History of Philosophy* 18 (July 1980): 299–317.

LeRider, Jacques. *Modernité viennoise et crises de l'identité*. Paris: 1990.

Levinson, Marjorie. *The Romantic Fragment Poem: A Critique of Form*. Chapel Hill: University of North Carolina Press, 1986.

Lewis, Matthew. *The Monk*. Oxford: Oxford University Press, 1980.

Leys, Ruth. "The Real Ms. Beauchamp: Gender and the Subject of Imitation." In *Feminists Theorize the Political*. Ed. Judith Butler and Joan Scott, 167–214. New York: Routledge, 1992.

Lunbeck, Elizabeth. *The Psychiatric Persuasion: Knowledge, Gender, and Power in Modern America*. Princeton: Princeton University Press, 1994.

MacPherson, C. B. *The Political Theory of Possessive Individualism: Hobbes to Locke*. Oxford: Clarendon Press, 1964.

Maertz, Gregory. "To Criticize the Critic: George Saintsbury on Goethe." *Papers on Language and Literature* 30.2 (Spring 1994): 115–31.

Mahoney, Patrick. "Friendship and Its Discontents." *Contemporary Psychoanalysis* XV (1979): 55–109.

Marchand, Leslie. *Byron: A Biography*. 3 vols. New York: Knopf, 1957.

Marcuse, Herbert. "A Note on the Dialectic." In *The Essential Frankfurt School Reader*. Ed. Andrew Arato and Eike Gebhardt, 444–51. New York: Continuum, 1988.

Martin, Robert K. "Knights-Errant and Gothic Seducers: The Representation of Male Friendship in Mid-Nineteenth-Century America." In *Hidden from History: Reclaiming the Gay and Lesbian Past*. Ed. Martin Duberman, Martha Vicinus, and George Chauncey, Jr., 169–82. New York: New American Library, 1989.

Massé, Michelle. *In the Name of Love: Women, Masochism and the Gothic*. Ithaca: Cornell University Press, 1992.

Masson, Jeffrey Moussaiff. *The Assault on Truth: Freud's Suppression of the Seduction Theory*. New York: Farrar, Straus, and Giroux, 1984.

Matlak, Richard. "*Licentia Biographica*: or, Biographical Sketches of Coleridge's Literary Life and Plagiarisms." *European Romantic Review* 4.1 (Summer 1993): 57–70.

Maturin, Charles. *Melmoth the Wanderer*. Oxford: Oxford University Press, 1989.

McFarland, Thomas. *Romanticism and the Forms of Ruin: Wordsworth, Coleridge, and Modalities of Fragmentation*. Princeton: Princeton University Press, 1981.

McGann, Jerome. "Byron, Mobility and the Poetics of Historical Ventriloquism." *Romanticism, Past and Present* 9.1 (1985): 67–82.

———. *Fiery Dust*. Chicago: University of Chicago Press, 1968.

Meer, Theo van der. "Sodomy and the Pursuit of a Third Sex in the Early Modern

Period." In *Third Sex Third Gender: Beyond Sexual Dimorphism in Culture and History.* Ed. Gilbert Herdt, 137–212. New York: Zone Books, 1994.

Mellor, Anne. *Romanticism and Gender.* New York: Routledge, 1993.

Meyer, Eric. "'I Know Thee Not, I Loathe Thy Race': Romantic Orientalism in the Eye of the Other." *ELH* 58 (1991): 657–99.

Micale, Mark. *Approaching Hysteria: Disease and its Interpretations.* Princeton: Princeton University Press, 1995.

———. "Hysteria Male/Hysteria Female: Reflections of Comparative Gender Constructions in Nineteenth-Century France and Britain." In *Science and Sensibility: Gender and Scientific Inquiry, 1780–1945.* Ed. Marina Benjamin, 200–39. Cambridge: Blackwell, 1991.

Miles, Robert. *Gothic Writing 1750–1820.* New York: Routledge, 1993.

Miller, D. A. "Secret Subjects, Open Secrets." *The Dickens Studies Annual* 14 (New York: AMS Press, 1985): 17–38.

Moers, Ellen. *Literary Women.* Garden City, N.Y.: Doubleday, 1977.

Moore, Dorothy Langley. *Lord Byron: Accounts Rendered.* New York: Harper, 1974.

Moretti, Franco. *Signs Taken for Wonders. Essays in the Sociology of Literary Forms.* Trans. Susan Fischer, David Forgacs, and David Miller. London: Verso, 1983.

Morrison, Paul. "End Pleasure." *GLQ* 1 (1993): 53–78.

Nietzsche, Friedrich. *Nachgelassene Fragmente. Werke.* Ed. Giorgio Colli and Mazzino Montinari. Vol. 8, Part 2. Berlin: Walter de Gruyter, 1970.

Nunokawa, Jeff. "Homosexual Desire and the Effacement of Self in *The Picture of Dorian Gray.*" *American Imago* 49.3 (1992): 31–38.

Nussbaum, Felicity. "Heteroclites: The Gender of Character in the Scandalous Memoirs." In *The New Eighteenth Century.* Ed. Felicity Nussbaum and Laura Brown, 144–67. New York: Routledge, 1987.

Ochojski, P. M. "S. W. Scott's Continuous Interest in Germany." *Studies in Scottish Literature* 3 (1966): 164–73.

Oppenheim, Janet. *Shattered Nerves: Doctors, Patients, and Depression in Victorian England.* New York: Oxford University Press, 1991.

Parker, Reeve. "'O Could You Hear His Voice!': Wordsworth, Coleridge, and Ventriloquism." In *Romanticism and Language.* Ed. Arden Reed, 125–43. Ithaca: Cornell University Press, 1984.

Paulson, Ronald. "Gothic Fiction and the French Revolution." *ELH* 48 (1981): 532–54.

Peel, Ellen. "Psychoanalysis and the Uncanny." *Comparative Literature Studies* 17.4 (December 1980): 410–17.

Peters, Edward. *Torture.* Oxford: Oxford University Press, 1985.

Phillips, Adam. *On Kissing, Tickling, and Being Bored.* Cambridge: Harvard University Press, 1993.

———. *Terrors and Experts.* Cambridge: Harvard University Press, 1996.

Plasa, Carl. "Revision and Repression in Keats's *Hyperion*: 'Pure Creations of the Poet's Brain.'" *Keats-Shelley Journal* 44 (1995): 117–46.

Pocock, J.G.A. *Virtue, Commerce, and History: Essays on Political Thought and History, Chiefly in the Eighteenth Century.* New York: Cambridge University Press, 1985.

Poovey, Mary. "Ideology and *The Mysteries of Udolpho.*" *Criticism* 21 (1979): 307–30.

Potkay, Adam. "Beckford's Heaven of Boys." *Raritan* 13.1 (Summer 1993): 73–86.

Punter, David. *Gothic Pathologies: The Text, the Body, and the Law.* New York: St. Martin's Press, 1998.

———. *The Literature of Terror: A History of Gothic Fictions from 1765 to the Present Day.* 2nd edition. 2 vols. New York: Longman, 1996.

"Quellentexte." *Luzifer-Amor* 1.1 (1988): 156–75.

Rajan, Tillotama. "Coleridge, Wordsworth, and the Textual Abject." *The Wordsworth Circle* 24.2 (Spring 1993): 61–68.

Railo, Eino. *The Haunted Castle: A Study of the Elements of English Romanticism.* New York: Dutton & Co., 1927.

Rand, Richard. "Geraldine." *Glyph* 5 (1978): 74–97.

Rashkin, Esther. *Family Secrets and the Psychoanalysis of Narrative.* Princeton: Princeton University Press, 1992.

Restuccia, Frances. "Female Gothic Writing: 'Under Cover to Alice.'" *Genre* 19.3 (Fall 1986): 245–66.

Richardson, Alan. "Escape from the Seraglio: Cultural Transvestism in *Don Juan.*" In *Rereading Byron.* Ed. Alice Levine and Robert N. Keane, 175–85. New York: Garland Press, 1993.

Roe, Nicholas. "Keats's Lisping Sedition." *Essays in Criticism* 42.1 (January 1992): 36–55.

Romanticism and Consciousness. Ed. Harold Bloom. New York: Norton, 1970.

Romanticism and Feminism. Ed. Anne Mellor. Bloomington: Indiana University Press, 1988.

The Romantics Reviewed. Ed. Donald Reiman. New York: Garland, 1972.

Rosenkranz, Karl. *Georg Wilhelm Friedrich Hegel's Leben.* Berlin: Dunker und Humblot, 1844.

Ross, Marlon. "Beyond the Fragmented Word: Keats at the Limits of Patrilineal Language." In *Out of Bounds: Male Writers and Gender[ed] Criticism.* Ed. Laura Claridge and Elizabeth Langland, 110–31. Amherst: University of Massachusetts Press, 1990.

———. *The Contours of Masculine Desire: Romanticism and the Rise of Women's Poetry.* Oxford: Oxford University Press, 1989.

Rousseau, G. S. "The Pursuit of Homosexuality in the Eighteenth Century: 'Utterly Confused Category' and/or Rich Repository?" In *'Tis Nature's Fault: Unauthorized Sexuality during the Enlightenment.* Ed. Robert Purks Maccubbin, 132–68. New York: Cambridge University Press, 1987.

Roustang, Francois. *Psychoanalysis never lets go.* Baltimore: Johns Hopkins University Press, 1983.

Rzepka, Charles L. "*Christabel*'s 'Wandering Mother' and the Discourse of the Self: A Lacanian Reading of Repressed Narration." *Romanticism Past and Present* 10.1 (1986): 17–43.

Savigny, Karl Friedrich von. *Das Recht des Besitzes. Eine civilistische Abhandlung.* Vienna: Carl Gerold, 1865.

———. *Von Savigny's Treatise on Possession; or the Jus Possessionis of the Civil Law.* Trans. Sir Erskine Perry. London: Sweet, 1848.

Scarry, Elaine. *The Body in Pain: The Making and Unmaking of the World*. New York: Oxford University Press, 1985.

Schama, Simon. *The Embarrassment of Riches*. New York: Knopf, 1987.

Schiller, Friedrich. *Gedichte*. Ed. Gerhard Fricke. Stuttgart: Reclam, 1978.

———. *Schillers Werke*. Ed. Hans Heinrich Borchert. Weimar: Hermann Böhlaus Nachfolger, 1954.

Schur, Max. "Some Additional 'Day Residues' of 'The Specimen Dream of Psychoanalysis.'" In *Psychoanalysis—A General Psychology: Essays in Honor of Heinz Hartmann*. Ed. Rudolph M. Loewenstein et al., 45–85. New York: International Universities Press, 1960.

Secret Sexualities. A Sourcebook of 17th- and 18th-Century Writing. Ed. Ian McCormick. New York: Routledge, 1997.

Sedgwick, Eve. *Between Men: English Literature and Male Homosocial Desire*. New York: Columbia University Press, 1985.

———. "The Character in the Veil: Imagery of the Surface in the Gothic Novel." *PMLA* 96.2 (March 1981): 255–70.

———. *The Coherence of Gothic Conventions*. New York: Methuen, 1986.

———. *The Epistemology of the Closet*. Berkeley: University of California Press, 1990.

———. "A Poem is Being Written." *Representations* 17 (Winter 1987): 110–43.

Seed, David. "'Disjointed Fragments': Concealment and Revelation in *The Giaour*." *The Byron Journal* 18 (1991): 14–27.

Shapiro, Barbara. "'Christabel': The Problem of Ambivalent Love." *Literature and Psychology* 30.3–4 (1980): 119–32.

Showalter, Elaine. *The Female Malady: Women, Madness, and English Culture, 1830–1980*. New York: Pantheon, 1985.

———. *Sexual Anarchy: Gender and Culture at the Fin-de-siècle*. New York: Viking, 1990.

Silverman, Kaja. *Male Subjectivity at the Margins*. New York: Routledge, 1992.

Simpson, David. *Romanticism, Nationalism, and the Revolt against Theory*. Chicago: University of Chicago Press, 1993.

Smith-Rosenberg, Carroll. *Disorderly Conduct: Visions of Gender in Victorian America*. New York: Knopf, 1985.

Sprengnether, Madelon. "Enforcing Oedipus: Freud and Dora." In *In Dora's Case*. Ed. Charles Bernheimer and Claire Kahane, 254–75. New York: Columbia University Press, 1985.

———. *The Spectral Mother*. Ithaca: Cornell University Press, 1990.

Stockley, V. *German Literature as Known in England, 1750–1830*. London: Routledge, 1929.

Stokoe, F. W. "The Appreciation of German Literature in England before 1820." *Publications of the English Goethe Society* NS, 3 (1926): 122–42.

———. *German Influence in the English Romantic Period, 1788–1818, with Special Reference to Scott, Coleridge, Shelley, and Byron*. Cambridge: Cambridge University Press, 1926.

Stone, Lawrence. *The Family, Sex, and Marriage in England, 1500–1800*. New York: Penguin, 1978.

Sulloway, Frank J. *Freud: Biologist of the Mind: Beyond the Psychoanalytic Legend*. New York: Basic Books, 1983.

Swann, Karen. "'Christabel': The Wandering Mother and the Enigma of Form." *Studies in Romanticism* 23 (Winter 1984): 533–53.

———. "Harassing the Muse." *Romanticism and Feminism*. Ed. Anne Mellor, 81–92. Bloomington: Indiana University Press, 1988.

———. "Literary Gentlemen and Lovely Ladies: The Debate on the Character of *Christabel*." *ELH* 52 (Spring 1985): 397–418.

Tatar, Maria M. "The Houses of Fiction: Toward a Definition of the Uncanny." *Comparative Literature* 33.2 (Spring 1981): 167–82.

Taussig, Michael. *Mimesis and Alterity: A Particular History of the Senses*. New York: Routledge, 1993.

Thorslev, Peter. *The Byronic Hero: Types and Prototypes*. Minneapolis: University of Minnesota Press, 1962.

Thurn, David. "Fideikomißbibliothek: Freud's 'Demonological Neurosis.'" *MLN* 108 (1993): 849–74.

Toews, John. "Fashioning the Self in the Story of the 'Other': The Transformation of Freud's Masculine Identity between 'Studies on Hysteria' and 'Dora.'" In *Proof and Persuasion*. Ed. Suzanne Marchand and Elizabeth Lunbeck, 196–218. Turnhout, Belgium: Brepols, 1997.

Tooke, Andrew. *The Pantheon*. London: Bathurst, 1784.

Tosh, John. "The Old Adam and the New Man: Emerging Themes in the History of English Masculinities, 1750–1850." In *English Masculinities, 1660–1800*. Ed. Tim Hitchcock and Michele Cohen, 217–38. New York: Longman, 1999.

Trumbach, Randolph. "The Birth of the Queen: Sodomy and the Emergence of Gender Equality in Modern Culture, 1660–1750." In *Hidden from History: Reclaiming the Gay and Lesbian Past*. Ed. Martin Duberman, Martha Vicinus, and George Chauncey, Jr., 129–40. New York: New American Library, 1989.

———. "Gender and the Homosexual Role in Modern Western Culture: The Eighteenth and Nineteenth Centuries Compared." In *Homosexuality, Which Homosexuality*. Ed. Dennis Altman et al., 149–70. London: GMP, 1989.

———. "London's Sapphists: From Three Sexes to Four Genders in the Making of Modern Culture." In *Body Guards: The Cultural Politics of Gender Ambiguity*. Ed. Judith Epstein and Kristina Straub, 112–41. New York: Routledge, 1991.

———. *The Rise of the Egalitarian Family*. New York: Academic Press, 1978.

———. "Sodomitical Assaults, Gender Role, and Sexual Development in Eighteenth-Century London." In *The Pursuit of Sodomy: Male Homosexuality in Renaissance and Enlightenment Europe*. Ed. Kent Gerard and Gert Hekma, 407–32. New York: Harrington Park, 1989.

———. "Sodomy Transformed: Aristocratic Libertinage, Public Reputation and the Gender Revolution of the Eighteenth Century." In *Love Letters Between a Certain Late Nobleman and the Famous Mr. Wilson*. Ed. Michael S. Kimmel, 105–24. New York: Harrington Park, 1990.

Tuttle, Donald. "*Christabel*'s Sources in Percy's *Reliques* and Gothic Romance." *PMLA* 53 (1938): 445–74.

Varma, Devendra. *The Gothic Flame*. London: Arthur Barker, 1957.

Ver Eecke, Wilfried. "Negation and Desire in Freud and Hegel." *The Owl of Minerva* 15.1 (Fall 1983): 11–22.

Verene, Donald. *Hegel's Recollection: A Study of Images in the Phenomenology of Spirit*. Albany: State University of New York, 1985.

Vidler, Anthony. *The Architectural Uncanny: Essays in the Modern Unhomely*. Cambridge: MIT Press, 1992.

Vital, Anthony. "Lord Byron's Embarrassment: Poesy and the Feminine." *Bulletin of Research in the Humanities* 86.3 (1983–85): 269–90.

Vitale, Marina. "The Domesticated Heroine in Byron's *Corsair* and William Hone's Prose Adaption." *Literature & History* 10 (1984): 72–94.

Walpole, Horace. *The Castle of Otranto*. Ed. W. S. Lewis. New York: Oxford University Press, 1996.

Warner, Michael. "Homo-narcissism; or, Heterosexuality." In *Engendering Men: The Question of Male Feminist Criticism*. Ed. Joseph A. Boone and Michael Cadden, 190–206. New York: Routledge, 1991.

Watkins, Daniel. *Social Relations in Byron's Eastern Tales*. Rutherford: Fairleigh Dickinson University Press, 1987.

Watt, Ian. "Time and Family in the Gothic Novel: *The Castle of Otranto*." *Eighteenth-Century Life* 10.3 (October 1986): 159–71.

Watt, James. *Contesting the Gothic: Fiction, Genre, and Cultural Conflict, 1764–1832*. New York: Cambridge University Press, 1999.

Weeks, Jeffrey. *Sex, Politics, & Society*. 2nd edition. London: Longman, 1989.

Whale, John. "Sacred Objects and the Sublime Ruins of Art." In *Beyond Romanticism*. Ed. Stephen Copley and John Whale, 218–36. London: Routledge, 1982.

Williams, Anne. *Art of Darkness: A Poetics of the Gothic*. Chicago: University of Chicago Press, 1995.

A Wiltshire Parson and His Friends: The Correspondence of William Lisle Bowles, Together with Four Hitherto Unidentified Reviews of Coleridge. Ed. Garland Greever. London: Constable, 1926.

Wolfenstein, Eugene Victor. "He Who Loses His Self Shall Find It: Self-Certainty and Freedom in Hegel's *Phenomenology of Spirit* and Psychoanalytic Practice." *Discours social/ social Discourse* 2.1–2 (Spring-Summer 1989): 279–309.

Wolfson, Susan. "Feminizing Keats." In *Critical Essays on John Keats*. Ed. Hermione de Almeida, 317–56. Boston: G. K. Hall & Co., 1990.

———. *Formal Charges: The Shaping of Poetry in British Romanticism*. Stanford: Stanford University Press, 1996.

———. "Keats and the Manhood of the Poet." *European Romantic Review* 6.1 (1995): 1–37.

———. "The Magic Hand of Chance." *Review* 14 (1992): 213–24.

———. *The Questioning Presence: Wordsworth, Keats, and the Interrogative Mode in Romantic Poetry*. Ithaca: Cornell University Press, 1986.

———. "'Their She Condition': Cross-Dressing and the Politics of Gender in *Don Juan*." *ELH* 54 (Fall 1987): 585–617.

Wolff, Cynthia Griffin. "The Radcliffean Gothic Model: A Form for Feminine Sexuality." *Modern Language Studies* 9.3 (1979): 98–113.

Žižek, Slavoj. *For They Do Not Know What They Do: Enjoyment as a Political Factor*. London: Verso, 1991.

———. "Grimaces of the Real." *October* 58 (1992): 44–68.

———. *Looking Awry: An Introduction to Jacques Lacan Through Popular Culture*. Cambridge: MIT Press, 1991.

———. *The Sublime Object of Ideology*. London: Verso, 1989.

———. *Tarrying with the Negative. Kant, Hegel, and the Critique of Ideology*. Durham: Duke University Press, 1993.

Index

213